n

Booktalks and Beyond

Booktalks and Beyond

Promoting Great Genre Reads to Teens

Lucy Schall

LIBRARIES
UNLIMITED
A Member of the Greenwood Publishing Group

Westport, Connecticut • London

Library of Congress Cataloging-in-Publication Data
Schall, Lucy.
    Booktalks and beyond : promoting great genre reads to teens / Lucy Schall.
      p. cm.
    Includes bibliographical references (p.) and index.
    ISBN-13: 978–1–59158–466–7 (alk. paper)
    ISBN-10: 1–59158–466–3 (alk. paper)
    1. Teenagers—Books and reading—United States. 2. Book talks—United States.
3. Reading promotion—United States. 4. Young adult literature—Bibliography. I. Title.
Z1037.A1S267   2007
028.5'5—dc22   2006037492

British Library Cataloguing in Publication Data is available.

Library of Congress Catalog Card Number: 2006037492
ISBN: 978–1–59158–466–7

First published in 2007

Libraries Unlimited, 88 Post Road West, Westport, CT 06881
A Member of the Greenwood Publishing Group, Inc.
www.lu.com

Printed in the United States of America

∞™

The paper used in this book complies with the
Permanent Paper Standard issued by the National
Information Standards Organization (Z39.48–1984).

10 9 8 7 6 5 4 3 2 1

To Bob Schall, my supportive husband,
an excellent classroom teacher and teacher educator.

Contents

Acknowledgments

I wish to thank Barbara Ittner, my editor, for her insight, encouragement, and patience; Linda Benson, from VOYA, for the generous sharing of her expertise; and Diana Tixier Herald for my organizational model.

The following libraries and media centers have provided me with resources and staff support: St. Petersburg Public Libraries in St. Petersburg, Florida; the Meadville Public Library and the Meadville Middle School and High School Media Center in Meadville, Pennsylvania.

Introduction

Booktalks and Beyond suggests high-quality books for booktalks, reading aloud, discussion groups, coordinated displays, book club programs, lesson plans, and just enjoyment. These books motivate readers, and lead them to insights about themselves and others, past and present. Families and professionals who live and work with teens will find a wide range of reading choices that encourage teenagers to think about and explore their interests, perhaps even discover a few new ones. Teen literature opens doors to classics, more difficult writing styles, and thoughtful conversation. The seven chapters follow the same order as those in *Teen Genre Connections: From Booktalking to Booklearning* (2004): Issues, Contemporary, Adventure/Survival, Mystery/Suspense, Fantasy/Science Fiction/Paranormal, History, and Multiple Cultures. More specific topics and themes divide each chapter.

The bibliographic information for featured books and "Related Works" includes the author name; book title; publisher and date of publication; number of pages; price and ISBN; a bracketed fiction, nonfiction, graphic novel, or reference designation; and a reading level suggestion.

M   = middle school
J   = junior high
S   = senior high
A   = adult

Remember! Because teen readers, like adults, have a broad range of purpose and preference in their reading, these reading level designations are only *suggestions*. The abbreviation "pa." indicates paperback. It is my hope that the designations and suggestions for these books published between 2001 and 2006, as well as the theme/topic designations, summaries, read aloud/reader response, booktalks, and related works will aid any professional or nonprofessional working with young people to match books, readers, and researchers.

Following the theme/topic designations and summary, each selection includes a Read Aloud/Reader Response section. The section lists at least five specific passages for sharing aloud, reflecting for discussion or writing, or preparing dramatic readings or performances. The Read Aloud/Reader Response entries include a chapter, section, or division where possible, page designation, a beginning and ending phrase to locate the passage, and a brief comment on the content. A book like *Letting Go of Bobby James, or How I Found My Self of Steam* has no chapter designations and will use page numbers only. The graphic novel, *Marvel 1602: # 1 to 8* uses part, page, and panel designations. Some passages are attention-getting statements for classroom or book display posters. Others are natural springboards for discussions or substitutions for booktalks.

Booktalks highlight good books teens might overlook in a well-developed library collection. They advertise both the book and the library. Teachers supplementing textbook information will find that booktalking makes that supplemental reading list a personalized reference document as students note their preferences during the presentation. Booktalks in this volume can be considered "ready-mades" or springboards for writing another booktalk according to personal style or purpose. Presenter directions for some of the booktalks are shown in italics. Short enough to hold a teen audience's attention, several booktalks from different genres can be included in one forty-five-minute program. Individual booktalks might introduce or conclude a class period or library program. Easily adapted for a school's morning announcements or the school newspaper, the booktalks are also appropriate for local public service announcements, newsletters, or Web sites. Nonprofit use is permitted and encouraged.

Every booktalker has a distinct style and favorite methods. The following are some suggestions I can pass on from my own experience. Read every book you booktalk. Booktalk only the books you respect. Include books from several genres. Tell your audience how a book from one genre relates to a book in another. If you are planning a full program of booktalks, invite your audience to select the books they want to hear about from the books that you bring. Display the books so that the covers hold the audience's attention. Hand out an annotated list at the beginning of the program for the audience to refer to and visit later. In any booktalk situation, keep the booktalk short. Hold the book while you speak. Have extra copies so that (if you are lucky) you will have a replacement for the one snatched by an eager reader. Involve your audience, if only with a rhetorical question, at least every five minutes. For more guidelines and tips on booktalking, refer to another publication from Libraries Unlimited, *The Booktalker's Bible: How to Talk about the Books You Love to Any Audience* (2003) by Chapple Langemack.

"Learning Opportunities" follow each booktalk. These sections suggest individual and group projects based on the book and "Related Works." The "Opportunities" include discussion topics; ideas for journals; longer papers; poems or other creative writing; panel discussions; or presentations—visual, oral, or both. Some may provide a basis for independent studies, portfolios, or senior projects. The discussion questions will promote lively exchanges in any reading group—teenage or teen/adult—or family. All will improve reading, writing, and speaking skills. Any works mentioned in "Learning Opportunities" are listed in "Related Works."

"Related Works" include sources for expanded learning, further reading, and inter-genre relationships. The listings include books as well as graphic novels, short stories, plays, poems, reference books, and Web sites. These sections will help build book displays, book programs, and units of study. Several of the sections include graphic novels. Including the graphic novels in displays or programs with related traditional books, some from other genres, may surprise readers and expand their reading interest. "Related Works" also will guide instructors, librarians, and parents to additional reading or information sources. The index includes authors, titles, and topics for a quick overview of a work's relationships to others mentioned in this volume.

As the quantity and quality of teen literature continues to grow, the professional recommendations from *VOYA, Booklist, School Library Journal,* the *ALAN Review,* as well as award lists and YALSA's "best" booklists become even more valuable to me. Personal reactions from my reading family, friends, and audiences influenced my final choices, too. It is my hope that this volume gives you useful tools for advertising the great collections you have, motivating more readers to explore recent texts, and encouraging your "customers" to tell their own important stories.

Issues

These selections focus on intense mental, emotional, moral, and spiritual issues. "Confronting the Bully" means facing up to abusive people and the fears they exploit. "Defining Love" explores the love and passion that can surprise us. "Living on the Edge" describes out-of-control situations that may trap us. "Finding Inner Peace or Spiritual Clarification" deals with why bad things happen and how we might deal with them, even in the afterlife.

Confronting the Bully

Bowler, Tim. **Firmament.**

New York: Simon & Schuster/Margaret K. McElderry Books, 2002. 306p. $16.95. ISBN 0 689 86161 3. [fiction] MJ

Themes/Topics: death, fathers/sons, music, blindness, intergenerational relationships, physical appearance, personal responsibility, loneliness

Summary/Description

Pushed by a local gang to break into the house of Mrs. Little, an ugly, old, unpopular woman who recently moved to town, fourteen-year-old Luke Stanton discovers a blind, weeping child living in the house. Like his deceased father, Luke is a musical genius. Mrs. Little discovers his break-in and lets him go, but, knowing his reputation, asks him to play the piano for the girl whom she claims is her grand-daughter. The girl responds to his music. He becomes close to the pair and refuses to steal from them even though the gang threatens his life.

Discovering that Mrs. Little is not the grandmother, he finds the parents and arranges for the girl's return without police intervention but then is trapped by the gang. Rescued by his mother's boyfriend, whom he hates, he discovers that acceptance is better than division. He draws Mrs. Little into the community, approves of his mother's dating, and finds a girlfriend of his own.

Read Aloud/Reader Response

1. Chapter 8, page 69, beginning " . . .he found himself . . . " and ending " . . . to bad use." Luke recalls his father's comments about Luke's good hands.
2. Chapter 11, pages 94 to 95, beginning "His mouth dropped open . . . " and ending " . . . glowered up at the wall." Sending a computer message to his deceased father, Luke receives a commercial reply and believes heaven is mocking him.
3. Chapter 19, pages 163 to 164, beginning "The firmament?" and ending " . . . human soul." Luke and his mother discuss the meaning of the firmament.
4. Chapter 20, page 168, beginning "Another stone . . . " and ending with the paragraph. The passage describes the stalking and threatening gang members.
5. Chapter 20, pages 171, beginning "He thought over . . . " and ending " . . . hate himself." Luke realizes how debilitating his grieving has been.
6. Chapter 22, page 191, beginning " . . . if you strike . . . " and ending " . . . same frequency." Mr. Harding's cryptic comment about the tuning fork applies to personal actions.
7. Chapter 29, pages 250, beginning "Luke waited . . . " and ending with the paragraph. Luke realizes that Roger, his mother's boyfriend, saved his life. Luke also understands his own personal journey, mentioned on page 191.

Booktalk

Ask how many in the group know what firmament means. If no one is familiar with it, explain it in your own words or refer to Read Aloud/ Reader Response 3.

Luke's father heard sounds. He talked about those sounds as a way of rising to the *Firmament*. Two years ago, Luke Stanton's father died. Something died in Luke too. Luke doesn't like to think about his father as part of the wonderful *Firmament*. He thinks just about his father not being there. Now Luke is fourteen. He lies to his mother, hates her boyfriend, makes trouble in school, and ignores his music—the gift of genius from his father. Instead of using his hands to play the piano, he uses them to climb trees where he can sit for hours and shut off the world. Luke has some new friends too. He hangs with the local troublemakers, the town gang. They want Luke to use his hands to climb into an old lady's house. The lady is rich, ugly, isolated, and new in town—an easy mark. He agrees. But when he climbs into that house, he climbs into a world more complicated than he could have imagined. He finds a small blind girl who cries and a tough old lady who demands that he help her. The cry haunts him. The lady stalks him. Luke wants to protect them, but if he doesn't deliver to the gang, Luke is the one who is going to need protection. What can he do? The answer is in his hands, and suddenly, with his father, he too is part of the *Firmament*.

Learning Opportunities

1. Using your library's resources, find copies of the musical pieces mentioned in the novel. Play them for the group and discuss the mood each suggests.
2. Discuss the role of Roger Gilmore. Be sure to consider his career as an artist.
3. The gang is punished for their crimes. Mrs. Little is not. Discuss why.
4. How does Natalie change Luke?
5. How does the concert function in the story? What does it say about sharing talents publicly?

Related Works

1. Almond, David. **Secret Heart.** New York: Delacorte Press, 2001. 199p. $17.99. ISBN 0 385 90065 1. [fiction] JS Bullied Joe Maloney finds a new perspective on life when a circus, which sees him as its savior, comes to town.
2. Cross, Gillian. **Tightrope.** New York: Holiday House, 1999. 216p. $16.95. ISBN 0 8234 1512 0. [fiction] MJS (See full booktalk in *Booktalks and More*, 2003, pages 130 to 132.) Fourteen-year-old Ashley Putnam takes care of her invalid mother and becomes drawn into and pressured by a neighborhood gang.
3. Freymann-Weyr, Garret. **The Kings Are Already Here.** Boston, MA: Houghton Mifflin Company, 2003. 149p. $15.00. ISBN 0 618 26363 2. [fiction] JS Two unusually talented teenagers decide how their talents will shape their lives.
4. Gaiman, Neil, and Mike Dringenberg, et al. **Death: The High Cost of Living.** New York: DC Comics, 1994. 104p. $22.20.

ISBN 1 4046 1368 4. [graphic novel] JS Death, personified as a friendly young girl, inspires a young man to choose life. Strong language may be considered controversial.

5. Wynne-Jones, Tim. **Stephen Fair.** New York: DK Ink, 1998. 218p. $15.95. ISBN 0 7894 2495 9. [fiction] MJ (See full booktalk in *Booktalks Plus*, 2001, pages 56 to 59.) Plagued with nightmares and a disintegrating family, Stephen discovers that his troubled mother stole him from his abusive birth parents.

ॐॐ

Brooks, Kevin. **Lucas: A Story of Love and Hate.**
New York: Chicken House, 2002. 432p. $16.95. ISBN 0 439 45698 3. [fiction] JS

Themes/Topics: loss, prejudice, personal responsibility, love, risk, England

Summary/Description

Sixteen-year-old Caitlin McCann, who lives with her father and older brother on Hale Island, recalls how knowing Lucas changed her life. Lucas, a teenager, appears on the island with no friends, family, or last name. A wild teen group led by the son of a wealthy landowner and the daughter of the local detective intend to drive brave and handsome Lucas off the island. They physically threaten him and spread rumors about his "crimes." Caitlin, befriending Lucas and defending him from the gang and eventually an island mob, rediscovers her brother who was part of the teen crowd. When Lucas kills himself, she understands her father's grief over her mother's accidental death.

Read Aloud/Reader Response

1. Chapter 1, pages 8 to 11, beginning "That was the moment . . . " and ending " . . . not be there." Caitlin describes the first time she sees Lucas.
2. Chapter 2, pages 70 to 71, beginning "That night . . . " and ending with the chapter. Caitlin describes the dream that she has about Lucas running from the mob.
3. Chapter 4, pages 104 to 105, beginning "I don't think . . . " and ending " . . . can't be changed." Caitlin reflects on Lucas's warning about danger.
4. Chapter 19, page 362, beginning "I'm trying to do . . ." and ending "going wrong." Caitlin expresses her frustration over her good intentions going wrong.

5. Chapter 23, pages 414 to 415, beginning " . . . getting over it . . . " and ending " . . . all it's got." Caitlin's father shares his perception of grief with her.

Booktalk

Read Caitlin McCann's introduction to her own story. It appears just before Chapter 1. Then begin the booktalk.

Sixteen-year-old Caitlin McCann lives on Hale Island. Like the rest of the world, the island has some bad people, some good people, and some who let others make their choices for them. But good or bad, the island residents don't see many strangers. When a strange, almost enchanted, young man shows up during Caitlin's fifteenth summer, Caitlin thinks he is probably the most fascinating person she has ever met. Others disagree. Will she side with the popular, wild group, the one her older brother chooses, and drive the stranger off the island? Will she join the goody-goodies and get lost in some cause that allows her to forget he even exists? Or will she seek a very dangerous path and befriend this mysterious and mystical boy called *Lucas*? Her decision changes her life, her home, and her island—forever.

Learning Opportunities

1. In the first chapter, Caitlin describes Lucas's walk as communicating his character and personality. Describe the walk of someone you know and communicate as much as possible about the person in your description.

2. *Lucas* says a great deal about the power of peer pressure over personal choice. Begin a personal decisions reading journal. List the decisions in the novel you feel are most significant. Explain why each is significant. As you read other literature, continue to note characters' decisions and their significance. At the end of each month, read what you have written. Try to describe your beliefs and values.

3. The novel ends with Lucas's death, a possible suicide, and Caitlin's grief and growth. Agree and/or disagree with the appropriateness of that ending.

4. At the end of the eighth chapter, Mr. McCann realizes that Lucas has alluded to a quote from Marcus Valerius Martialis. Discuss the meaning of the quotation and what the allusion reveals about Lucas.

5. Identify points in the story where non-verbal communication is central. Using your library's resources, research non-verbal communication. Choose one behavior you discover in your research. Use it and write about its effect on those around you.

Related Works

1. Brooks, Kevin. **Martyn Pig.** [fiction] JS (See full booktalk in "Mystery/Suspense"/ "Contemporary," pages 114 to 116.) Like *Lucas,* the novel involves young people making moral choices and learning to live with the consequences.
2. George, Jean Craighead. **My Side of the Mountain.** New York: Puffin Books, 1988. 177p. $5.99pa. ISBN 0 14 034810 7. [fiction] MJ Tired of living in a crowded New York apartment, Sam Gribley decides to live with nature. His romantic experience contrasts Lucas's.
3. Muharrar, Aisha. Elizabeth Verdick (ed.). **More Than a Label: Why What You Wear or Who You're With Doesn't Define Who You Are.** Minneapolis, MN: Free Spirit Publishing Inc., 2002. 144p. $13.95. ISBN 1 57542 110 0. [nonfiction] MJS Muharrar defines labeling, explains how labels make people feel, and suggests ways to deal with labels.
4. Singer, Marilyn (ed.). **I Believe in Water: Twelve Brushes with Religion.** New York: HarperCollins Publishers, 2000. 280p. $24.89. ISBN 0 06 028398 X. [fiction] JS Like Caitlin, the characters in these short stories decide whether or not to believe in something beyond themselves.
5. Schmidt, Gary D. **Lizzie Bright and the Buckminster Boy.** [fiction] MJS (See full booktalk in "Multiple Cultures"/"Learning from the Cultures within Our Country," pages 251 to 254.) When a minister's family moves to a new church, they are overcome with hate and prejudice.

ख़ॡॐ

Clements, Bruce. **What Erika Wants.**
New York: Farrar, Straus and Giroux, 2005. 216p. $16.00.
ISBN 0 374 32304 6. [fiction] MJS

Themes/Topics: family problems, lawyers, acting, divorce, personal choices

Summary/Description

Fifteen-year-old Erika lives with her emotional and indecisive father. Her manipulative mother, back after five years, wants Erika to live with her. Twenty-five-year-old Karen, Erika's half-sister, claims that Erika should care for their mother. Karen wants to move in with Bernie, a petty criminal. Erika's friend, Carrie Ives, is already part of the juvenile court system. Jean Rostow-Kaplan, a court appointed lawyer, gives Erika a diary to record her thoughts and feelings. She supports Erika's desire to try out for the school play, an activity both Erika's mother and friend discourage, and encourages Erika's father to support her also. Erika experiences a successful performance, understands her mother's manipulation, rejects the life Karen chooses, realizes that Carrie is no longer her friend, finds a possible boyfriend who shares her drama interest, acknowledges that she is not strong enough to make everyone happy, and decides to stay with her father. Jean Rostow-Kaplan affirms that she will help Erika through future decisions.

Read Aloud/Reader Response

1. Chapter 1, page 4, beginning "It's always better . . . " and ending with the paragraph. The courthouse policeman explains the difference between criminal and family court.
2. Chapter 1, page 11, beginning, "Jean smiled." and ending " . . . their plans for you." Erika wonders if Jean is really for her client.
3. Chapter 3, pages 40 and 41, beginning with the chapter and ending " . . . with no place to go." Erika realizes that Bernie could destroy her entire family.
4. Chapter 9, pages 99 to 100, beginning "Sitting on the bus" . . . and ending with the chapter. The dialogue reveals Erika's inability to stand up to her mother.
5. Chapters 10 and 11, pages 101 to 105, beginning with Chapter 10 and ending " . . . I'll punch his lights out." The father expresses fear and anger over losing Erika.
6. Chapter 12, pages 109 and 110. Karen's letter reveals her motives for pressuring Erika.
7. Chapter 27, pages 186 to 187, beginning "As soon as they were settled . . . " and ending "Jean grabbed her coat." Carrie wants to control Erika, and Jean responds.

Booktalk

Fifteen-year-old Erika lives with her father. Mom left for Arizona five years ago. Now Mom is back, and she wants Erika back. Erika doesn't know what to do. Her older sister Karen says that Erika owes Mom. Erika's dad wonders why she even considers her mom her mom. But Erika has lots of people to help her decide what to do besides her fighting family. The court appoints an attorney for her. The woman lawyer talks like a New Yorker. She doesn't look—well, she doesn't look that good. Carrie, Erika's best friend, says that court appointed lawyers are losers. Carrie should know. She has been in the court system quite awhile. Carrie has some plans for Erika too. Bernie, Karen's boyfriend, wants to give Erika presents and some pills to smooth out her feelings a little. The drama teacher wants Erika to star in his play. Erika has acted for her family and friends all her life. And the play's leading man is somebody she wants to get to know a little better. Erika would like to tell everybody "yes." Then everyone will be happy. But how happy will Erika be if what everyone else wants isn't *What Erika Wants?*

Learning Opportunities

1. When Jean Rostow-Kaplan explains ideas, she uses stories. List three of your beliefs. Then tell a personal story that illustrates that belief or why you hold it.
2. Using your library and possibly your local legal resources, research the responsibilities of a family court lawyer. Share your information with the group.
3. Many other characters, besides Erika, are "acting." Cite as many instances as you can. Explain how each is hurtful or harmful.
4. When Erika tries out for the play, she learns about herself and others. List all the things that you think she learns.
5. List three events in the novel that reveal Erika's character.
6. Do you think Erika made the right decision in staying with her father?

Related Works

1. Aydt, Rachel. **Why Me?: A Teen Guide to Divorce and Your Feelings.** New York: The Rosen Publishing Group, 2000. 64p. (The Divorce Resource Series.) $19.95. ISBN 0 8239 3113 7. [nonfiction] MJS The Divorce Resource Series uses stories, definitions, and examples to explain how to cope with the many aspects of divorce including feelings, property, the law, and independence.
2. Ferris, Jean. **Bad.** New York: Farrar, Straus and Giroux, 1998. 182p. $16.00. ISBN 0 374 30479 3. [fiction] JS (See full booktalk in *Booktalks and More*, pages 137 to 139.) Sixteen-year-old Dallas Carpenter decides on placement in a foster home instead of her father's home after she is arrested for robbery and sentenced to rehabilitation.
3. McNeal, Laura, and Tom McNeal. **Crooked.** New York: Alfred A. Knopf, 1999. 346p. $16.95. ISBN 0 679 89300 8. [fiction] MJ (See

full booktalk in *Booktalks and More,* 2003, pages 3 to 5.) Fourteen-year-old Clara Wilson develops her own interests and cultivates new friends to cope with her parents' separation and her own lack of confidence.

4. Monthei, Betty. **Looking for Normal.** New York: HarperCollins Publishers, 2005. 185p. $15.99. ISBN 0 06 072505 2. [fiction] JS After their father kills their mother and commits suicide, a brother and sister move in with their dysfunctional grandparents and suffer abuse from their alcoholic grandmother.

5. Pearson, Mary E. **A Room on Lorelei Street.** New York: Henry Holt and Company, 2005. 266p. $16.95. ISBN 0 8050 7667 0. [fiction] JS A young girl believes that she can escape her dysfunctional family by renting a room of her own, but the dream goes sour when she prostitutes herself to pay the rent.

ᘇᘇ

Curtis, Christopher Paul. **Bucking the Sarge.**

New York: Wendy Lamb Books, 2004. $15.95. ISBN 0 385 32307 7. [fiction] MJS

Themes/Topics: business, fraud, group homes, mothers, mental disabilities, African-Americans, integrity, identity

Summary/Description

Fourteen-year-old Luther T. Farrell wants a third school Science Fair win. He completes his schoolwork while running a group home, owned by his slumlord mother, for mentally disabled men. Like Shayla Dawn, his main Science Fair competitor and secret love interest, he is envied for his family's wealth. Luther's mother discourages academics and wants him to take over her empire, which involves him in painful evictions and government scams. A new home resident, Chester X, encourages Luther to break free of his mother, escape with him to Florida, and build a new life. Luther and Shayla tie for the Science Fair prize. His project explains the dangers of lead paint, catches the attention of the authorities, and will inevitably highlight the illegal stash his mother uses to paint her properties. Knowing she will take revenge, he uses business money and assets to help some of the people she exploited; gives the previous year's science medal, which he discovers he won through his mother's pressure, to Shayla; and leaves Flint, Michigan, with a grateful Chester X.

Read Aloud/Reader Response

1. Chapter 1, pages 6 and 8, beginning "Sparky said, 'Naw, Luther . . . '" and ending "I changed the subject." Sparky and Luther review Luther's life.
2. Chapter 4, pages 38 to 39, beginning "In the Sarge's eyes . . . " and ending ". . . and two hallways." Luther describes the fast and sloppy painting techniques of Darnell Dixon, the Sarge's enforcer.
3. Chapter 6, pages 44 to 63. Luther describes evicting tenants and discovers that the latest victim is the third-place winner in last year's science competition.
4. Chapter 8, pages 97 to 102, beginning "She just didn't understand me . . . " and ending with the chapter. Sarge gives her rationale for exploitation.
5. Chapter 13, pages 177 to 181, beginning "I know I've got . . . " and ending with the chapter. Chester X warns Luther not to let his possessions define him.

Booktalk

Fourteen-year-old Luther T. Farrell lives in Flint, Michigan. His mother, the Sarge, owns most of it. She is the toughest loan shark, slum landlord, and government scam artist around. She has enough money and clout to give Luther anything he wants. What other fourteen-year-old has a driver's license, a wallet full of credit cards, and more than ninety-thousand dollars in his education fund? But that sweet life comes with a price. Luther is in charge of a group home for old, mentally disabled men. He has been changing their diapers since he was in third grade. He uses his driver's license only to drive the home's van. He also evicts people from his mother's houses—rats and all. His money and credit cards are for business emergencies, and his education fund comes right from his hourly wage. He isn't exactly the poster boy for "Got It Made." And his personal ambitions are a little different from his mother's. He wants to be a great American philosopher. The first step toward that goal is coming up. He could win first place in the school Science Competition for the third year in a row. Colleges would want him then. His only obstacle is that beautiful, brilliant, hard-to-get-along-with Shayla Dawn, the mortician's daughter. She almost beat him out for the medal last year. But Luther is ready with the goods and focused on the goal. Unfortunately the goods put him on a collision course with Sarge, the queen of the Evil Empire and her hit man, Darnell Dixon. Then there is Chester X, the new and mysterious inmate at the home. He has ideas that Luther likes but doesn't want to hear. Chester is convinced that Sarge will kill them both. And Chester might just be right. Life gets a whole lot more dangerous when Luther stops being Loser and decides to go after his own dreams—even if it means *Bucking the Sarge.*

Learning Opportunities

1. Discuss the title. How many ways could it be interpreted?
2. When Sparky lists the items in Luther's wallet, and Luther goes through the items in Bo Travis's house, discuss what the reader learns about each boy.
3. Choose a wallet, closet, desk, or home of someone you know. Characterize the person in terms of what you find.
4. Using your library's resources, research the effects of lead paint. Share the information with the group.
5. List the positive people in Luther's life. Explain the importance of each.

Related Works

1. Fleischman, Paul. **Seek.** Chicago, IL: Cricket Books/A Marcato Book, 2001. 167p. $16.95. ISBN 0 8126 4900 1. [fiction] JS Writing his autobiography for his senior English class, Robert Radkovitz discovers that his father, who left, is an unnecessary part of his life.
2. Myers, William Dean. **The Dream Bearer.** New York: HarperCollins Publishers, 2003. 181p. $16.89. ISBN 0 06 029522 8. [fiction] MJS Twelve-year-old David Curry learns, from a man who claims to be more than 300 years old, that young men build their own dreams rather than live the dreams of others.
3. Nelson, Blake. **The New Rules of High School.** New York: Viking Press, 2003. 227p. $16.99. ISBN 0 670 03644 7. [fiction] JS Seventeen-year-old Max Caldwell decides, in his senior year, that he will build a life based on his own feelings and ambitions rather than his parents' expectations.
4. Rottman, S. L. **Stetson.** New York: Viking Press, 2002. 192p. $16.99. ISBN 0 670 03542 4. [fiction] JS (See full booktalk in *Teen Genre Connections,* pages 23 to 25.) Seventeen-year-old Stetson and his newly discovered fourteen-year-old sister Kayla decide to leave home and build lives independent of their alcoholic father.
5. Smith, Sherri L. **Lucy the Giant.** New York: Delacorte Press, 2002. 217p. $15.95. ISBN 0 385 72940 5. [fiction] MJS (See full booktalk in *Teen Genre Connections,* 2005, pages 121 to 123.)

Fifteen-year-old Lucy Otswego leaves her alcoholic father and signs up for a crabbing expedition under a false identity. She discovers a new life and independence.

℘℘

Flinn, Alex. Breaking Point.

New York: Harper Tempest, 2002. 240p. $6.99pa. ISBN 006 447371 6. [fiction] JS

Themes/Topics: high school, bullies, friendship, in-group/out-group, social exploitation

Summary/Description

Now eighteen, Paul Richmond reflects on his experience in an exclusive school where his divorced mother found a job in the school's office. Charlie Good, a charismatic and manipulative student, made Paul, a lonely computer nerd, his "friend." The conditions for friendship included Paul's breaking into the school and changing a low grade that Charlie received. Paul watched David Blanco, the janitor's son, pressured to suicide. David had been Charlie's former "friend," but Paul still believed that Charlie was the only one who understood Paul's negative feelings about school and home. Eventually, Charlie persuaded Paul to set a bomb in the classroom of the teacher who gave Charlie the poor grade. The teacher discovered the plot. Paul confessed and implicated Charlie. Charlie's mother, an attorney, secured Charlie's release. Paul went to jail, and Charlie realized a successful tennis career.

Read Aloud/Reader Response

1. "Prologue," One page before page 1, the entire prologue. At eighteen, Paul, released from jail, reflects on how he arrived there.
2. Chapter 3, pages 20 to 21, beginning "Why can't I . . . " and ending at the bottom of page 21. Paul makes the case for going to public school, but his mother won't listen.
3. Chapter 5, page 32, beginning "Show me . . . " and ending " . . . ten-year reunion." Binky comments on high school popularity.
4. Chapter 7, pages 49 to 51, beginning "David wasn't . . . " and ending " . . . father to clean." David Blanco expresses his anger about all the sick pranks played on him and his parents and compares the situation to Nazi Germany.
5. Chapter 20, pages 136 to 137, beginning "I'm sick of him." and ending " . . . other way around." St. John defines Paul's relationship with the in-group and taps an overwhelming anger in Paul.

Booktalk

Paul is fifteen. Most of his life, he has been homeschooled. His family traveled around because Paul's father is in the service. Learning at home was just easier than being the new kid in school—constantly. Now his dad is gone. He left Paul and Paul's mother to start a new life. Mom has to get a job, and she finds one in a private school in Miami, Florida—Brickell Christian. The big job perk is that Paul can attend. This school is bursting with rich kids. Paul is not only the new poor kid, but also a six one, skinny, computer nerd. The first person to say hello to him at Brickell Christian looks just about as nerdy as he does. Then life gets interesting. The most popular boy in school, the leader of the pack, the guy who doesn't seem to have to follow school rules—that guy wants to get to know Paul. So Paul finds Charlie Good. Charlie is smart. He is handsome. He is rich, and all the kids do what he says. He is what Paul wants to be, and he is Paul's ticket to belonging. But Charlie Good is going to charge for that ticket. The price is going to be high—so high that it might drive Paul to the *Breaking Point.*

Learning Opportunities

1. Why is David Blanco important?
2. Discuss where Paul fails to take responsibility for his actions.
3. How does Charlie manipulate Paul?
4. Identify each sermon topic mentioned. Choose one and write the sermon that you feel would be most appropriate for the Brickell Christian School audience.
5. Identify each setting. Discuss the effectiveness of each.
6. Using your library's resources, research student violence. Discuss how the information that you find makes this story more or less believable.

Related Works

1. Going, K. L. **Fat Kid Rules the World.** New York: G. P. Putnam's Sons, 2003. 183p. $17.99. ISBN 0 399 23990 1. [fiction] JS (See full booktalk in *Teen Genre Connections,* 2005, pages 4 to 6.) The friendship between an outcast and a popular student makes both stronger.
2. Korman, Gordon. **Jake, Reinvented.** New York: Hyperion, 2003. 213p. $15.99. ISBN 0 786 81957 X. [fiction] JS Through Rick, the reader learns about Jake, a brainy, social outsider who manufactures a new persona to capture the cold, popular girl he adores.
3. Myers, Walter Dean. **Shooter.** New York: Harper Tempest, 2004. 223p. $16.89. ISBN 0 06 029520 1. [fiction] JS A friendship among

three school outcasts and unchecked bullying in the school lead to
a fatal shooting.

4. Schwarz, Ted. **Kids and Guns.** New York: Franklin Watts, 1999.
    128p. $24.00. ISBN 0 531 11723 5. [nonfiction] JS Schwarz reviews
    recent shootings and considers the attacks in the framework of
    Americans' attitudes toward guns.

5. Strasser, Todd. **Give a Boy a Gun.** New York: Simon & Schuster,
    2000. 146p. $16.00. ISBN 0 689 81112 8. [fiction] MJS (See full
    booktalk in *Booktalks and More*, 2003, pages 116 to 118.) Two boys,
    bullied and teased by the school jocks, plan and execute a terrorist
    act in their school.

Defining Love

ဢ

Beard, Philip. **Dear Zoe.**
New York: Viking Press, 2005. 196p. $21.95. ISBN 0 670 03401 0. [fiction] JS

Themes/Topics: sisters, loss, fathers and daughters, blended
families, personal vs. public tragedy, illegal drugs, love

Summary/Description

Fifteen-year-old Tess lives with her mother and stepfather, David. Her
younger stepsister dies in an auto accident on September 11, 2001,
and each family member experiences deep grief. The mother sleeps constantly, and the stepfather works long hours. Tess, who feels responsible
for the death, helps her other sister, seven-year-old Em, cope. But when
Tess thinks that her mother is having an affair, she goes to live with her
biological father, a drug dealer, whom her mother married at nineteen.
The father, compassionate but irresponsible, forbids her to see the boy
next door, Jimmy Freeze, a juvenile delinquent who helps the father sell
drugs. Jimmy and Tess, however, develop both friendship and romance.
Jimmy blames his conflict with his father and his own delinquent behavior
on his mother's death and his father's remarriage. Eventually, Tess works
through her feelings of isolation instead of imitating Jimmy's negative
pattern of behavior and returns home. Tess, her mother, stepfather, and
sister attend counseling and become a stronger family unit. The content,
involving drugs and sex, requires a mature audience.

Read Aloud/Reader Response

1. "Naming You," page 1, beginning "I have . . ." and ending " . . . now with David." This opening paragraph focuses on the importance of names and Tess's realization that her mother fears they are too much alike.
2. "Anniversary," pages 13 and 14. The chapter discusses the difference for her between national (deaths of September 11, 2001) and personal (Zoe's death) grief.
3. "Roller Coaster," page 22, beginning "For me . . ." and ending "We have to." Tess questions opening up about her feelings, especially in therapy.
4. "My Face," and "Yours," pages 26 to 30. In "My Face," Tess describes the meticulous detail of her morning routine that puts her in conflict with her stepfather. In "Yours," she describes Zoe's naturally beautiful face.
5. "Z," pages 195 to 196, beginning "Remember how I said . . ." and ending with the chapter. Tess reflects on how love helps people cope with change.

Booktalk

Sixteen-year-old Tess lives in a great house with loving parents and two sisters. Then things change. Her little sister dies, the one Tess was supposed to be watching. No one blames Tess. Maybe that is part of the problem. She knows they know how it happened and when—exactly the day the Twin Towers went down in New York—September 11, 2001. The day Tess was distracted by big and terrible news. The silence builds. Tess can't stand it. This family doesn't seem like hers anymore, or anyone else's. So she goes to live with her real father, the one her mother married at nineteen and left shortly after Tess was born. No great house there. Dad doesn't seem to care where he lives. He is usually in a beer sleep or gone. The only one from her own family she wants to go back and see is her sister Em, but Tess can still visit her at school. Then Tess meets Jimmy Freeze. He lives next door. Don't let the name fool you. Jimmy is the hottest item on the block. He gives her plenty to do when Dad isn't looking, and it's nothing any parent, even her laid-back dad, would want for her. But Tess knows that this is her life, and if her sister is any example, she may not have long to live it. She has to think it all through. Maybe she'll just tell all her thoughts and feelings to her dead three-year-old sister. No one else wants to listen. And maybe she'll start, *Dear Zoe*.

Learning Opportunities

1. Tess believes her mother fears that Tess will repeat the mother's mistakes and marry too young and for the wrong reasons. After reading the story, do you agree?
2. Discuss the role of make-up and the roller coaster in the story.
3. Discuss how Tess changes by the end of the story.
4. Cite the instances of loss and near loss and examine how each supports the writer's purpose.
5. Using your library's resources, find out as much as you can about the grief process. Share your information with the group.

Related Works

1. Frank, Hillary. **Better Than Running at Night.** New York: Houghton Mifflin Company, 2002. 263p. $17.00. ISBN 0 618 10439 9. [fiction] JS Eighteen-year-old Ladybug (Ellie) Yelinsky frees herself of men who offer her negative and destructive life choices.
2. Holt, Kimberly Willis. **Keeper of the Night.** New York: Henry Holt and Company, 2003. 308p. $16.95. ISBN 0 8050 6361 7. [fiction] MJS (See full booktalk in *Teen Genre Connections*, 2005, pages 278 to 280.) Thirteen-year-old Isabel tries to protect her family from their grief after her mother's suicide, but the overwrought family must learn to face their problems.
3. Pearson, Mary E. **A Room on Lorelei Street.** New York: Henry Holt and Company, 2005. 266p. $16.95. 0 8050 7667 0. [fiction] JS Zoe Buckman eventually decides to free herself of her destructive family and bad choices after she prostitutes herself for rent money.
4. Walker, Pamela. **Pray Hard.** New York: Scholastic, 2001. 176p. $15.95. ISBN 0 439 21586 2. [fiction] MJ Twelve-year-old Amelia believes the popper toy she put in her father's plan caused his death.
5. Woodson, Jacqueline. **Miracle's Boys.** New York: G. P. Putnam's Sons, 2000.131p. $15.99. ISBN 0 399 23113 7. [fiction] MJS (See full booktalk in *Teen Genre Connections*, 2005, pages 28 to 30.) Three brothers deal with the guilt of their mother's death in both constructive and destructive ways.

☙❧

Blackman, Malorie. Naughts & Crosses.

New York: Simon & Schuster Books for Young Readers, 2005. 387p. $15.95.
ISBN 1 4169 0016 0. [fiction] JS

Themes/Topics: love, racism, prejudice, conduct of life, terrorism

Summary/Description

Sephy Hadley, a dark-skinned cross, and Callum McGregor, a light-skinned naught, become friends when Callum's mother does domestic work for the Hadleys. After Mrs. McGregor loses her job, Sephy and Callum maintain contact, and Sephy tutors him for the entrance exams to a previously all-cross school. Sephy's father is a high government official. Callum's older brother and father, like other naughts, hold low-level jobs and work for a terrorist group. Callum encounters prejudice at school, and Sephy is beaten up and ostracized because of their friendship. Callum's father and brother help plant a bomb in a local shopping center. The father is arrested and tried. Sephy's mother anonymously hires a famous trial lawyer who gets Mr. McGregor a life sentence rather than a death sentence, but Mr. McGregor dies of electrocution while supposedly trying to escape prison. Bitter against all crosses, Callum joins the terrorists. Eventually, he is assigned to kidnap Sephy, and discovers that he still loves her. They make love, and he helps her escape. Sephy discovers that she is pregnant. When Callum is captured, her father offers to save Callum's life if Sephy agrees to destroy the baby. Sephy refuses. Callum hangs, and their baby girl, Callie Rose McGregor, is born after his death. The story is told by Sephy and Callum in alternating chapters.

Read Aloud/Reader Response

1. Chapter 7, pages 47 to 48, beginning "It's just a word, . . . " and ending " . . . of his or her armpit." When Sephy uses the word *blanker,* a slang insult for naught, she learns that emotional hurt might be greater than physical hurt.
2. Chapter 14, page 66, beginning "I was trying . . . " and ending "But why?" Callum reflects on cross/naught classifications.
3. Chapter 28, page 112, beginning "I put down . . . " and ending with the chapter. After Callum is invited to Sephy's birthday party, he begins to think that she considers him a political symbol rather than a person about whom she cares.
4. Chapter 38, pages 143 to 144, beginning "Dear Callum," and ending "Lynette." Lynette explains that she commits suicide because, as a naught, she will never be good enough.
5. Chapter 83, pages 274 to 275. Sephy writes a letter to God in which she wonders who is responsible for hatred.

6.   Chapter 94, page 310, beginning *"Be what . . . and ending " . . . what you are."* Callum tries to overcome his feelings for Sehpy.

Booktalk

Show large pictures of zeroes and crosses. Ask what the group associates with these images.

Naughts & Crosses, zeroes and pluses. These symbols make us think of games or math problems. Where Callum McGregor and Sephy Hadley live, these symbols stand for races. The games and the problems are deadly serious. Callum is a naught. He is light skinned. Sephy is a cross. She has a beautiful dark skin. More color is a plus. No color means a zero life. Callum's mother works for Sephy's family, the rich and powerful Hadleys. Callum and Sephy grow up together in the Hadley house. They think they are friends. But *Naughts & Crosses* can't be friends. *Naughts & Crosses* feel fear and hate for one another, but seldom friendship and never love. The crosses want to keep the naughts down. The naughts want to blow up the crosses. Callum and Sephy would just like to be together, but that wish is against the rules. Can this couple let society think they are playing the game, without going to their graves? Maybe, if they can look at each other and see Callum and Sephy instead of what others want them to see—*Naughts & Crosses*.

Learning Opportunities

1.   Skin color is the basis of prejudice in the book. Using your library's resources, research characteristics of racial prejudice. Share your information with the group.

2.   Which family, the Hadleys or the McGregors, suffer more as a result of prejudice?

3.   Describe the response of each McGregor family member to prejudice.

4.   Do you agree with Sephy's decision to keep the baby and let Callum die?

5.   How is Mr. Jason, a biracial person, important to the story?

Related Works

1.   Adlington, L. J. **The Diary of Pelly D.** [fiction] JS (See full booktalk in "Fantasy/Science Fiction/Paranormal"/ "Meeting the Challenges of the Future," pages 178 to 181.). A worker finds the diary of a privileged young woman who was shunned, betrayed by the boy she loves, and exterminated because of her genetic make-up.

2.   Jordan, Sherryl. **The Raging Quiet.** New York: Simon & Schuster, 1999. 226p. $17.00. ISBN 0 689 82140 9.[fiction] JS (See full

booktalk in *Booktalks and More,* 2003, pages 15 to 17.) Marnie and Raven fall in love in spite of the prejudices and taboos of their community.

3. Lester, Julius. **Time's Memory.** New York: Farrar, Straus and Giroux, 2006. 230p. $17.00. ISBN 0 374 37178 4. [fiction] JS Nathanial, the slave, and Ellen, the slave owner's daughter, cannot express their love until they are re-incarnated.
4. Spiegler, Louise. **The Amethyst Road.** New York: Clarion Books, 2005. 328p. $16.00. ISBN 0 618 38572 4. [fiction] MJ A young girl living in a prejudiced society finds love and self-respect as she works to bring her family together.
5. Woodson, Jacqueline. **If You Come Softly.** New York: G. P. Putnam's Sons, 1998. 181p. $15.99. ISBN 0 399 23112 9. [fiction] JS Jeremiah and Ellie decide to date even though they know they will encounter resistance and condemnation. At the end of the novel, Jeremiah is shot and killed.

Flake, Sharon G. Who Am I without Him?: Short Stories about Girls and the Boys in Their Lives.
New York: Hyperion Books for Children/Jump at the Sun, 2004. 168p. $15.99. ISBN 078680693 1. [fiction, short stories] JS

Themes/Topics: fathers/daughters, boyfriends, self-esteem, conduct of life

Summary/Description

Ten short stories explore the female/male relationship. In "So I Ain't No Good Girl," a girl demeans herself to hold on to a good-looking, exploitive boyfriend. "The Ugly One" has disfiguring bumps on her face and lives a romantic fantasy. "Wanted: A Thug" involves the risk of taking a juvenile delinquent boyfriend away from a good friend. In "I Know a Stupid Boy When I See One," the main character uses her attraction and her unborn baby to exploit a mentally challenged boy who strangles her when he discovers that she sold her baby. "Mookie in Love" tells about a girl finding a male focus for a female-dominated family so that she can date the only male offspring. "Don't Be Disrespecting Me" illustrates that stealing to look good will get a person in jail instead of the prom. In "I Like White Boys," a scholarship student in a predominantly white school feels attracted to white boys instead of the black boys. High school students in "Jacob's Rules" learn the difference between lust and love. The girls of the Calvary Church of God's Blessed Example discover that "Hunting for Boys" may involve taking on the boys' would-be girlfriends. A father, in "A Letter to My Daughter," encourages the daughter he abandoned to avoid choosing a boy like him.

Read Aloud/Reader Response

1. "So I Ain't No Good Girl," pages 4 and 5, beginning "I give in." and ending "That's all that counts right?" The narrator accepts an abusive relationship.
2. "The Ugly One," pages 10 to 14, beginning with the chapter and ending " . . . run just as fast as I can." Asia Calloway describes her appearance and the bullying she experiences because of it.
3. "Jacob's Rules," page 109, beginning "Jonathan taps . . . " and ending " . . . not fitting and stuff." A boy tries to characterize the problems girls have with boys.
4. "Hunting for Boys," pages 136 to 137, beginning "My friends and I . . . " and ending " . . . tired of missing out." The narrator explains the strict situation the girls are in, as well as how and why they want to break out of it.
5. "A Letter to My Daughter," pages 157 to 168. A father who abandoned his daughter writes a letter to her and explains how she should respect herself.

Booktalk

Ask the group if they think that boys or girls are more difficult in a dating situation.

In these short stories, Sharon G. Flake kind of answers that question. Most of her characters are girls. She includes stories about girls who will do anything to keep a boyfriend happy, girls who are looking for a boyfriend, and girls who have fantasy boyfriends. She even lets a father explain why his daughter shouldn't choose a boyfriend like him. It seems like finding someone to date is as difficult as finding a good friend. But all these stories kind of suggest that the whole process might be smoother if girls would ask themselves one not-so-simple question, *Who Am I without Him?*

Learning Opportunities

1. Write a short story that answers the question "Who am I without her?"
2. Using your library's resources, find self-help books about boy/girl relationships. Share the information that you find with the class.

3. Using the information from Learning Opportunity 2, discuss what advice applies to each story.
4. Choose your favorite story from the collection. Explain why it is your favorite.
5. Discuss the order in which the stories are placed. Would you have chosen the same order? Why or why not?

Related Works

1. Dessen, Sarah. **Dreamland.** New York: Viking Press, 2000. 250p. $15.99. ISBN 0 670 89122 3. [fiction] JS (See full booktalk in *Booktalks and More*, 2003, pages 73 to 75.) To assert her identity, Caitlin O'Koren dates a brilliant boy who manipulates and abuses her until she discovers her own value as a person.
2. Flake, Sharon G. **Begging for Change.** New York: Hyperion Books for Children/Jump at the Sun, 2003. 235p. $15.99. ISBN 0 786 80601 X. [fiction] MJS (See full booktalk in *Teen Genre Connections*, 2005, pages 286 to 289.) Raspberry Hill deals with stealing, becomes a couple with Sato, and realizes her own mother's mistake in choosing her father.
3. McDonald, Janet. **Chill Wind.** New York: Farrar, Straus and Giroux/Frances Foster Books, 2002. 134p. $16.00. ISBN 0 374 39958 1 [fiction] MJS In this sequel to *Spellbound,* nineteen-year-old Aisha, single mother of two, is more focused on boyfriends and welfare payments than on her personal skills.
4. McDonald, Janet. **Spellbound.** New York: Farrar, Straus and Giroux/Frances Foster Books, 2001. 138p. $16.00. ISBN 0 374 37140 7. [fiction] MJS Raven Jefferson faces the responsibility of her pregnancy and developing her own life.
5. Myers, Walter Dean. **145th Street: Short Stories.** New York: Delacorte Press, 2000. 151p. $15.95. ISBN 0 385 32137 6. [fiction] JS (See full booktalk in *Booktalks and More*, 2003, pages 91 to 93.) In ten short stories, Myers portrays tragedy, frustration, achievement, and compassion on 145th Street.

꧁꧂

Frost, Helen. Keesha's House.

New York: Farrar, Straus and Giroux/Frances Foster Books, 2003. 116p. $16.00.
ISBN 0 374 34064 1. [poetry] JS

Themes/Topics: homelessness, unwanted pregnancy, foster care, alcoholism, homosexuality

Summary/Description

Joe, accepted into this house when he was twelve by a lady named Aunt Annie, now offers refuge to troubled teens. Keesha left her alcoholic father's home, moved in with Joe, and encourages others to join her. Each resident expresses fears and concerns in either sestinas or sonnets. The forms are explained in "Notes on the Forms" at the end of the book. Stephanie and Jason struggle with unwanted pregnancy. Dontay suffers in foster care while his parents are in jail. Carmen, raised by her grandmother, is arrested for DUI and waits for a judge to hear her case. Harris is disowned by his family for being gay. Katie escapes her abusive stepfather through school and work.

Read Aloud/Reader Response

This book lends itself to a complete dramatic reading, each part being a separate act. Five passages that may draw further reflection are listed below.

1. Part I, "That one word," pages 12 and 13. Harris recounts telling his parents he is gay.
2. Part II, "Some little thing," pages 10 and 11. Carmen explains her arrest.
3. Part II, "Questions about Joe," pages 22 to 23. Keesha explains her position in the house.
4. Part II, "Look around and wonder," pages 28 to 29. Harris reflects on labels.
5. Part IV, "Across whatever secret," pages 44 to 45. Stephie looks at a single mother's future.

Booktalk

Seven teenagers don't have much in common except trouble. They find *Keesha's House*. Keesha doesn't own the house. It belongs to Joe, a man who grew up with trouble too. That's why he shares his house with down-on-their luck young people. That's why he understands Keesha inviting more and more people to live there. Some just visit. Others stay a little while, and a few make it home. They discover that a house can protect a person from rain, wind, and snow. But a house can't shelter anyone from life storms like drinking, unwanted pregnancy, abuse, and abandonment. Only families can give a little shelter from those storms. Listen to the voices trying to build one in *Keesha's House*.

Learning Opportunities

1. Consider each of the eight parts as acts in a play. Recruit members of the group to read out loud the poems within the parts.

2. Discuss the relationship of each part's title to the purpose of the part.
3. Write one more sonnet and one more sestina for one of the characters.
4. Both *Keesha's House* and *A Face in Every Window* (Related Work 5) deal with blended families. Read both novels and compare them.
5. Using your library's resources, continue to research poetic forms. You may wish to start with *How to Write Poetry* (Related Work 2). Then create a fictional character of your own to tell his or her story through poetic forms that you choose.

Related Works

1. Frost, Helen. **The Braid.** New York: Farrar, Straus and Giroux/ Frances Foster Books, 2006. 95p. $16.00. ISBN 0 374 30962 0. [historical fiction, poetry] JS Jeannie and Sarah, two sisters, tell their stories in alternating narrative poems. Jeannie leaves Scotland with her family during the nineteenth-century Highland Clearances. Sarah hides so that she can remain in Scotland with her grandmother. Frost emphasizes the inter-relationship of their lives through a braided poetic form that mimics Celtic knots. She explains the structure on pages 91 and 92.
2. Janeczko, Paul B. **How to Write Poetry.** New York: Scholastic, 1999. 117p. (Scholastic Guides). $12.95. ISBN 0 590 10077 7. (See full booktalk in *Booktalks Plus*, 2001, pages 215 to 217.) Janeczko explains the poetry-writing process, from gathering the ideas and words to sharing finished poems.
3. Muharrar, Aisha. Elizabeth Verdick (ed.). **More Than a Label: Why What You Wear or Who You're With Doesn't Define Who You Are.** Minneapolis, MN: Free Spirit Publishing Inc., 2002. 144p. $13.95. ISBN 1 57542 110 0. [nonfiction] JS Written when the author was seventeen, the book talks about the effects of high school labels.
4. Myers, Walter Dean. **The Beast.** New York: Scholastic Press, 2003. 176p. $16.95. ISBN 0 439 36841 3. [fiction] JS A senior at an exclusive prep school returns to his Harlem home and discovers that his girlfriend is a drug addict.
5. Nolan, Han. **A Face in Every Window.** New York: Harcourt Brace and Company, 1999. 264p. $16.00. ISBN 0 15 201915 4. [fiction] JS (See full booktalk in *Booktalks and More*, 2003, pages 17 to 19.) James Patrick O'Brian adjusts to a blended family of troubled strangers his mother invites to live with them.

6. Pearson, Mary E. **A Room on Lorelei Street.** New York: Henry Holt and Co., 2005. 266p. $16.95. ISBN 0 8050 7667 0. [fiction] JS Zoe Buckman leaves her dysfunctional and manipulative family, rents a room from a positive, eccentric old woman, but seeks another home when she prostitutes herself to pay rent.

CG'EO

Johnson, Angela. The First Part Last.
New York: Simon & Schuster Books for Young Readers, 2003. 131p. $15.95. ISBN 0 689 84922 2. [fiction] JS

Themes/Topics: teenage father, family, responsibility, manhood

Summary/Description
In four parts, Bobby tells about his journey to fatherhood with "then" (before the baby) and "now" (with his new daughter) chapters. After the baby's mother, Nia, slips into an irreversible coma, Bobby keeps his daughter even though the couple agreed to put her up for adoption. Both sets of grandparents oppose his decision. Bobby's divorced mother does little to support him. Exhausted and discouraged, Bobby struggles to meet his obligations. He moves in with his father briefly but eventually moves to a small Ohio town where his older, understanding brother lives with his own two children.

Read Aloud/Reader Response
1. Part I, "now," pages 3 to 4. Bobby realizes how reassuring his own mother's presence was for him.
2. Part I, "now," pages 14 to 17. The rules and the list reveal Bobby's difficult life.
3. Part II, "now," pages 32 to 35. Bobby confronts caring for a sick baby.
4. Part III, "now," pages 80 to 81. Bobby feels old.
5. Part IV, "now," pages 116 to 118. Bobby tells his baby about Nia, her mother.

Booktalk
Bobby hopes to graduate from high school this year. He won't be the typical graduate though. Bobby is living in two worlds. One world is a teenager's world. His mother and father pay most of his expenses. He goes to class, but sometimes cuts class. He likes to hang with his friends. He is protected. The other world is an adult world. On his sixteenth

birthday, Bobby found out that he was going to be a father. Now he takes care of his new daughter, Feather, 24/7. The crying baby, the sick baby, is all his. His mother isn't helping. She already raised three sons and has her own career. His friends come over, but hanging on corners or going out for a ballgame—that part of life, that first part, is finished. Bobby's world is backward and mixed up. And he knows that he made it that way. He thinks that nature got it all wrong. According to Bobby, people should start out with the wisdom and work backward—to babyhood. Maybe life wouldn't be such a mess if we could all just live *The First Part Last.*

Learning Opportunities

1. How does Johnson's organization support her purpose?
2. List all the parents in the story. Discuss the role each plays.
3. Using your library's resources, research a father's responsibility and rights.
4. Discuss the significance of the title.
5. After reading both *The First Part Last* and *Hanging on to Max* (Related Work 1), compare the decisions.

Related Works

1. Bechard, Margaret. **Hanging on to Max.** Brookfield, CT: Roaring Brook Press, 2002. 142p. $15.95. ISBN 0 7613 1579 9. [fiction] JS Spending his senior year taking care of his new son, Sam Pettigrew decides his baby needs a stable family.
2. Gantos, Jack. **Hole in My Life.** New York: Farrar, Straus and Giroux, 2002. 200p. $16.00. ISBN 0 374 39988 3. [nonfiction] JS. (See full booktalk in *Teen Genre Connections*, 2005, pages 1 to 3.) Gantos explains how deciding to deal in drugs in his teens sent him to jail and changed his life.
3. Haruf, Kent. **Plainsong.** New York: Alfred A. Knopf, 1999. 320p. $27.50. ISBN 0 375 40618 2. [fiction] S/A A young girl decides to raise her baby with the support of an odd combination of adults.
4. Rottman, S. L. **Stetson.** New York: Viking Press, 2002. 192p. $16.99. ISBN 0 670 03542 4. [fiction] JS (See full booktalk in *Teen Genre Connections*, 2005, pages 23 to 25.) A young man takes responsibility for himself and a sister whom he never knew existed.
5. Sparks, Beatrice (ed.). **Annie's Baby: The Diary of Anonymous, A Pregnant Teenager.** New York: Avon Books, 1998. 245p. $4.50pa. ISBN 0 380 79141 2. [fiction] JS Fourteen-year-old Annie, pregnant by an abusive boyfriend, decides to give up her baby for adoption.

Living on the Edge

ೞೞ

Flinn, Alex. Nothing to Lose.

New York: HarperCollins Publishers/Harper Tempest, 2004. 277p. $16.89.
ISBN 0 06 051751 4. [fiction] JS

Themes/Topics: runaways, wife abuse, murder,
mother and sons, trials, Florida

Summary/Description

Seventeen-year-old Michael Days runs away with a carnival after
killing his stepfather. When Michael returns to Miami, his mother
is on trial for the murder. With the help of his childhood friend, Julian
Karpe and Julian's attorney stepmother, Michael confesses. The book is
organized in alternating "This Year," "Last Year" chapters that explain
the abuse, the mother's victim behavior, and Michael's relationship with
an independent older girl who teaches him about personal responsibility. Ironically, Michael's decisions inspire the girl to return to her own
dysfunctional family. The mother is released, and the killing is ruled a
justifiable homicide. Michael goes free, but mother and son need new
individual lives and a new relationship with each other.

Read Aloud/Reader Response

1. "Last Year," pages 112 to 116, beginning, "The rest of the morning . . . " and ending " . . . to the fair." Michael is changing, in part
   because of the persistent Karpe.
2. "This Year," page 121, *"Am I innocent? Am I really?"* Michael's
   question suggests his involvement, and raises questions about the
   meaning of innocent.
3. "Last Year," page 132, beginning "The marks . . . " and ending " . . .
   of their own eyes." Cricket describes the town people seeing carnies
   as untouchables while ignoring their own problems.
4. "Last Year," pages 137 to 139, beginning "She took me . . . " to
   " . . . nothing to lose!" Kirstie explains the advantages of a "nothing
   to lose" life.
5. "Last Year," page 154. " . . . sometimes you have to help yourself
   because that's the only one you can help." Kirstie justifies not getting involved.
6. "Three Hours Later," pages 270 to 272. Angela and Michael talk
   about what comes next and abuse's lingering effects.

Booktalk

Seventeen-year-old Michael Daye looks like a carnie. He is. But his name isn't Michael Daye anymore. It's Robert Frost. A year ago this carnie was a star athlete who lived in an expensive Miami, Florida, house with his beautiful mother and a rich stepfather who beat up Michael's mother whenever the mood hit him. Michael decided to get out and join the carnival. Now he is back in Miami, and his mother's picture is in the newspaper for killing Michael's stepfather. She is claiming self-defense and spousal abuse. But because her story doesn't quite add up, lots of people think she is a gold-digging trophy wife. Michael knows differently. Should he go to court and tell them about life with Dad? Should he move on before someone recognizes him? Or should he make another choice? A more dangerous one—one that could leave him and his mother with absolutely *Nothing to Lose.*

Learning Opportunities

1. Michael's stepfather is obviously abusive. Is Michael's mother abusive also?
2. Julian Karpe is a significant character in the novel. Why?
3. Kristie is a love interest. What other reasons might Flinn have for including her?
4. "Destiny" and free will are significant elements in the novel. On pages 111 and 112, Michael applies those concepts to his reading of *The Great Gatsby* (See Related Work 1). After reading Michael's comments on Gatsby, discuss how they apply to *Nothing to Lose.*
5. Using your library's resources, find out the effects of domestic violence and how it can be prevented. Share the information you find with the group.

Related Works

1. Fitzgerald, F. Scott. **The Great Gatsby.** New York: Scribner Paperback Fiction, 1995. 240p. $12.00pa. ISBN 0 684 80152 3. [classic fiction] S/A First published in 1925, the novel tells about the mysterious Gatsby who loves the elusive, upper-class Daisy.
2. Flinn, Alex. **Fade to Black.** New York: Harper Tempest, 2005. 192p. $16.99. ISBN 0 06 05 6839 9. [fiction] JS A young man attacked because he is HIV-positive decides whether to clear his enemy falsely accused of the attack.
3. Hobbs, Valerie. **Letting Go of Bobby James, or How I Found My Self of Steam.** [fiction] JS (See full booktalk in "Contemporary"/ "Finding Our Talents and Friends," pages 50 to 52.) A young teenager leaves her abusive husband and finds a bigger, safer world.

4. Klass, David. **You Don't Know Me.** New York: Farrar, Straus and Giroux/ Frances Foster Books, 2001. 262p. $17.00. ISBN 0 374 38706 0. [fiction] JS (See full booktalk in *Booktalks and More,* 2003, pages 31 to 33.) Fourteen-year-old John lives with his mother and her boyfriend, who secretly abuses and degrades him.

5. Oates, Joyce Carol. **Freaky Green Eyes.** New York: Harper Tempest, 2003. 341p. $17.89. ISBN 0 06 623757 2. [fiction] MJS (See full booktalk in *Teen Genre Connections,* 2005, pages 140 to 142.) Fourteen-year-old Franky (Francesca) Pierson is the daughter of a famous sports announcer who abuses and kills her mother.

ඟ

Leavitt, Martine. Heck Superhero.

Asheville, NC: Front Street, 2004. 144p. $16.95. ISBN 1 886910 94 4. [fiction] MJ

Themes/Topics: abandoned children, comics, mental illness, art, friendship, Canada

Summary/Description

Thirteen-year-old Heck, abandoned by his depression-prone mother, searches for her while surviving on the street and dealing with the pain of a badly infected tooth. He copes by moving back and forth between real and comic book worlds. Heck sees himself in a pre-super-hero state and perceives his mother as trapped in hypertime. He believes that doing Good Deeds for others, instead of asking for help from people he trusts, will solve his problems. A talented artist, he wants to retrieve his portfolio and art assignment from the apartment from which he and his mother have been evicted. He knows that Mr. Bandras, his art teacher, believes in him and wants him to succeed. In his encounters with street life, Heck steals from his friend and takes drugs. He befriends and protects eighteen-year-old mentally ill Marion Ewald who believes that Heck can free the spores that Marion talks to. Not able to fulfill his superhero promise, Heck paints Marion's portrait instead. Marion jumps off a building to free the spores and dies. Heck, trying to explain the situation to the police, passes out. At the hospital, he finds his mother being treated for mental problems. He realizes that they must ask for help to solve their own problems in the real world or be lost, like Marion, in a fantasy.

Read Aloud/Reader Response

1. "Monday, May 2," pages 9 to 10, beginning with the chapter and ending "He just didn't want to know." The passage establishes how Heck's situation developed from avoidance and denial.

2. "Tuesday, May 3," page 51, beginning "It works . . . " and ending
    " . . . couldn't see them anymore." Heck examines his "Theory
    of Everything" that tells him Good Deeds will change a person's
    reality.
3. "Wednesday, May 4," pages 80 to 81, beginning "I'm afraid . . . " and
    ending " . . . speak anyway." Heck, turned down for a steady gallery
    job, realizes he is considered a charity case.
4. "Thursday, May 5," page 123, beginning "Maybe the . . . " and
    ending " . . . has to be today." Heck distinguishes between fantasy
    and reality. Marion does not.
5. "Friday, May 6," pages 139 to 141, beginning "Looking in her
    eyes . . . " and ending " . . . the one they were in." Heck confronts
    his mother about needing help and living in the real world.

Booktalk

Heck is an eighth-grade superhero. Actually he is kind of a superhero
in training. He doesn't have his costumes or muscles yet. Right now he
is still just the stick man on the page. But Heck believes in the "Theory
of Everything," Good Deeds rule. No matter how much trouble comes
to a superhero or superhero in training, his Good Deeds will eventually
save him. And does Heck ever have trouble. His mother is gone. He's
out on the street because the rent is overdue. His tooth is one screaming
pain, and his stomach is a gaping monster that keeps repeating, "Feed
me." Heck just stole twenty dollars from his best friend, and the landlord won't let him have his art project—due Friday. The bad forces are
winning this round. Good Deeds are going down for the count, but then
KA-POW—enter *Heck Superhero.*

Learning Opportunities

1. Spencer, Mr. Bandras, and Marion Ewald are central to the story.
    Why?
2. Do you agree with Heck's Good Deeds theory?
3. Is Heck a "superkid"?
4. Should Heck stay with his mother?
5. Using your library's resources, learn more about Will Eisner or
    another graphic artist and author. Share your information with the
    group. (See Related Work 1)

Related Works

1. Greenberger, Robert. **Will Eisner**. New York: The Rosen
    Publishing Group, 2005. 112p. (The Library of Graphic Novelists)
    $31.95. ISBN 1 4042 0286 2. [nonfiction] JS In examining
    Eisner's career, this professional biography also explores the

history of the graphic novel, which Eisner originated, shaped, and changed.

2. Hartnett, Sonya. **What the Birds See.** Cambridge, MA: Candlewick Press, 2002. 196p. $15.99. ISBN 0 7636 2092 0. [fiction] JS Surrounded by irresponsible adults, nine-year-old Adrian is drawn into a neighbor girl's tragic fantasy.

3. Lubar, David. **Flip.** New York: Tom Doherty Associates Books, 2003. 304p. $5.98pa. ISBN 0 765 34048 8. [fiction] MJ In this humorous exploration of heroism, twins Ryan and Taylor discover disks from another planet that allow them to take on identities of earth's heroes and bring them into conflict with the school bully and their father. The reader's guide includes a plot summary, author information, writing and research activities, and discussion questions.

4. Kupperberg, Paul. **The Creation of SPIDER-MAN.** New York: The Rosen Publishing Group, 2007. 48p. (Action Heroes). $29.25. ISBN 1 4042 0763 5. [nonfiction] MJ Spider-Man embodies the qualities of the modern superhero: a vulnerable, thoughtful person who receives the privilege and responsibility of superpowers, but who still deals with personal human problems. Other books in the series describe the creation of Captain America, the Fantastic Four, the Incredible Hulk, Iron Man, and the X-Men.

5. Munroe, Kevin. **Olympus Heights.** San Diego, CA: IDW Publishing, 2005. 149p. $19.99. ISBN 19238255 0. [graphic] JS/A Oliver Dobbs discovers that his secretive next-door neighbor is actually Zeus who requires Oliver's help in waging a battle against evil.

6. Walker, Virginia (text), and Katrina Roechelein (graphics). **Making Up Megaboy.** New York: DK Ink/Richard Jackson, 1998. 63p. $16.95. ISBN 0 7894 2488 6. [fiction] MJ (See full booktalk in *Booktalks Plus*, 2001, pages 82 to 84.) Robbie Jones, on his thirteenth birthday, acts on what he believes the superhero Megaboy would do and kills the elderly owner of a liquor store.

ℭℑ

Rapp, Adam. Timothy Basil Ering (illus.).
33 Snowfish.

Cambridge, MA: Candlewick Press, 2003. 179p. $15.99. ISBN 0 7636 1874 8. [fiction] S

Themes/Topics: homeless persons, sexual abuse, babies, friendship, drug-addiction, murder, pyromania, kidnapping

Summary/Description

Custis, who is about ten, runs from the law with Curl, a fifteen-year-old prostitute, and Boobie, a seventeen-year-old boy who murdered his parents and plans to sell his baby brother. Custis's life with his "owner," who used him for sex and pornographic films, drove him to join Curl and Boobie. As the trio runs and hides from the law, Curl deteriorates from addiction. After her death, Boobie, a pyromaniac and pedophile, attempts suicide and leaves their broken-down van, their hide-out. While trying to save Curl's life, Custis encounters Seldom, a black man with a small farm, who forces Custis to clean up the yard after Custis tries to steal Seldom's chicken. Seldom then discovers Custis and the baby alone in the van, takes them in, and offers them a new life that Custis struggles to understand and accept.

Read Aloud/Reader Response

1. "The Skylark," "Custis," pages 7 to 9, beginning "Curl thinks . . ." and ending " . . . started owning me." Custis explains how Bob Motley began owning him.
2. "The otel Motel," "Custis," pages 65 to 73, beginning "Whatchu doin' in here, Bruce Maloney?" and ending with the chapter. Custis encounters a boy in the motel room. Boobie intends to molest him, but Custis releases him. Custis's motivation would be an interesting discussion topic.
3. "The Van," "Custis," pages 97, beginning "All Earth's got . . . " and ending " . . . light up and shit." Custis reflects on why outer space would be better than earth.
4. "The Van," "Custis," page 116, "Once we reached the Skylark . . . " to " . . . didn't seem right without Curl." Custis describes the mood after Curl's death.
5. "The Itty Bitty Farm." "Custis," pages 152 to 154, beginning "You a character." to the end of the chapter. Custis finds support in Seldom.

Booktalk

Custis is about ten. Bob Motley owns him. Well, Bob Motley owns him until Custis learns that Bob is going to put him in another one of his homemade films. Only this time, the film is going to be a snuff film. Custis doesn't want to disappear like the boys that Bob Motley's friends own, so Custis decides to skate. If Bob Motley finds him, he'll cut off Custis's hands—for real. Custis finds himself a ride with Darrin Flowers A.K.A Reggie, A.K.A. Boobie, and the beautiful Curl. She can finance their trip with all those wealthy men who want her company. Their trip, though, isn't the most pleasant. Boobie killed his parents. The police are looking for him. Custis's job is to watch for pig cars—marked or unmarked. Their ace in the hole is a baby. When Boobie killed his parents, he took his little brother. Now they can sell him for maybe five-hundred dollars. With that money, they will be set. But Curl just can't leave the drugs alone. The baby cries, and Boobie keeps acting stranger and stranger. When Custis gets stressed, he does the thirty-threes. Some nun told him that counting to thirty-three would calm him down and keep him out of trouble. He is doing a bunch of thirty-threes now. The weather is getting colder. It's scary, but Custis lives scared all the time. So Custis will try to count thirty-three *something*, even if that something is as unreal as *33 Snowfish*.

Learning Opportunities

1. Explain how each setting aids the author's purpose.
2. Discuss how the title applies to the story.
3. Using your library's resources, continue to research drug abuse. Share the information with the group. Discuss how that information adds to your understanding of the novel.
4. Using your library's resources, continue to research sexually trans-mitted diseases. Share the information with the group. Discuss how that information adds to your understanding of the novel.
5. Describe Custis. Use specific references from the novel. Is he a reliable narrator?
6. Artwork appears throughout the novel. Examine the pictures away from the text. Discuss their function.
7. The song "Hushabye Mountain" is a central allusion in the novel. Discuss its importance.

Related Works

1. Burgess, Melvin. **Smack.** New York: Henry Holt and Company, 1998. 327p. $16.95. ISBN 0 8050 5801. [fiction] JS Set in the 1980s, the novel describes the lives of teenage heroin addicts who have formed kind of a family.
2. Clarke, Judith. **The Lost Day.** New York: Henry Holt and Company, 1997. 154p. $16.95. ISBN 0 8050 6152 5. [fiction] S Nineteen-year-old Vinny mysteriously disappears during an evening of nightclubbing and ends up drugged and molested.
3. Curran, Christian Perdan. **Sexually Transmitted Diseases.** Berkeley Heights, NJ: Enslow Publishers, 1998. 128p. (Diseases and People). $18.95. ISBN 0 7660 1050 3. [nonfiction] MJS The book defines STDs and explains their escalation.

4. Myers, Walter Dean. **The Beast.** New York: Scholastic Press, 2003. 176p. $16.95. ISBN 0 439 36841 3. [fiction] JS A senior in an exclusive prep school returns to his old neighborhood and realizes how fragile lives are when trapped in crime, addiction, poverty, and despair.

5. Nolan, Han. **Born Blue.** New York: Harcourt Brace and Company, 2001. 177p. $17.00. ISBN 0 15 201916 2. [fiction] JS (See full booktalk in *Teen Genre Connections*, 2005, pages 13 to 15.) Born to a heroin addict, Janie grows up in foster care and pursues a destructive life pattern, but decides to leave her own baby with a stable family.

ৎৡৡ৾

Waltman, Kevin. **Learning the Game.**
New York: Scholastic Press, 2005. 224p. $16.95. ISBN 0 439 73109 7. [fiction] JS

Themes/Topics: loyalty, moral choices, peer pressure, hidden guilt, family, risk-taking

Summary/Description

Practicing for his senior season on the local court, Nate Gilman, whose family is one of the most affluent in town, helps the team rob a college fraternity. The team, dominated by a bully team member promising to fence the goods, swears secrecy. Throughout the story, Nate wrestles with the secret. His brother, who killed a young friend in a shooting accident five years before and is estranged from the family, pressures him to tell. Jackson, his friend and team member, who refused to participate, tells him to make a decision and live with it. Lorrie, his girlfriend, demands that he keep the secret to protect his image. Eventually, he confesses, sees his brother move on with his life, gains true friendship, and loses his girlfriend, but he resolves to live with the consequences of any decision he makes.

Read Aloud/Reader Response

1. Chapter 9, pages 99 to 101, beginning "The key is to keep my head down." And ending " . . . where I usually sit." Nate feels paranoid about the school's social stratification and pressure.

2. Chapter 9, page 110, beginning "It's just that . . . " and ending "I won't ever do that again." Jackson reacts to lying for the team.

3. Chapter 10, pages 115 to 122, beginning "I walk in the house . . . " and ending " . . . post-accident are forgeries." Nate reflects on the

relationship between a player's breakdown on the basketball court and the change in Marvin.

4. Chapter 11, pages 125 to 130, beginning with the chapter and ending " . . . away into the morning haze." Marvin tries to persuade Nate to confess.
5. Chapter 15, pages 194 and 195, beginning "I pat Saveen on . . . " and ending with the chapter. Nate realizes he lost the trust of the team, and Branson lost control of it.
6. Chapter 17, pages 208 to 217. Going to the opening game, Nate realizes the implications of his actions and the need to go on with his life.

Booktalk

Nate Gilman is almost a winner. He'll be a senior next year. He comes from one of the wealthiest families in town, and he has a great girl-friend. If he practices enough and gets the help of his good friend Jackson, he'll be a starter on the basketball team. In his small town of Cheneysburg, Indiana, it doesn't get any better than that. So, over the summer, he practices. But after one of those practices, the team decides to pull off a little robbery. After all, they all aren't rich. Nate joins in, to be one of the guys. Nate takes the code of silence, to be one of the guys. He thinks that if he follows the team rules, if he is one of the guys, they can keep the game going. But team's rules can be different than life's rules. And, as far as life's rules go, he has only started *Learning the Game*.

Learning Opportunities

1. Marvin, Jackson, and Lorrie present different views of life. Describe each one, and compare each one to your own.
2. What does each character teach Nate about himself?
3. Trey is a minor character with a major impact. Explain his role.
4. How does the small town setting affect the story?
5. Risk-taking is a major issue. Cite all the risks, and, when possible, their outcomes.
6. Using your library's resources, research positive and negative risk-taking.

Related Works

1. Coy, John. **Crackback.** New York: Scholastic Press, 2005. 208p. $16.99. ISBN 0 439 69733 6. [fiction] JS Pressured by his coach, teammates, and father to perform well in football, junior Miles Manning considers taking steroids.

2. Gantos, Jack. **Hole in My Life.** New York: Farrar, Straus and Giroux, 2002. 200p. $16.00. ISBN 0 374 39988 3. [nonfiction] JS (See full booktalk in *Teen Genre Connections*, 2005, pages 1 to 3.) Gantos tells about his decision, as a teenager, to transport drugs and the consequences that decision had for his life.
3. Klass, David. **Dark Angel.** New York: Farrar, Straus and Giroux/ Frances Foster Books, 2005. 320p. $17.00. ISBN 0 374 39950 6. [fiction] JS Seventeen-year-old Jeff may lose his family, friends, and home, when his older brother Troy, a convicted killer, returns from prison to supposedly build a new life.
4. McDonald, Joyce. **Swallowing Stones.** New York: Laurel-Leaf Books, 1997. 245p. $4.50. ISBN 0 440 22672 4. [fiction] JS (See full booktalk in *Booktalks and More*, 2003, pages 97 to 99.) Michael MacKenzie accidentally kills a man, and decides to take responsibility for his actions.
5. Wallace, Rich. **Playing without the Ball.** New York: Random House Books, 2002. 224p. $5.99pa. ISBN 978 0 440 22972 8. [fiction] S Seventeen-year-old Jay McLeod lives in a single room above Shorty's Bar and seeks stability in his life.

Finding Inner Peace or Spiritual Clarification

Albom, Mitch. The **Five People You Meet in Heaven.**

New York: Hyperion, 2003. 196p. $19.95. ISBN 0 7868 6871 6. [fiction] JS/A

Themes/Topics: accident victims, amusement parks, aging, death, heaven, after-life, love, interconnectedness

Summary/Description

Eighty-three-year-old Eddie dies saving a little girl's life during an amusement park accident. His journey to the after-life includes visits to five people: the Blue Man from the freak show, his World War II army Captain, the wife of the amusement park owner, Eddie's wife, and a little girl he didn't save from a fire set when he was an escaping prisoner of war. In these visits he learns that there are no random acts, sacrifice brings reward, letting go of anger allows one to move on, love lasts through memories, and responsibility and integrity bring redemption and salvation. The book includes the encounters, the lessons, and Eddie's birthdays that relate to them. The opening chapters set the scene and describe Eddie's character. In the last chapter, Eddie finds home with those he loves and discovers his life's meaning. The epilogue shows life moving on and explains the source of the accident.

Read Aloud/Reader Response

1. "The First Lesson," pages 47 to 50. The Blue Man illustrates that there are no random acts.
2. "The Second Lesson," pages 91 to 96. The Captain confesses that he shot Eddie in the leg to save him.
3. "The Third Lesson," pages 132 to 144. Ruby, the amusement park owner's wife, explains the importance of loyalty and letting go of anger.
4. "The Fourth Lesson," pages 172 to 178. Marguerite tells Eddie that although he lost his wife early in their married life, he still had her memory.
5. "The Last Lesson," pages 185 to 194. Tala, the girl Eddie burned while escaping the prisoner of war camp, reveals that she pulled him into heaven because he made up for the act so many times in his life by keeping the children safe.

Booktalk

Why are we alive? Do our lives mean anything? Do we ever make a difference? Is everybody bogged down by the same routine day in and day out? Maybe these are questions that all of us ask. Eddie, when he dies at eighty-three, finds the answers. He fought in World War II. He came home to work in a has-been amusement park where his father worked. He never made enough money to say to his wife before she died, "Go get anything you want." He never had any children. His brother was the one with the big job and condo. And he really didn't have that many friends. His companions were bitterness and regret. Then, finally, the day comes, that last day. A horrible accident at the park that already took most of his life kills him. He moves on, takes his final journey—the journey that might leave you a little curious about *The Five People You Meet in Heaven*.

Learning Opportunities

1. Continue to research the circumstances of World War II and the people who fought it. You might wish to start with Brokow's *The Greatest Generation* (Related Work 1).
2. Describe Eddie from the details that you learn about him.

3. Discuss the purpose of each person Eddie meets in heaven.
4. List the people that you would wish to see in heaven.
5. After reading the novel, write a definition of a successful life. Include examples that both illustrate and contradict your definition.

Related Works

1. Brokaw, Tom. **The Greatest Generation.** New York: Random House, 1998. 412p. $24.95. ISBN 0 375 50202 5. [nonfiction] S/A. Soldiers from World War II tell their wartime experiences and often include their joys and regrets.
2. Fraustino, Lisa Rowe (ed.). **Soul Searching: Thirteen Stories about Faith and Belief.** New York: Simon & Schuster Books for Young Readers, 2002. 267p. $17.95. ISBN 0 689 83484 5. [fiction] MJS The stories illustrate the great faith required in all cultures to face life's problems and responsibilities.
3. Greene, Bob. **Once Upon a Town: The Miracle of the North Platte Canteen.** New York: HarperCollins Publishers/William Morrow, 2002. 264p. $24.95. ISBN 0 06 008196 1. [nonfiction] S/A. Greene tells the story of the incredible World War II volunteer project that daily fed and heartened thousands of young soldiers. It reinforces the idea of "no random acts."
4. Rylant, Cynthia. **The Heavenly Village.** New York: The Blue Sky Press, 1999. 95p. $15.95. ISBN 0 439 04096 5. [fiction] MJS. (See full booktalk in *Booktalks Plus,* 2001, pages 52 to 54.) In this village between heaven and earth, homebodies complete unfinished business on earth.
5. Zevin, Gabrielle. **Elsewhere.** [fiction] MJS (See full booktalk in "Fantasy/Science Fiction/Paranormal"/"Meeting the Challenges of the Future," pages 188 to 190.) Fifteen-year-old Liz dies and discovers a new world and her true spirit in *Elsewhere.*

ᘓᘔ

Green, John. **Looking for Alaska.**

New York: Dutton Books, 2005. 224p. $15.99. ISBN 0 525 47506 0. [fiction] S

Themes/Topics: interpersonal relations, boarding schools, conduct of life, death, grieving

Summary/Description

Sixteen-year-old Miles Halter, bored and isolated in his local high school, attends his father's alma mater, Culver Creek, to seek what

François Rabelais described in his last words as "a Great Perhaps." At Culver, he finds a prank-filled dorm society focused on drugs, alcohol, sex, and cigarettes but also challenged by rigorous academics. Three students, the Colonel, Takumi, and Alaska, support and befriend him. Although the beautiful, brilliant, and emotionally damaged Alaska is dating someone else, he falls in love with her. Miles's favorite class is World Religions, and because famous last words fascinate him, he is drawn into the question of life after death. The first 133 pages before Alaska's fatal car crash relate the four students bonding around academic studies, drinking sessions, prank plans, and dating. The rest of the novel deals with the grief process after her death and the responsibility each boy feels for letting her drive drunk. The material and language require a mature audience.

Read Aloud/Reader Response

1. "one hundred thirty-six days before," page 5, beginning "Mom was not particularly . . . " and ending " . . . seeking a Great Perhaps." Miles explains to his parents why he is going to Culver Creek.
2. "one hundred twenty-six days before," page 32, beginning "This year, . . . " and ending " . . . might we best play it?" Doctor Hyde opens his first class.
3. "one hundred twenty-six days before," page 33, beginning "I learned that *myth* . . . " and ending " . . . hold sacred." Miles relates the meaning of myth.
4. "one hundred days before," pages 52 to 53, beginning "NOT TO ASK . . . " and ending " . . . just like I wanted to be." Alaska explains her name.
5. "two days before," pages 114 to 119, beginning "Everybody tells the story . . . " and ending " . . . without lifting her head from the hay." Each person tells the best and worst day in their lives. The friends discover Alaska's guilt over her mother.
6. "one hundred thirty-six days after," pages 219 to 221, beginning "Before I got here, . . . " and ending " . . . hope it's beautiful." Miles explains what he has learned.

Booktalk

Choose some famous last words either from the novel, a biography, or a reference. Read the words and/or their circumstances out loud. Discuss the group's reaction to the words themselves or the person who spoke them.

Miles Halter is sixteen and about the most invisible kid in his school. He keeps himself interested in life by learning famous last words like the ones we just talked about. When he decides to go to Culver Creek, a boarding school in Alabama, his going away party consists of two guests he barely knows and a mountain of avocado dip. So Miles is ready for something new, something that a famous dying poet described as the "Great Perhaps." And he finds it or at least starts looking for it. At Culver Creek, the work is hard and the dorm life is wild. The pranks run from funny to fatal. In fact, Miles comes close to getting killed his first night there. Cigarettes, liquor, and drugs are popular too, but the greatest "perhaps" at Culver Creek is a girl who is as different as her name—Alaska. She may be messed up, but she is so funny, smart, and sexy that Miles tends to forget about that first thing. He wants to be with her all the time, in every way. Learning about Alaska means learning about cigarettes, liquor, drugs, and some other things Alaska so easily teaches. But each time he thinks he knows Alaska, his illusions about her vanish in a "poof." And each time he starts over, the search, like those pranks, gets a little more dangerous. So he starts to wonder what his own famous last words will be, if he fails, if someone dies—*Looking for Alaska.*

Learning Opportunities

1. Using the library's resources, research the mythological meaning of the labyrinth. Discuss how that information impacts the story.
2. Miles focuses on biography and last words. Choose a biography that you might be interested in reading. Discuss what other aspects of the person's life you might highlight instead of the person's death or last words.
3. Note each mention of religion or any act or situation that seems religious or spiritual in the novel. Discuss what these specifics say about spiritual experience.
4. List each character and discuss what each contributes to the novel.
5. Alaska points out that what a person surrounds himself or herself with communicates that person's values. Explain yourself or someone whom you know in terms of what surrounds that person or what he or she possesses.

Related Works

1. Bronte, Emily. **Wuthering Heights.** New York: Bantam Books, 1983. 336p. $4.95pa. ISBN 0 553 21258 3. [classic fiction] S/A Originally published in 1847, this violent romance deals with the themes of social class, self-destruction, and the power of the after-life. Like *Looking for Alaska,* it includes a revealing "best day" conversation.

2. Earls, Nick. **48 Shades of Brown.** New York: Houghton Mifflin Company, 1999, 2004. 288p. $6.99pa. ISBN 0 618 45295 8. [fiction] S. (See full booktalk in *Teen Genre Connections,* 2005, pages 75 to 77.) Sixteen-year-old Dan, the narrator, tells about the year he comes of age by staying with his young and liberal Aunt Jacq.
3. Korman, Gordon. **Jake, Reinvented.** New York: Hyperion, 2003. 213p. $15.99. ISBN 0 786 81957 X. [fiction] JS Through Rick, the reader learns about Jake, a brainy, social outsider who manufactures a new persona to capture the cold, popular girl he adores. A high school version of *The Great Gatsby,* the story has parallels to *Looking for Alaska.*
4. Spinelli, Jerry. **Stargirl.** New York: Alfred A. Knopf, 2000. 186p. $15.95. ISBN 0 679 88637 0. [fiction] MJ (See full booktalk in *Booktalks and More,* pages 8 to10.) Leo Borlock recalls the mystical and mysterious tenth grader, Stargirl, who captivated, alienated, and hypnotized him and the rest of the student body.
5. Wallace, Rich. **Playing without the Ball.** New York: Alfred A. Knopf, 2002. 224p. $5.99pa. ISBN 978 0 440 22972 8. [fiction] S Seventeen-year-old Jay McLeod, deserted by his mother and father, lives in a single room above Shorty's Bar and tries to build stability in his life through basketball and girlfriends.

Koja, Kathe. **Buddha Boy.**

New York: Farrar, Straus and Giroux/Frances Foster Books, 2003. 117p. $16.00.
ISBN 0 374 30998 1. [fiction] MJS

Themes/Topics: conduct of life, peer pressure, artists, Buddhism, high schools, orphans

Summary/Description

Justin attends affluent Edward Rucher High School dominated by an outstanding student named McManus and his bullies. A new student named Jinsen, an obvious misfit, is their target. Jinsen wears old clothes, begs like a monk, and dares to outshine McManus in art class. McManus nicknames him Buddha Boy. Justin, who would like to stay out of any conflict, is assigned to work with Jinsen in a school project. Justin discovers that Jinsen, intelligent and talented, is an orphan living with and helping a great aunt. Even though the harassment escalates, Jinsen refuses to retaliate or report it. Finally, he reveals to Justin that he was also a bully. After his parents' death, therapy with a Buddhist art teacher changed his life. He fears that retaliation will reduce him to McManus's level. When Jinsen completes an outstanding mural and receives recognition for it, McManus and his gang destroy it before it can be submitted to a magnet art school. Justin openly defends Jinsen. The bullies are punished, and Jinsen is accepted into the art program every Edward Rucher art student hopes for. Justin fears that he will lose a wonderful friend when Jinsen moves on, but appreciates his own divorced parents more and realizes his actions make a difference.

Read Aloud/Reader Response

1. Chapter 5, pages 47 to 49, beginning with Jinsen's question "Are you Christian?" to the end of the chapter. Justin is introduced to Jinsen's perception of religion.
2. Chapter 9, page 75, beginning with "No, I— . . . " and ending with the paragraph. Justin realizes that he is an "ordinary" citizen called to do the "extraordinary."
3. Chapter 10, pages 81 to 86, beginning "At the door . . . " and ending " . . . *not going to fight.*" Jinsen explains his background and why he won't fight.
4. Chapter 11, pages 89 to 91, beginning with "My heart jumped, . . . " and ending " . . . maybe it doesn't really—" McManus reveals that Jinsen and being the bully are getting to him.
5. Chapter 14, page 117. "You want to see karma coming? Go look in the mirror, right now." The passage suggests that actions determine reactions.

Booktalk

Justin goes to Edward Rucher High School. It is upscale—big homes, nice cars, lots of money. It should be perfect. Everybody knows where he or she fits in the popularity scale and who belongs to which group. If such a school isn't perfect, it should be predictable. But stories are about the unpredictable, and the unpredictable at Edward Rucher is the new kid, Jinsen. Let me read to you a little about him. (*Read the opening paragraph of Chapter 1.*) Jinsen doesn't dress up. He doesn't have a car, and at Rucher, he doesn't have a friend. Is he miserable? No. He is probably one of the happiest people there. He has a fantastic talent. He has hope, and he has a mind that tells him to listen to his heart instead of the crowd—all good things. But the "[k]ings of the school" don't think so. They want control and stardom. If the group is paying attention to a kid who doesn't fit the mold, who looks like some kind of Buddhist monk, well, the mold might break. They might lose their crowns. So the kings decide to wage war against the boy who just appeared one day, the boy who is their enemy, the *Buddha Boy*.

Learning Opportunities

1. Using your library's resources, continue to research Buddhism. Share your findings with the group. You might wish to start with *The Way of Youth: Buddhist Common Sense for Handling Life's Questions* (Related Work 4) or *The Illustrated Encyclopedia of Zen Buddhism* (Related Work 2).
2. Discuss how the journey Jinsen brings to Justin effects a change.
3. Discuss the part that parents play in the story.
4. Are teachers responsible for the bullying going on as long as it did?
5. Interpret the sign "RUCHER CAN'T SUCCEED WITHOUT *U* !" Was Justin right in tearing it down?

Related Works

1. Anderson, M. T. **Feed.** Cambridge, MA: Candlewick Press, 2003. 235p. $16.99. ISBN 0 7636 1726 1. [fiction] JS (See full booktalk in *Teen Genre Connections*, pages 201 to 203.) This science fiction novel projects what our world will be like if it centers on consumerism instead of spiritual growth.
2. Baroni, Ph.D., Helen J. **The Illustrated Encyclopedia of Zen Buddhism.** New York: The Rosen Publishing Group, 2002. 426p. $95.00. ISBN 0 8239 2240 5. [reference] MJS This reference provides a history of Zen and the vocabulary to understand further discussions of the topic.
3. Carter, Alden R. **Love, Football, and Other Contact Sports.** New York: Holiday House, 2006. 261p. $16.95. ISBN 0 8234 1975 4. [related short stories] JS In a series of short stories, Carter portrays the football team as the hub confronting the high school issues of bullying, belonging, and identity.
4. Ikeda, DaiSaku. **The Way of Youth: Buddhist Common Sense for Handling Life's Questions.** Santa Monica, CA: Middleway Press, 2000. 188p. $14.95. ISBN 0 9674697 08. [nonfiction] JS This book explains how one can apply Buddhist principles to friendship, ownership, individuality, parents, teachers, and self-discipline.
5. Martel, Yann. **Life of Pi.** [fiction] S/A (See full booktalk in "Adventure/Survival"/"Sea," pages 91 to 93.) A young man who embraces all faiths finds he must survive alone in a life boat with a Bengal tiger.

6. Spinelli, Jerry. **Stargirl.** New York: Alfred A. Knopf, 2000. 186p. $15.95. ISBN 0 679 88637 0. [fiction] MJ (See full booktalk in *Booktalks and More,* 2003, pages 8 to 10.) Leo Borlock recalls the mystical and mysterious tenth grader named Stargirl who captivated, alienated, and, then once again, hypnotized him and the rest of the student body.

လ

Woodson, Jacqueline. **Behind You.**
New York: G. P. Putnam's Sons, 2004. 128p. $15.99. ISBN 0 399 23988 X. [fiction] JS

Themes/Topics: grief, interpersonal relations, African-Americans, after-life

Summary/Description

*B*ehind You is a series of first-person essays in which Jeremiah ("Miah") Roselind, the African-American young man mistakenly killed in *If You Come Softly,* and the people who love him, work through their losses and transitions. Miah, encouraged by his already deceased grandmother to move on, still focuses on earth and wants his girlfriend, friends, and family to know that he loves them. His spirit helps them to move on. Ellie, Miah's Jewish girlfriend, realizes that knowing Jeremiah opened an entirely new world of friends for her and gave her insight into her own problematic, sometimes hypocritical family. Nelia, Miah's mother, begins to write again as she focuses on the happy moments with her son. Norman Roselind, Miah's father, rediscovers his ex-wife as a friend. Carlton, Miah's friend, decides to declare his homosexuality so that he can live as fully and authentically as possible. Kennedy, an acquaintance, reflects on Miah's death in relation to racism and follows through on the desire of both boys to win basketball games. All characters work toward the next step after a death.

Read Aloud/Reader Response

The entire book, with separate readers taking the various parts, would create a powerful group reading. Below are particularly strong selections.

1. "Jeremiah," pages 3 to 5. Jeremiah describes the transition from life to death.
2. "Nelia," pages 11 to 13. Jeremiah's mother reacts to his death.
3. "Norman Roselind," pages 18 to 21. Jeremiah's father reacts to his death.

4. "Desire Viola Roselind," pages 24 to 27. Jeremiah's grandmother recalls Jeremiah and their relationship.
5. "Ellie" and "Jeremiah," pages 115 to 118. Each person is adjusting to new worlds.

Booktalk

Fifteen-year-old Miah is dead. Two policemen saw him running in Central Park. They had a description of an African-American man committing a crime in the area. They called to Miah to stop. He didn't hear them and kept running. They shot and killed him. But Miah wasn't ready to die. He looked forward to life with Ellie, the white girlfriend who many condemned him for loving. He wanted to shelter his mother from his father's affair and his parents' subsequent divorce. He planned to watch his dad make more films with beautiful people. He wanted to make sure his friend Carlton got to live the life he desired. And he had to help his high school basketball team have a winning season. So he stuck around awhile, even though his grandmother told him to keep moving toward eternity. No one living knew he was there. Oh, some suspected. But after all, they weren't dead yet. They didn't realize that passing to the other side still meant that every once in a while you have to stop, and maybe just for a moment, look *Behind You*.

Learning Opportunities

1. Each essay reveals something about the speaker. Using Woodson's style, write a first-person essay revealing the attitudes of one of Ellie's parents. You may decide to allow your essay to agree with Ellie's opinions of them or not.
2. Central to the book's theme is the grandmother's favorite saying, "The soul looks back and wonders." Discuss how that statement applies to each of the characters.
3. List the settings that Woodson chooses for her novel. Explain how each contributes to her purpose.
4. Jeremiah refers to "Stopping by the Woods" (Related Work 1) by Robert Frost. Read the poem and then discuss its application to the novel.
5. Using your library's resources, look for poems that deal with the subject of death or the after-life. Choose two, read them to the group, and compare the poets' points of view.
6. Discuss how inter-racial dating and homosexuality affect the novel.

Related Works

1. Frost, Robert. "Stopping by the Woods." American Poems. Available: http://www.americanpoems.com/poets/robertfrost/12103. (Accessed August 2006). The poem involves the reader deciding to stay in the quiet and dark woods (death) or return to the everyday world (life).

2. Rylant, Cynthia. **God Went to Beauty School.** New York: HarperCollins Publishers , 2003. 64p. $14.99. ISBN 0 06 009433 8. [poetry] MJS (See full booktalk in *Teen Genre Connections*, 2005, pages 84 to 85.) In twenty-three poems, Rylant characterizes God as an almighty being who puts the world in motion and then discovers, when getting involved, the pain and beauty in His creation.

3. Rylant, Cynthia. **Heavenly Village.** New York: The Blue Sky Press, 1999. 95p. $15.95. ISBN 0 439 04096 5. [fiction] MJS (See full booktalk in *Booktalks Plus*, pages 52 to 54.) These essays describe souls who hesitate between heaven and earth to take care of unfinished business.

4. Soto, Gary. **The Afterlife.** New York: Harcourt Brace and Company, 2003. 161p. $16.00. ISBN 0 15 204774 3. [fiction] JS. (See full booktalk in *Teen Genre Connections*, 2005, pages 294 to 296.) Stabbed to death in a restroom, eighteen-year-old Jesús, having grown up in a Mexican/Hmong Fresno neighborhood, moves from life to the after-life and briefly touches those left behind.

5. Woodson, Jacqueline. **If You Come Softly.** New York: G. P. Putnam's Sons, 1998. 181p. $15.99. ISBN 0 399 23112 9. [fiction] JS Jeremiah and Ellie decide to date even when they encounter resistance and condemnation. At the end of the novel, Jeremiah is shot and killed.

Contemporary

Contemporary books deal with growing up. "Finding Our Talents and Friends" concentrates on the complicated process of discovering what we can achieve and who will support us in accomplishment and accept us in failure. "Laughing" reminds us that this often difficult process has a light side, and "Competing" points out that those games, and the skills we develop in playing them, teach us about ourselves and life.

Finding Our Talents and Friends

☙☙

Brooks, Martha. **True Confessions of a Heartless Girl.**

New York: Farrar, Straus and Giroux/Melanie Kroupa Books, 2003.
181p. $16.00. ISBN 0 374 37806 1. [fiction] JS

Themes/Topics: restitution, conduct of life, love, community

Summary/Description

Pregnant seventeen-year-old Noreen Stall steals her boyfriend's truck and money, drives to the small community of Pembina Lake, and persuades Lynda Bradley, the owner of an almost-bankrupt café and the single mother of a five-year-old boy, to let her stay the night. The mistakes Noreen makes—feeding chicken bones to the Bradley dog, setting fire to a local cabin, and pulling large plaster chunks off the café walls—unite the residents of the town living secretly with their own demons. Noreen reminds seventy-six-year-old Dolores Harper, who spearheads the help for Noreen, of her flawed relationship with her own daughter who died of leukemia. Mary Reed, Dolores's best friend admits the physical problems she has been coping with alone. Del Armstrong, a middle-aged bachelor farmer and recovering alcoholic, reveals the guilt he feels over his brother's death, and with Noreen's encouragement, admits his love for Lynda and her son. The healing residents help Noreen accept responsibility and encourage her to return to her boyfriend whom she loves. The situations and language demand a mature reader.

Read Aloud/Reader Response

1. Part One, Chapter 4, pages 11 to 13, beginning "At seventy-six, . . . " and ending " . . . on the hottest days." Delores receives condolences after her daughter dies.
2. Part Two, Chapter 5, page 39, "As long as . . . feel lonely." Wesley tells her to rely on the stars.
3. Part Three, Chapter 1, pp. 51–52. Dolores confronts Noreen in the diner.
4. Part Four, Chapter 4, pages 112 to 114, beginning "I'm sorry . . . " and ending with the chapter. Noreen and Del discuss restitution.
5. Part Four, Chapter 30, pages 180 to 181, beginning "In the living room . . ." and ending with the chapter. Noreen writes Del a good-bye.

Booktalk

Seventeen-year-old Noreen Stall is a doer-not-thinker-take-charge kind of girl. She skips school to watch her favorite television shows. She steals her latest boyfriend's truck and money. She starts fires without even trying, and she can rip walls apart faster than most people can walk across a room. When she drives into the town of Pembina Lake one dark and stormy night, the residents don't realize that she is the storm. They befriend her, find out about her, and try to help her out. But the *True Confessions of a Heartless Girl* tear apart and rearrange their lives. Hate, sorrow, and trouble follow Noreen and anyone standing next to her. But as Noreen disrupts others' lives, her own life gets her attention. All that throwing up probably means she is pregnant. If she decides to blow this town and put more distance between herself and her boyfriend, she doesn't know where to go. Since the boyfriend caught up with her, then took the truck and most of the money back, she can't travel very far—without help from another stranger who might kill her and dump her body on the road. Noreen has to make some tough decisions pretty fast, and this *heartless girl* might have to learn to use what she does have—her head.

Learning Opportunities

1. Discuss how Noreen changes from the beginning to the end of the novel and what each character contributes to that change.
2. The title of each part of the novel has a religious connotation. How is each title appropriate? How do the titles carry out the book's religious motif?
3. How would the baby's survival have changed the story?
4. *Being with Henry* (Related Work 1), also by Martha Brooks, involves a runaway, an older advisor, and falling in love. After reading *Being with Henry* and *True Confessions of a Heartless Girl*, discuss how Brooks uses these elements to develop family and personal responsibility themes.
5. Dolores watches part of an Oprah Winfrey show that features Dr. Phil. She wonders why people can't model their own communication after the communication used on the program. Research communication techniques. Try some of them in actual situations. Then share your results with the group.

Related Works

1. Brooks, Martha. **Being with Henry.** New York: DK, Ink, 2000. 216p. $17.95. ISBN 0 7894 2588 2.[fiction] JS Sixteen-year-old Laker Wyatt, thrown out of his house after fighting his second step-father, finds a home with eighty-four-year-old Henry Olsen.
2. Ferris, Jean. **Bad.** New York: Farrar, Straus and Giroux, 1998. 182p. $16.00. ISBN 0 374 30479 3. [fiction] JS (See full booktalk in *Booktalks and More,* 2003, pages 137 to 139.) Sentenced to "Juvie" for robbery, sixteen-year-old Dallas Carpenter decides that actions, not genes, determine her future.
3. Haruf, Kent. **Plainsong.** New York: Random House/Vintage Books, 1999. 301p. $13.95pa. ISBN 0 375 70585 6. [fiction] S/A Citizens of a small rural community change their lives by helping an unmarried, pregnant teenager.
4. McGraw, Jay. **Life Strategies for Teens.** New York: Fireside Press, 2000. 236p. $14.00. ISBN 0 7432 1546 X. [nonfiction] JS (See full booktalk in *Teen Genre Connections,* 2005, pages 52 to 54.) Jay McGraw adapts *Life Strategies* by his father, Phillip C. McGraw, for teenagers. The book deals with taking responsibility for one's actions and communicating with others about those actions.
5. Nolan, Han. **Born Blue.** New York: Harcourt Brace and Company, 2001. 177p. $17.00. ISBN 0 15 201916 2. (See full booktalk in *Teen Genre Connections,* 2005, pages 13 to 15.) Janie lives

a complicated and destructive life of stealing, lying, drugs, and sex as she deals with betrayal, unusual talent, and the pain she holds inside.

ᆺ ᆺ

Hobbs, Valerie. **Letting Go of Bobby James, or How I Found My Self of Steam.**

New York: Farrar, Straus and Giroux/Frances Foster Books, 2004.
136p. $16.00. ISBN 0 374 34384 5. [fiction] JS

Themes/Topics: coming-of-age, self-esteem, wife abuse, friendship, change

Summary/Description

Married for thirteen weeks, Jody hides from her husband in a Florida restroom. He blackened her eye and now abandons her. She rides a bus to the end of the line, briefly lives a homeless life, and gets a dishwasher's job at Thelma's Café in Jackson Beach. Mentally challenged Dooley, who sweeps out the Cineplex, allows her to sleep there. Effaline, pregnant and alone, encourages her to rent an apartment and be her neighbor. Effaline claims to be waiting for her boyfriend but depends on Jody to help her break away from Kirby, the abusive apartment manager. Effaline's baby comes during a hurricane that drives Kirby away. Jody and Effaline manage the apartments, and Jody replaces Thelma's cook. When Bobby James shows up, Jody resists both him and the pressure from her own abused mother to reconcile.

Read Aloud/Reader Response

1. Page 6, beginning "We were at a picnic table . . . " and ending "popped me winded." Jody describes Bobby James hitting her.
2. Page 28, beginning "Mama says . . . " and ending "Only two days . . . " Jody realizes that she could go back with Bobby James.
3. Page 37, beginning "Did you ever wonder what happens . . . " and ending "From here, up looked like a long, long way." Jody doubts that she can live independently.
4. Pages 53 to 55, beginning "If you have ever looked . . . " and ending " . . . I wondered how long that would be." Jody resolves to stay on her own.
5. Page 104, beginning "I left that hospital, . . . " and ending with the paragraph. Jody reflects on her new strength.

Booktalk

Jody is sixteen and married thirteen weeks. Suddenly, her husband backhands her. She blames it on bad coleslaw. They were eating at the time. So she writes a complaint to the owner of the store where she bought it. His bad coleslaw gives her a big life jolt, and she wants to tell him about it. But there is another man influencing her life too. Do you know who Willie Nelson is? Well, he sings a song that Jody can't help thinking about. "Forgiving you is easy, but forgetting seems to take the longest time." Forgetting takes Jody so much time, in fact, that her husband just leaves her in a Florida restroom, with nothing. But she does have one thing he didn't know about—a twenty-dollar bill. She uses that to ride a bus as far as it will take her. That's how she starts a new life journey, a journey titled *Letting Go of Bobby James, or How I Found My Self of Steam.*

Learning Opportunities

1. Discuss why Hobbs alludes to *The Great Gatsby* and *A Streetcar Named Desire.*
2. Write Jody's description of ideal married life at the beginning and end of the novel.
3. Discuss what each character reveals about Jody.
4. Why is coleslaw central to the story?
5. By the end of the novel, do you think that Jody is successful? Explain your answer.
6. Research wife and girlfriend abuse. Share the information that you find with the group.

Related Works

1. Dessen, Sarah. **Dreamland.** New York: Viking Press, 2000. 250p. $15.99. ISBN 0 670 89122 3. [fiction] JS (See full booktalk in *Booktalks and More,* 2003, pages 73 to 75.) Caitlin O'Koren dates an abusive young man and eventually enters a recovery center.
2. Fitzgerald, F. Scott. **The Great Gatsby.** New York: Scribner Paperback Fiction, 1995. 240p. $12.00pa. ISBN 0 684 80152 3. [fiction] S/A First published in 1925, the novel tells the story of the mysterious Gatsby and the beautiful people with whom he wished to belong.
3. Flinn, Alex. **Breathing Underwater.** New York: HarperCollins Publishers, 2001. 263p. $15.95. ISBN 0 06 029198 2. [fiction] JS (See full booktalk in *Teen Genre Connections,* 2005, pages 19 to 21.) Sixteen-year-old Nick Andreas is sentenced to family violence and anger management classes for beating up on his girlfriend.

4. Oates, Joyce Carol. **Freaky Green Eyes.** New York: Harper Tempest, 2003. 341p. $17.89. ISBN 0 06 623757 2. [fiction] MJS (See full booktalk in *Teen Genre Connections,* 2005, pages 140 to 142.) Fourteen-year-old Franky Pierson discovers that her abusive, celebrity father killed her mother.
5. Williams, Tennessee. **A Streetcar Named Desire.** New York: Signet, 1975. 144p. $7.99pa. ISBN 0 451 16778 3. [drama] S/A First performed in 1946, the play deals with an abusive relationship between a working-class man and his wife.

ය ෙ

Marchetta, Melina. **Saving Francesca.**
New York: Alfred A. Knopf, 2004. 243p. $17.99. ISBN 0 375 92982 7. [fiction] JS

Themes/Topics: gender roles, Catholic schools, depression (mental illness), family life, Australia (Sydney), peer pressure, friendship

Summary/Description

Sixteen-year-old Francesca has been a student at St. Sebastian's, a traditionally all-boys school, for one semester. Popular friends from her former school, St. Stella's, attend Pius Senior College, another girls' school. Francesca deals with her new school, her mother's severe depression, and the strain in her family. Gradually, she bonds with other female students, who were the St. Stella's out-group. They all learn about themselves and develop relationships with the male students. Francesca works through her problems with significant help from her family and staff, discovers real friendship, a new love, and her own strength and identity.

Read Aloud/Reader Response

1. Chapter 2, page 13, beginning with "My theory . . . " and ending " . . . being an outcast." Francesca resists approaching her new school with open hostility or a spirit of change.
2. Chapter 4, pages 28 to 30, beginning "I see familiar . . . " and ending "It's a good night." The St. Stella's in-group reunites with Francesca.
3. Chapter 11, pages 89 to 91, beginning "Angelina takes . . . " and ending with the chapter. Francesca learns to love her extended family, but to preserve her family and personal identity.
4. Chapter 26, pages 182 to 183, beginning with "The next day . . . " and ending with the chapter. Francesca recalls how the popular

group from St. Stella's sabotaged her chance to try out for the school musical.

5. Chapter 32, pages 226 to 228, beginning with "And it's that . . . " and ending with "*The* guy." Francesca discovers that her anger toward her father is tied to her fear of losing him and that she has real friends.

Booktalk

Sixteen-year-old Francesca is having a big year. One of the oldest boys' schools in Sydney, Australia, is admitting girls. She is one of them. At her old school, St. Stella's, she was in the most popular group. Now, at Saint Sebastian's, she is surrounded by all the girls in the St. Stella's out-group and a bunch of ignorant, arrogant boys who could care less—about anything. Her mother insisted that Francesca should go to Sebastian's instead of Pius Senior College with all of her friends. Francesca feels that her mother should make up for the mess she created or at least help out. But Mom can't solve problems right now. She is too depressed to get out of bed. Dad is a stranger to family matters. He is just confused. Francesca's little brother is scared to death. And Francesca, well Francesca is angry—at everyone. She doesn't want turmoil and trouble just when her life is supposed to start the way she wants it. Who can help her? Who will take on the job of *Saving Francesca?*

Learning Opportunities

1. Choose one friend from either the St. Stella's friends or the St. Sebastian's friends. Describe that friend by writing, drawing, or a dramatic presentation.
2. Using your library's resources, research depression. Share your information with the rest of the group.
3. Using your library's resources, research labeling. Share your information with the rest of the group. You may wish to start by reading *More Than a Label* (Related Work 4).
4. Discuss how Francesca changes during the course of the novel.
5. Examine the role of one family member in Francesca's life.

Related Works

1. Fredericks, Mariah. **The True Meaning of Cleavage.** New York: Atheneum Books for Young Readers/A Richard Jackson Book, 2003. 211p. $15.95. ISBN 0 689 85092 1. [fiction] MJ In their freshman year, two close friends, separated by popularity issues, decide how important their friendship is to them.
2. konigsburg, e. l. **Outcasts of 19 Schuyler Place.** [fiction] MJS (See full booktalk in "History"/"Choosing in Peace," pages 199

to 202.) Twelve-year-old Margaret confronts bullies in summer camp and helps her uncles save towers they have built for forty-five years.

3. McGraw, Jay. **Life Strategies for Teens.** New York: Fireside Press, 2000. 236p. $14.00. ISBN 0 7432 1546 X. [nonfiction] JS (See full booktalk in *Teen Genre Connections,* 2005, pages 52 to 54.) Jay McGraw adapts his father's *Life Strategies* for the teen audience and explains how a person can positively manage life.

4. Muharrar, Aisha. **More Than a Label.** Minneapolis, MN: Free Spirit Publishing Inc., 2002. 144p. $13.95pa. ISBN 1 57542 110 0. [nonfiction] JS Muharrar distinguishes between labels and slurs and explains how each is a form of peer pressure. She provides extensive references for dealing with bullying and peer acceptance.

5. Quarles, Heather. **A Door Near Here.** New York: Delacorte Press, 1998. 231p. $13.95. ISBN 0 385 32595 9. [fiction] JS (See full book-talk in *Booktalks Plus,* 2001, pages 54 to 56.) As the oldest of three, fifteen-year-old Katherine tries to keep her family from disintegrating in reaction to her mother's depression.

෴

Simmons, Michael. **Pool Boy.**
Brookfield, CT: Roaring Brook Press/A Neal Porter Book, 2003.
164p. $23.90. ISBN 0 7613 2924 2. [fiction] JS

Themes/Topics: fathers/sons, wealth, prisoners, family life, California, working

Summary/Description

After his father is convicted of insider trading, fifteen-year-old Brett works for Alfie Moore, the family's former pool man. A self-proclaimed "wiseass," Brett gives his family, especially his father, a hard time. Alfie listens to Brett's complaints and slowly teaches him hard work and its satisfactions. When Alfie has a heart attack, Brett meets the daughter, whom Alfie deserted and who accepts her father as he is. Alfie dies. He leaves Brett money to continue the pool business and his education. Brett begins to drop his defenses with his family, who support him in grief, and shares his experiences with his father.

Read Aloud/Reader Response

1. Chapter 1, pages 1 to 3. Brett introduces himself and explains his situation. This opening chapter would be an excellent booktalk.

2. Chapter 8, pages 20 to 22. Brett explains how his school life changed.
3. Chapter 10, pages 31 to 33, beginning with "One of my coworkers . . ." and ending with the chapter. Brett explains losing his fast food job.
4. Chapter 15, page 45, beginning with "If there's one thing I learned . . ." and ending ".to learn." Brett's mother reflects on how people should approach difficult situations.
5. Chapter 43, page 147, beginning with "After he said . . ." to the end of the paragraph. Alfie's daughter explains how she learned to accept her father.
6. Chapter 47, page 162, beginning " . . . I guess . . ." to " . . . with a list." Brett is beginning to separate disagreement and unconditional love.

Booktalk

Fifteen-year-old Brett has a problem. He isn't rich. He used to be, but his dad messed up, did some insider trading, got caught, and went to jail. Being rich and then not being rich is about more than money. Your friends are different because you can't afford to hang out at the same places. Your clothes are different. They aren't as expensive. You don't have as much time because you're working—and in Brett's case—going to the prisoners' visiting day. And since Brett has a rich kid attitude, he is having trouble holding a job at all. Then he runs into Alfie Moore. Alfie cleans pools. In fact, he used to clean Brett's pool. He needs some extra help. Brett needs a job. It seems like a perfect match—perfect until Brett's name becomes *Pool Boy*.

Learning Opportunities

1. Explain how Brett, Brett's father, Brett's mother, Aunt Mary, and Alfie each might define wealth.
2. Using your library's resources, research the qualities that employers value in an employee. Share the information with the group.
3. List and discuss the story events that change Brett.
4. Describe Alfie's character. Why does he appeal to Brett?
5. Why are the two-hundred-dollar bathing suit and the party important to the story?

Related Works

1. Cohn, Rachel. **Gingerbread.** New York: Simon & Schuster Books for Young Readers, 2002. 172p. $15.95. ISBN 0 689 84337 2. [fiction] JS After a disappointing visit with her biological father

about whom she fantasizes, Cyd Charisse returns to her more traditional and loving blended family.

2. Fleischman, Paul. **Seek.** Chicago, IL: Cricket Books/ A Marcato Book, 2001. 167p. $16.95. ISBN 0 8126 4900 1. [fiction] JS Senior Robert Radkovitz creates his own sense of worth as he seeks his biological father on the airways.

3. Garfinkle, D. L. **Storky: How I Lost My Nickname and Won the Girl.** [fiction] MJ (See full booktalk in "Contemporary"/ "Laughing," pages 63 to 65.) A high school freshman finds happiness with down-to-earth people instead of glitzy, demanding ones.

4. Lubar, David. **Dunk.** New York: Clarion, 2002. 249p. $15.00. ISBN 0 618 19455 X. [fiction] JS (See full booktalk in *Teen Genre Connections,* 2005, pages 79 to 81.) Fifteen-year-old bad attitude Chad learns to be a Bozo from one of the best who has lost his own family and career.

5. Rottman, S. L. **Hero.** Atlanta, GA: Peachtree Publishers, 1997. 134p. $14.95. ISBN 1 56145 159 2. [fiction] JS (See full booktalk in *Booktalks Plus,* 2001, pages 223 to 225.) An intelligent but troubled ninth grader is sentenced to community service and meets a tough World War II hero who shows him the value of hard work and responsibility.

Laughing

ርያ ጮ

Anderson, Laurie Halse. **Prom.**

New York: Viking Press, 2005. 215p. $16.99. ISBN 0 670 05974 9. [fiction] JS

Themes/Topics: proms, urban high schools, self-realization, family life, Pennsylvania, boyfriends

Summary/Description

Eighteen-year-old Ashley Hannigan, the oldest of four in a dysfunctional urban family, focuses on her exploitive juvenile delinquent boyfriend, tolerates school and ignores the prom. When the advisor steals the prom funds, however, Ashley decides to help her best friend plan a prom in the school gym. Dodging detentions, working after school, helping at home, and overcoming her own poor choices, Ashley plans a beautiful event and discovers her leadership abilities and a pride in her work. She learns that her father, pregnant mother, aunts, and even her best friend's senile grandmother, want her to have a fairy tale prom evening. Her boyfriend is more interested in having sex, smoking pot, and planning for their apartment that she will work two jobs to support. The assistant principal, ignoring her positive efforts, blocks her attendance. Making it into the prom and enjoying the evening, she realizes what she doesn't need and what she can overcome. She decides to move in with her best friend, the prom chairman, and, next year, attend the community college.

Read Aloud/Reader Response

1. Chapter 9, page 7. Ashley's description of Carceras High suggests the school's problems.
2. Chapter 33, pages 37 and 38. Ashley's description of her home reveals its dysfunction.
3. Chapter 95, pages 124 to 128. TJ reveals his character and selfish expectations.
4. Chapter 133, pages 177 to 178. The neighborhood stages a prom send off.
5. Chapter 142, pages 190 to 193. Ashley realizes how self-centered TJ's affections are.

Booktalk

Eighteen-year-old Ashley Hannigan is the oldest of four children, and her mother is about to make it five. Ashley has a job after school, a slew of detentions, and a to-die-for boyfriend she plans to live with after graduation. Home, work, and school make her life practically a blur. Like all other normal kids, she doesn't have the time or money for a prom—even if her best friend and next-door neighbor is chairman. Then the new math teacher steals the prom money. The prom plans are history. Who cares? Maybe Ashley. When disaster strikes, she sees life differently. *Read the passage in Chapter 22, on page 26, beginning "I had been saying . . ." and ending ". . . what to say or do."* The dance still isn't so important, but her friends sure are. So she volunteers for the out-of-funds emergency committee. Can a prom happen without money? Ashley has been making things happen without money for years. She just thought that's what normal people did. Being the oldest in her family, she gets people to do what she wants all the time. She thought that was normal too. But Ashley isn't normal anymore. Now she is a prom fiend. She'll plan it, run it, and maybe even go to it. Her crazy family, her friends, the principal, and even her best friend's senile grandmother are right behind her. Is that good? Ashley finds out what she can do, what she wants, and who and what she can live without, just because she decides to go to the *Prom.*

Learning Opportunities

1. Discuss why TJ and the assistant principal are so important to the story.
2. Ashley sees her family as dysfunctional. Would you agree?
3. How does the urban setting affect the story?
4. Using your library's resources, research the cost of a prom. Discuss, with the group, how that cost might be cut.
5. Ashley insists that she is normal. Define normal from her point of view. Then define normal from your point of view.

Related Works

1. Brashares, Ann. **Girls in Pants: The Third Summer of the Sisterhood.** New York: Delacorte Press, 2005. 338p. $17.99. ISBN 0 385 90919 5. [fiction] JS With new people in their lives, the four girlfriends plan their futures and preserve their relationship.
2. Dessen, Sarah. **Someone Like You.** New York: Viking Press, 1998. 281p. $15.99. ISBN 0 670 87778 6. [fiction] JS (See full booktalk in *Booktalks and More,* 2003, pages 219 to 221.) Scarlett and Halley attend the prom they have fantasized about for years in spite of boyfriend pressures and an unplanned pregnancy.
3. Graham, Stedman. **Teens Can Make It Happen: Nine Steps to Success.** New York: Scholastic Press, 2000. 250p. $6.95pa. ISBN 0 439 40498 3. [nonfiction] JS This teen adaptation of the adult *You Can Make It Happen: A Nine Step Plan for Success* focuses on "active optimism" and three "success circles"—Career, Personal Development, and Relationships.
4. Osa, Nancy. **Cuba 15.** New York: Delacorte Press, 2003. 277p. $17.99. ISBN 0 385 90086 4. [fiction] JS Fifteen-year-old Violet Paz discovers her own strengths and her family roots as she plans her Cuban womanhood ceremony.
5. Levithan, David (ed.) and Daniel Ehrenheft (ed.). **21 Proms**. New York: Scholastic, 2007. 304p. $8.99pa. ISBN 13: 978 0 439 89029 8. [short stories] S Twenty-one short stories depict the coming-of-age power of the prom. some may be considered controversial.

✿✿

Blacker, Terence. Boy2Girl.

New York: Farrar, Straus and Giroux, 2004. 295p. $16.00.
ISBN 0 374 30926 4. [fiction] MJ

Themes/Topics: cousins, death, cross-dressing, peer pressure, American students, British students, gender roles

Summary/Description

Thirteen-year-old cousins, Matthew Burton and Sam Lopez, have never met. Sam's mother, who moved to the United States at eighteen, dies in a car crash. Mrs. Burton, her sister, brings Sam, whose petty criminal father is in jail, back to England to live. Sam's behavior leads Matthew and his friends to reject him, but Sam promises to make amends by undergoing an initiation. He will pose as a girl, Samantha, for the first week of school and spy on the "Bitches," three girls that Matthew and his friends harass. Sam carries off the charade and bonds with the girls. Newly released from jail, Sam's father remarries, learns Sam inherited money, and heads to England to get Sam. The Burtons and Sam foil the father's plans. Sam reveals his disguise, gains a girlfriend from the "Bitches," and helps the boys find their feminine side. The story is told from multiple points of view.

Read Aloud/Reader Response

1. Chapter 1, pages 3 and 4. Matt describes Sam at their first meeting.
2. Chapter 2, page 20. The passage explains the history of the "Sheds" and the "Bitches."
3. Chapter 11, pages 150 to 153. The conversation between Sam and Zia reveals the reasons for Sam's obnoxious personality.
4. Chapter 17, page 241, beginning "Sometimes . . . " and ending " . . . adults." In his advice to Jake, Sam reveals his own tumultuous life and the responsibility that both adults and teenagers have for communication.
5. Chapter 19, pages 289 to 293. Sam explains why he thought he sent his father to jail.

Booktalk

Thirteen-year-old Sam Lopez doesn't have an ordinary life. In fact, no one intended him to have a life at all. His mother described him as an accident. After he was born, Sam learned to live on his own. When Sam was five, his dad went to jail. Now Sam is moving to London to live with his aunt, uncle, and cousin—"the Burtons." His mom was born in England. She just died in a car crash and specified that Sam will live with her sister, Mrs. Burton. When Sam arrives, Matt Burton, his cousin, gets one look and agrees that Sam is an accident. But Matt is sure that the real accident is still waiting to happen. He is right. Big time. Sam thinks the Burtons are absolutely weird. Mrs. Burton brings home the money. Mr. Burton takes care of the house, and Sam's cousin belongs to some loser group called the "Sheds." According to Sam, life in London "sucks." Then one of the Sheds makes a remark about Sam's father. Sam attacks and tears him apart. But he tears apart something else too. He's out of the group. Sam is alone. Suddenly, any group, even a loser group, seems better than nothing. Can Sam get back in? Only the hard way. But Sam just might be man enough to do it. His next life change is one that Sam never anticipated. The next change is from *Boy2Girl*.

Learning Opportunities

1. What does the character of Mark Kramer add to the story?
2. Sam notes that his mother is smarter than people thought she was. Is he right?
3. How does the experience of being a girl change Sam?
4. Using the library's resources, research gender roles and the expectations that come with them. Share the information with the group. Then discuss how those roles influenced the outcome of the novel.
5. List each adult in the novel. Explain how he or she supports the novel's purpose.

Related Works

1. Abrahams, George, and Sheila Ahlbrand. **Boy v. Girl?: How Gender Shapes Who We Are, What We Want, and How We Get Along.** Minneapolis, MN: Free Spirit Publishing, 2002. 193p. $14.95. ISBN 1 57542 104 6. [nonfiction] MJ Abrahams and Ahlbrand invite readers to examine their own identities in relation to the gender stereotypes surrounding them.
2. Bagdasarian, Adam. **First French Kiss and Other Traumas.** New York: Farrar, Straus and Giroux/Melanie Kroupa Books, 2002. 134p. $16.00. ISBN 0 374 32338 0. [fiction] JS (See full booktalk in *Teen Genre Connections,* 2005, pages 73 to 74.) In five groups of essays, a fictional character tells his traumatic and sometimes humorous life experiences in becoming a man.
3. McGraw, Jay. **Life Strategies for Teens.** New York: Fireside Press, 2000. 236p. $14.00. ISBN 0 7432 1546 X. [nonfiction] JS (See full booktalk in *Teen Genre Connections,* 2005, pages 52 to 54.) Jay McGraw presents "Ten Laws of Life" dealing with identity, independence, decision-making, and self-respect.
4. O'Connell, Tyne. **Dueling Princes.** New York: Bloomsbury Children's Books, 2005. 250p. $16.95. ISBN 1 58234 658 5. [fiction] MJ An American girl, attending an exclusive English school, makes friends while dealing with a demanding fencing coach and difficult parents who are about to divorce.

5. Paulsen, Gary. **The Glass Café.** New York: Wendy Lamb Books, 2003. 99p. $12.95. ISBN 0 385 90121 6. [fiction] MJ Twelve-year-old Tony Henson, a talented artist and the son of a stripper, finds himself and his mother in a custody battle after he sketches the other exotic dancers.

ᏨᏏ

Cabot, Meg. **Teen Idol.**
New York: HarperCollins Publishers, 2004. 293p. $16.89.
ISBN 0 06 009617 9. [fiction] MJS

Themes/Topics: high school, interpersonal relations, conduct of life, actors and actresses, bullies, Indiana, Hollywood star

Summary/Description

Junior Jenny Greenley guides movie star Luke Striker, researching an upcoming film, around her high school. Jen, known for smoothing over hurt feelings and difficult situations, anonymously writes a school newspaper advice column. Nineteen-year-old Striker, who never attended high school, is shocked by the school's conditions and attitudes. He tells Jenny to use her popularity to "effect social change." Taking Striker's advice, Jen advises and defends an outcast girl, stops participating in an extracurricular activity she was pushed into joining, tells her best friend off, and rescues a kidnapped doll prized by her Latin teacher. Each action brings positive results. She has more trouble with the complications from Striker's asking her to the Spring Fling, the school dance. Reporters hound her, and the boy whom she wants to date thinks he can't compete with a movie star. At the dance, she learns that Striker is dating the ex-girlfriend of the nonconformist Jen likes. Furious, Jen, with Striker's limousine at her disposal, leaves the dance, drives to an anti-Spring Fling party, and clarifies her romantic relationship. The experiences reveal her true friends and her people skills.

Read Aloud/Reader Response

1. Each "Ask Annie" letter. One introduces each chapter. The letters and advice reflect the problems that high school students face and Jen's growth throughout the novel.
2. Chapter 2, page 20, beginning "You are coming to my party!" and ending " . . . before anyone got hurt." Jen explains the role she plays in her high school and social group.

3. Chapter 10, pages 139 to 144, beginning "There was . . ." and
    ending with the chapter. Luke wants Jen to change the school.
4. Chapter 14, pages 228 to 229, beginning "Why'd you do that?" and
    ending " . . . had ever done for me." Jenny realizes that Scott is will-
    ing to put himself at risk to defend her.
5. Chapter 15, pages 233 to 234, beginning with the chapter and
    ending " . . . more power than I'd ever known." When Jen stands up
    to Kurt, the doll kidnapper, he backs down.

Booktalk

Hollywood, fame, teenage heart throbs. Those are the farthest things
from steady, level-headed Jenny Greenley's mind. She is too busy
solving everybody's problems. Jen writes an advice column called
"Ask Annie" for the school newspaper. Even the guidance counselor
confides in Jen. Anonymously, Jenny deals with it all—uncooperative
parents, friendships gone bad, unrequited love, and disloyal friends.
She is so busy that she doesn't have time to have a boyfriend herself.
But then the school she holds together gives her one job too many.
Nineteen-year-old Luke Striker, screen star extraordinaire, comes to
Clayton High School. Like "Ask Annie," Luke wants to be anonymous.
Jen is supposed to make sure that he stays that way. But this visitor is
hard to keep secret and even harder to keep secrets from. Almost right
away, he starts asking tough questions. Some are about her love life.
The more she listens, the more she believes that Striker is crazy as well
as famous. Mr. Striker gives Jen plenty of advice too. Can she take it
as well as hand it out? She'd better. This Hollywood star soon has Jen's
quiet Indiana town and her life in turmoil. Love is on its way, ready or
not, when Clayton High's Annie comes up against the guy every other
reporter except the one from National Geographic is writing about—
Luke Striker, *Teen Idol.*

Learning Opportunities

1. Bullies are a central issue in the novel. List each character who tries
    to bully another. Describe the method and the result.
2. Using your library's resources, research bullying and how to prevent
    or fight it. Share the information with the group.
3. Evaluate each character and the advice he or she gives.
4. Discuss the title, *Teen Idol,* and the many ways it can apply to the
    novel.
5. Performers and newspaper people conflict on several levels. How
    does Cabot use the conflict?

Related Works

1. Cabot, Meg. **The Princess Diaries.** New York: HarperCollins Publishers, 2000. 238p. $15.95. ISBN 0 380 97848 2. [fiction] MJS In this first book of the series, fourteen-year-old Mia Thermopolis discovers that the father who visits her from overseas is the Prince of Genovia and that she must deal seriously, and not so seriously, with her new identity.

2. Collins, Yvonne, and Sandy Rideout. **Introducing Vivien Leigh Reid: Daughter of the Diva.** New York: St. Martin's Griffin, 2005. 227p. $9.95pa. ISBN 0 312 33837 6. [fiction] JS Vivien Leigh Reid becomes reacquainted with the mother who left her for an acting career, but finds herself being drawn into acting.

3. Collins, Yvonne, and Sandy Rideout. **Now Starring Vivien Leigh Reid: Diva in Training.** New York: St. Martin's Griffin, 2006. 242p. $9.95pa. ISBN 0 312 33839 2. [fiction] JS In this sequel to Related Work 2, Leigh, in her second summer with Annika, enrolls in acting classes, lands a roll in a soap opera, and discovers that she can be an even more difficult diva than her mother.

4. Sachar, Louis. **Small Steps.** New York: Delacorte Press, 2006. 257p. $16.95. ISBN 0 385 73314 3. [fiction] MJS In this *Holes* sequel, seventeen-year-old Armpit is targeted in a murder/embezzlement plot when he becomes involved with a teen singing sensation.

5. Young, Karen Romano. **The Beetle and Me: A Love Story.** New York: Greenwillow Books, 1999. 181p. $15.00. ISBN 0 688 15922 2. [fiction] JS Fifteen-year-old Daisy Pandolfi, through car repair and participation in the school play, sorts out her feelings of love and infatuation.

Garfinkle, D. L. Storky: How I Lost My Nickname and Won the Girl.

New York: G. P. Putnam's Sons, 2005. 184p. $16.99. ISBN 0 399 24284 8. [fiction] MJ

Themes/Topics: diaries, high schools, dating, family life, divorce, popularity, friendship

Summary/Description

High school freshman Michael "Storky" Pomerantz seeks popularity in school, approval from his father who has left the family, and a dating relationship with Gina, a fellow gifted student. Instead of membership in the popular crowd, he finds one good friend and academic success. Instead of approval from his father, he acquires a stepfather, his dentist, who gives him attention and respect. Instead of his fantasy, the beautiful and loving Gina, he discovers a selfish and manipulative Gina, whom he eventually rejects for the quiet, loyal, and intelligent Sydney Holland. By the end of the year, his personal decisions, guided by Duke, Mike's nursing home Scrabble buddy, produce a future baby brother, two new friends, academic success, and the confidence to claim his own name instead of nicknames. Some of the humor, based on Michael's out-of-control penis, may be considered controversial.

Read Aloud/Reader Response

1. "Tuesday, November 9," pages 58 to 60. Mike realizes how "The Road Not Taken" relates to his relationship with his father.
2. "Thursday, November 18," pages 66 to 67. Mike sees himself as a "Total Loser" when he chooses and delivers Gina's birthday present.
3. "Thursday, January 20," pages 118 to 121. Mike realizes Gina's true personality.
4. "Monday, February 28," page 142. Mike reacts negatively to the "wonderful" plans for his mother's marriage and the new baby.
5. "Wednesday, March 16," "Friday, March 18," and "Sunday, March 20," pages 150 to 152. These entries explain Mike's feelings about Duke and his ability to relate to a group of people beyond high school.
6. "Monday, May 16," pages 183 to 184. After living through his freshman year, Mike makes up a list of rules for Mason, his future little brother.

Booktalk

Freshman year in high school is never easy, but for Mike Pomerantz, AKA "Storky," every day is a disaster. His older sister is the "Queen of Popularville." She doesn't want to be seen with a tall, scrawny, Scrabble nerd like Mike. Gina, one of his best friends in grade school, is dating "Hunk," the high school heart throb. Mike's chances of dating her are about as thin as he is. Mike's father is working on a new concept of family based on an old marriage contract concept—divorce. And Mike's mother is starting to date. Unfortunately, her date is also Mike's dentist. He likes to ruffle Mike's hair and call him Mikey—not Mike's favorite thing. So how can a guy live with all of this or through it? He tries drinking, girls, television, and even nursing homes—but he finally puts the success package together. He can tell you all about his secret formula. He wrote it all down, day by day in *Storky: How I Lost My Nickname and Won the Girl*.

Learning Opportunities

1. Read Robert Frost's "The Road Not Taken" (Related Work 1). Note how it affects Mike's life. Choose a poem that relates significantly to your own life. Read the poem to the group and explain your choice.
2. Nicknames are central to the story. List all the nicknames used and discuss what they reveal about both the namer and the named.
3. Using your library's resources, find more information about the importance of names. Share the information with the class. Relate what you have learned to the story.
4. Choose one literary work mentioned in the novel. Read it and discuss how the allusion aids the author's purpose.
5. Write a diary entry about Mike from another character's point of view.

Related Works

1. Frost, Robert. "The Road Not Taken." Poets.org. Available: http://www.poets.org/viewmedia.php/prmMID/15717. (Accessed August 2006). Frost's poem is the classic example of the power of individual choice.
2. Juby, Susan. **Alice I Think.** New York: Harper Tempest, 2003. 290p. $16.89. ISBN 0 06 051544 9. [fiction] JS Alice, homeschooled by her eccentric parents, decides to enter high school to please her therapist and becomes a misfit and target.
3. Klise, Kate. **Deliver Us from Normal.** New York: Scholastic Press, 2005. 240p. $16.95. ISBN 0 439 52322 2. [fiction] MJ After Charles Harrisong's older sister is maligned by the popular crowd of Normal, Charles and his eccentric family strike out for a new life.
4. Korman, Gordon. **Jake, Reinvented.** New York: Hyperion, 2003. 213p. $15.99. ISBN 078681957-X. [fiction] JS Thinking his happiness lies with a girl from the in-crowd, an academic nerd changes himself into a party animal with disastrous results.
5. Simmons, Michael. **Pool Boy.** [fiction] JS (See full booktalk in "Contemporary"/"Finding Our Talents and Friends," pages 54 to 56.) Like Storky, the main character finds maturity and guidance from an old man.

Competing

Averett, Edward. **The Rhyming Season.**
New York: Clarion Books, 2005. 214p. $16.00. ISBN 0 618 46948 6. [fiction] JS

Themes/Topics: grief, brothers, basketball, high school, coaches, poets, future orientation

Summary/Description

Senior Brenda Jacobsen lives in Hemlock, Washington, where life centers on logging and basketball. Last year, her brother Benny, the player who was to take the boys' team to a championship, died in a car crash. This year the girls' team plans to win a championship. Brenda, a star player, grieves for her brother and watches her parents' marriage fall apart. Then the logging mill closes down, and the coach of the girls' team resigns. The new coach, an eccentric English teacher, addresses each girl by a poet's name. The players must memorize one of the poet's poems and recite it before each foul shot. The team gains attention, skill, and insight as they work with the controversial coach, deal with the town's conflicts, and accept that they are spending their last year together. By the end of the novel, Brenda copes with her losses, builds on her strengths, and plans for the future. Her parents are mending their marriage, but the reader never learns, for sure, if the team wins the state championship.

Read Aloud/Reader Response

1. Chapter 1, pages 4 to 6, beginning "I live in a desperate town." and ending with the chapter. Brenda describes the town and her team's second-class status.
2. Chapter 2, page 14, beginning "As we drove . . . " and ending " . . . along with me." Brenda recognizes her inner feelings in her father's actions.
3. Chapter 5, pages 41 to 44, beginning "I groaned." and ending with the chapter. Mr. Hobbs introduces his team to the mix of basketball and poetry.
4. Chapter 6, pages 51 to 52, beginning "I sat down . . . " and ending " . . . going to grow?" Brenda realizes that her protection is gone but does not understand how to react.
5. Chapter 15, pages 139 to 140, beginning "He grinned and . . . " and ending " . . . the way life works." Darwin explains that normal is relative, and change is part of life.

Booktalk

It's Brenda Jacobsen's senior year and she stars on the school basketball team. Brenda lives in Hemlock, Washington, where tall people and basketball are two of the most important things in life. Brenda's year should be exciting and good, but exciting and good don't seem to be part of her game. First, Brenda plays on the girls' team. They have decided that they are going to states. But in Hemlock, home of tall trees and macho men, the girls' team is definitely second place. Second, Brenda's brother, Benny, was supposed to take the boys' team to states last year, but he died in a car crash. Making baskets just makes her miss him more. Third, Brenda is watching her parents' marriage fall apart. Benny seemed to be the glue that held them together. Fourth, the coach announces she is leaving. How can they win without her? Fifth, the lumber mill closes down. Sixth, their crazy English teacher, who thinks more about books than basketball, is the new coach. He gives each girl the name of a poet to replace her own name.

She has to recite that poet's lines while playing basketball. The world is going crazy, and when Brenda starts passing out and talking to dead people, she thinks that she might be going crazy too. Brenda's life is losing all its familiar rhythms, fast. Is there any hope to find some new ones in *The Rhyming Season?*

Learning Opportunities

1. Using your library's resources, research the poets Mr. Hobbs assigns to the team members. Share your information with the group and discuss his choices.
2. Choose a poet that you admire or with whom you identify. Memorize at least one work by that poet. Share your poem and explain your choice.
3. List each change in Brenda's life. Discuss how it affects both Brenda and the town.
4. Mr. Hobbs and Darwin are two of the most eccentric residents of the town. Why are they so important? Be sure of consider each man's name in your discussion.
5. How does vandalism to the Napavine tree and the Hemlock tree frame the story?

Related Works

1. Macy, Sue, and Jane Gottesman (ed.). **Play Like a Girl: A Celebration of Women in Sports.** New York: Henry Holt and Company, 1999. 32p. $15.95. ISBN 0 8050 6071 5. [photos] MJS Pictures of famous women athletes and quotations about winning, losing, and loving the game communicate the joy of women's sports.
2. Powell, Randy. **Three Clams and an Oyster.** New York: Farrar, Straus and Giroux, 2002. 216p. $16.00. ISBN 0 374 37526 7. [fiction] JS A touch football team finds new direction when they replace an unreliable male player with a girl.

3. Swanson, Julie A. **Going for the Record.** Grand Rapids, MI: Eerdmans Books for Young Readers, 2004. 217p. $8.00pa. ISBN 0 8028 5273 4. [fiction] JS (See full booktalk in *Teen Genre Connections*, 2005, pages 68 to 70.) Seventeen-year-old Leah Weiczynkowski, an Olympic-level soccer star, rethinks her relationship with sports when her father develops cancer.

4. Turner, Ann. **Hard Hit.** New York: Scholastic Press, 2006. 176p. $16.99. ISBN 0 439 29680 3. [poetry] JS In a novel of poems, Mark Warren, the star pitcher of his high school baseball team, questions the importance of sports in light of his father's terminal illness.

5. Watterson, Bill. **The Calvin and Hobbes Tenth Anniversary Book.** Kansas City, MO: Universal Press Syndicate, 1995. 208p. $14.95. ISBN 0 8362 04387. [graphic, cartoon collection] All ages. Hobbes is the off-beat advisor to the recalcitrant Calvin resisting change. Frames on pages 40 and 41 explore the shock and injustice of early death.

ぽ

de la Peña, Matt. **Ball Don't Lie.**
New York: Delacorte Press, 2005. 280p. $16.95. ISBN 0 385 73232 5. [fiction] JS

Themes/Topics: basketball, obsessive-compulsive disorder, foster home care, race relations

Summary/Description

Seventeen-year-old Sticky, a white foster child with obsessive-compulsive behavior, focuses his life in the Lincoln Rec, a basketball court/homeless shelter, where he is challenged, harassed, protected, and eventually accepted by outstanding black street ball players. As he works through a day in which he plans to buy and steal birthday gifts for his girlfriend, Anh-thu, the story flashes back to his abusive childhood, obsessive-compulsive disorder, unsuccessful foster care, his own poor judgments, incredible basketball talent, relationships at the Rec, and love for Anh-thu, who now worries she is pregnant. Deciding to steal the money for her present rather than shoplift it, Sticky chooses a drug dealer and finds himself in the emergency room. The incident, and Anh-thu's accepting presence, makes him release his grief over his mother's death and realize how much he has to lose. At the end of the novel, Sticky has Anh-thu's love, acceptance at the Rec, and a letter from UCLA. Situations and language can be controversial.

Read Aloud/Reader Response

1. "Dreadlock Man," pages 4 to 6, beginning "This is Lincoln Rec . . . " and ending with the chapter. The passage describes Lincoln Rec and Sticky's drive to play.
2. "I Could Tell," pages 52 to 55. The chapter describes the Lincoln Rec citizens.
3. "Sometimes I Think," pages 67 to 69. Basketball is Sticky's lifeline.
4. "Cheerleaders Screamed Out," pages 95 to 98, beginning *"Nine seconds on the clock . . . "* and ending *"white space-thing again."* Sticky plays under pressure.
5. "Lincoln Rec Shuts," pages 228 to 230, beginning "Dante picks up a stick . . . " and ending *"You three stones back."* Dante makes the case for stealing.

Booktalk

Seventeen-year-old Sticky lives in a foster home. His mom, Baby, died years ago. He isn't very good at school. He is fairly good at shoplifting. But in basketball?—The sky is the limit. That is because Sticky has a secret weapon. He knows that if he does something again and again, it will finally be right. He shoots baskets until that swish is just right. He is so good, that even though he is young and white, the old black guys at Lincoln Rec let him play. Sticky doesn't think too much about the race thing, and his teammates don't pay too much attention to the repeat thing he has going on, so everyone usually gets along fine. But then Sticky falls in love. He needs money to make him good enough for her. He moves off the court and to the street. He is ready to take what he deserves. But maybe he should think that he is good enough already. Maybe he is forgetting that *Ball Don't Lie.*

Learning Opportunities

1. Read Aloud/Reader Responses 1 and 2 describe Lincoln Rec. Is it an appropriate place for Sticky to be?
2. Using your library's resources, continue to research obsessive-compulsive disorder. Share your information with the group.
3. In "After the Good," pages 264 to 274, both Sticky and Anh-thu have realizations about themselves and their decisions. Explain the realizations and why each is important.
4. Using your library's resources, research the path to professional basketball. Share your information through either a presentation or a chart.
5. Explain why each character is important to understanding Sticky.

Related Works

1. Coy, John. **Crackback.** New York: Scholastic Press, 2005. 208p. $16.99. ISBN 0 439 69733 6. [fiction] JS Pressured by his coach, teammates, and father to perform well in football, junior Miles Manning considers taking steroids.

2. Hesser, Terry Spencer. **Kissing Doorknobs.** New York: Delacorte Press, 1998. 149p. $15.95. ISBN 0 385 32329 8. [fiction] JS (See full booktalk in *Booktalks Plus,* 2001, pages 148 to 150.) Tara Sullivan learns to deal with her obsessive-compulsive disorder and reach out to others with the same problem. The "Afterword" by A. J. Allen, M.D., Ph.D., explains OCD, its history, and treatment. Following the "Afterword" is an annotated list of resources.

3. Myers, Walter Dean. **The Beast.** New York: Scholastic Press, 2003. 176p. $16.95. ISBN 0 439 36841 3. [fiction] JS A young man escapes the streets by attending an exclusive academy, but sees his former girlfriend being taken over by its despair.

4. Nolan, Han. **Born Blue.** New York: Harcourt Brace and Company, 2001. 177p. $17.00. ISBN 0 15 201916 2. [fiction] JS (See full booktalk in *Teen Genre Connections,* 2005, pages 13 to 15.) Janie, a talented singer, tells about her life from the time she is four years old until she is sixteen. Like Sticky, she experiences an irresponsible mother, a series of foster homes, and acceptance by the African-American community.

5. Wallace, Rich. **Playing without the Ball.** New York: Random House, 2002. 224p. $5.99pa. ISBN 978 0 440 22972 8. [fiction] S Seventeen-year-old Jay McLeod, deserted by his mother and father, lives in a single room above Shorty's Bar and seeks stability in basketball and girlfriends.

ᘒᘓ

Deuker, Carl. **Runner.**
New York: Houghton Mifflin Company, 2005. 216p. $16.00.
ISBN 0 618 54298 1. [fiction] JS

Themes/Topics: smuggling, terrorism, father/son relationships, poverty, alcoholism, Puget Sound, running

Summary/Description

High school senior, Chance Taylor, deserted by his mother, lives on a broken down sailboat with his alcoholic father, a Gulf War veteran, and washes dishes to supplement their income. When his father loses his job, Chance accepts an offer to pick up packages and deposit them in the marina locker for two-hundred dollars per week. Melissa Watts, daughter of a prominent attorney who was a high school friend of Chance's father, befriends Chance, wants him to write for the school newspaper, and questions him about his daily runs. At first, Chance picks up drugs, but another customer will pay Chance an additional one-hundred dollars to handle packages marked with foreign writing and filled with plastic explosives. After his employer commits a questionable suicide, Chance knows the terrorists will come after him. The father discovers the problem, sends Chance to Watts, the father's high school friend, and dies a hero, in an explosion that foils the terrorists' plans. The Watts family offers to give Chance a home and send him to school, but Chance decides to join the army and stay faithful to his roots.

Read Aloud/Reader Response

1. Part One, Chapter 8, pages 24 to 27. Chance describes the *Tiny Dancer,* his home.
2. Part One, Chapter 14, pages 49 to 51, beginning "I was angry . . . " and ending with the chapter. Chance raises the question of only the poor serving in the military.
3. Part Two, Chapter 17, pages 128 to 129, beginning "As soon as I can . . . " and ending with the chapter. Chance cannot reach out to Melissa when she offers him help.
4. Part Three, Chapter 1, pages 133 to 134. Chance questions his taking the pick-up job.
5. Part Three, Chapter 22, page 213, beginning "When are they . . . " and ending " . . . out for yourself." Chance realizes that he must make restitution but won't go to jail.
6. Part Three, Chapter 22, pages 215 to 216. Chance explains his decision to enlist.

Booktalk

Easy money. That's what a fat man offers Chance Taylor. All Chance has to do is make a stop on his regular jogging run, pick up a package, and deliver it to the marina where he lives. He won't go out of his way, and he'll earn two-hundred dollars each week. Too good to be true? Oh yes. Even Chance knows that, but his dad lost his job and is drinking again. Chance's dishwashing job isn't going to pay the mooring fees for the pitiful boat they call home, or buy groceries. Since Chance is a senior this year, he would like to have a little put away to make the break when he graduates. If he doesn't like it, he can quit anytime, right? Maybe. But

Chance finds out that nothing good comes in hidden packages, and once he puts his feet on that path, maybe he'll always be a *Runner.*

Learning Opportunities

1. Using your library's resources, research how an ordinary citizen can fight terrorism. You may wish to start with *Coping with Terrorism* (Related Work 1).
2. Melissa asks the class speaker what he has read about the Middle East. Each week read one article about the Middle East. Share your information with the group. Ask others in the group to do the same. Keep a journal for new information and your reactions. You may wish to start with *Critical Perspectives on Islam and the Western World* (Related Work 4).
3. How does Dueker use the theme of personal responsibility?
4. Describe the best school for Chance.
5. Continue the discussion that Chance started in Mr. Arnold's class.
6. Discuss how many ways the title and Chance's name might apply to the story.

Related Works

1. Casil, Amy Sterling. **Coping with Terrorism.** New York: The Rosen Publishing Group, 2004. 96p. $27.95. ISBN 0 8239 4484 0. [nonfiction] MJS Casil lists terrorist strikes and explains how the private citizen might aid the government and cope emotionally.
2. Coy, John. **Crackback.** New York: Scholastic Press, 2005. 208p. $16.99. ISBN 0 439 69733 6. [fiction] JS Pressured by his coach, teammates, and father to perform well in football, junior Miles Manning considers taking steroids.
3. Gantos, Jack. **Hole in My Life.** New York: Farrar, Straus and Giroux, 2002. 200p. $16.00. ISBN 0 374 39988 3. [nonfiction] JS (See full booktalk in *Teen Genre Connections,* 2005, pages 1 to 3.) Gantos tells about his jail time for selling and delivering drugs.
4. Johansen, Jonathan (ed.). **Critical Perspectives on Islam and the Western World.** New York: The Rosen Publishing Group, 2006. 182p. (Critical Anthologies of Nonfiction Writing). $30.60. ISBN 1 4042 0538 1. [nonfiction] JS The selections explore some modern Muslim thinking and the unrest and upheaval it has produced.
5. Smith, Sherri L. **Lucy the Giant.** New York: Delacorte Press, 2002. 217p. $15.95. ISBN 0 385 72940 5. [fiction] MJS (See full booktalk in *Teen Genre Connections,* 2005, pages 121 to 122.) Fifteen-year-old Lucy Otswego leaves her alcoholic father and signs

up for a crabbing expedition where she finds family and proves herself physically, mentally, and emotionally fit.

❧❧

Koertge, Ron. **Shakespeare Bats Cleanup.**
Cambridge, MA: Candlewick Press, 2003. 116p. $15.99.
ISBN 0 7636 2116 1. [fiction, poems] MJS

Themes/Topics: grief, mono, baseball, poetry, father/son relationships, dating

Summary/Description

When fourteen-year-old Kevin Boland is diagnosed with mono, he stops playing baseball and starts writing poems. His poems reflect on his mother's death, his father's writing career, his initiation into dating, and the parallels between baseball and poetry. He recovers and is as hooked on writing as he was on baseball.

Read Aloud/Reader Response

1. "The Book I've Been Reading," page 23. Kevin explains revision and compares successful writing to being in the zone.
2. "Pantoum for Mom," page 29. Kevin uses the form to preserve his mother's memory. The next poem, "Just Not a Very Good Pantoum for Mom," reflects on how the structure helped focus Kevin's thoughts and how proud his mother would have been with his creation.
3. "After the Funeral," pages 37 and 38. The ballad describes his father's grief.
4. "Life in the Country," page 59. Kevin describes the beautiful game scene.
5. "Try, Try Again," pages 71 to 74. Kevin finally makes a connection with Mia. More than one person could participate in the reading.

Booktalk

Fourteen-year-old Kevin Boland now has an imaginary life and a real life. Let him tell you about them both. *Read the poem on page 1.* Lots of time on his hands means thinking about being sick, his mother dying, his father trying to adjust, going back to baseball, getting a girl, and, believe it or not, becoming a poet. Sometimes things that don't seem like they will ever fit, fit perfectly. That's just what happens when Kevin discovers that *Shakespeare Bats Cleanup.*

Learning Opportunities

1. Using your library's resources, find a definition for each poetry form that Kevin uses. Share the information in an oral or visual presentation.
2. Write a poem each day for thirty days about your own life.
3. Kevin thinks about poetry in terms of baseball. Complete the sentence, "Poetry is like . . . " Write a poem or paragraph explaining your sentence.
4. Discuss the appropriateness of the title.
5. Discuss the roles that Kevin's father and Mira play in the novel.

Related Works

1. Fletcher, Ralph. **A Writing Kind of Day: Poems for Young Poets.** Honesdale, PA: Wordsong/Boyds Mills Press, Inc., 2005. 32p. $17.95. ISBN 1 59078 276 3. [poetry] MJ This collection combines the topics of family, writing, and language.
2. Janeczko, Paul B. **How to Write Poetry.** New York: Scholastic Press, 1999. 117p. (Scholastic Guides). $12.95. ISBN 0 590 10077 7. [poetry] MJS This book provides step-by-step advice about the poetry-writing process, from gathering ideas and words to sharing finished poems.
3. Koertge, Ron. "Just a Couple of Girls Talking Haiku." In **Twice Told: Original Stories Inspired by Original Art.** Drawings by Scott Hunt. New York: Dutton/Penguin Putnam, 2006. 320p. $19.99. ISBN 0 525 46818 8. [fiction] MJS A haiku assignment in English class brings people together and helps them heal. The story appears on pages 59 to 69. The short stories focus on nine images by eighteen writers. A pair of writers reacts to each of the images.
4. Swanson, Julie A. **Going for the Record.** Grand Rapids, MI: Eerdmans Books for Young Readers, 2004. 217p. $8.00pa. ISBN 0 8028 5273 4. [fiction] JS (See full booktalk in *Teen Genre Connections*, 2005, pages 68 to 70.) Seventeen-year-old Leah Weiczynkowski qualifies for the Olympic soccer team at the same time that she finds out that her father has cancer, and decides to put more balance in her life away from competitive sports.
5. Turner, Ann. **Hard Hit.** New York: Scholastic Press, 2006. 176p. $16.99. ISBN 0 439 29680 3. [poetry] JS. In a series of poems, Mark Warren, a star high school pitcher, tells about playing baseball while his father dies of pancreatic cancer.

ɔʳʅɒ

Peet, Mal. **Keeper.**

Cambridge, MA: Candlewick Press, 2003. 225p. $15.99.
ISBN 0 7636 2749 6. [fiction] JS

Themes/Topics: soccer, rainforest, conservation, conduct of life

Summary/Description

El Gato, the world's best goalkeeper, gives an interview to Paul Faustino, the best soccer reporter in South America. He lets Faustino have the exclusive on his retirement with the condition that Faustino write an entire book about El Gato's life. As a boy, El Gato lives in the South American jungle where his father is a logger. El Gato, a poor soccer player, quits the game at twelve and begins to explore the jungle where he learns about wildlife and discovers a mysterious soccer field and a ghostly mentor who teaches him goalkeeping skills. The mentor, to whom he refers as the Keeper, teaches with comparisons to animal behavior. At fifteen, El Gato works in the logging company's tool shop. On payday the workers play and bet on a camp soccer game. El Gato is goalie, earns the name El Gato, and, eventually, a professional contract. When his professional team wins the gold cup, he decides to devote his life to saving the rainforest. In Faustino's files, El Gato discovers a picture of the Keeper, a member of the 1948 to 1950 national soccer team, never found after a jungle plane crash. El Gato returns to the forest to see the Keeper. The other Lost Ones emerge from the forest. El Gato lets them hold the gold cup, and they pass into the next life. What they were meant to do is accomplished.

Read Aloud/Reader Response

The novel's chapters have no number or title designation.

1. Pages 12 to 14, beginning "But when it came . . . " and ending " . . . for saying such a thing." The grandmother tells jungle horror stories that include the "Waiting Dead."
2. Pages 30 to 32, beginning "Try again, . . . " and ending with the chapter. The Keeper teaches the young El Gato to see like a hawk
3. Pages 46 to 47, beginning "'Yes,' I said . . . " and ending "They are all the same." The Keeper teaches El Gato that the soccer goal belongs to the goalkeeper as the spider web belongs to the spider.
4. Page 50, beginning "He was teaching me . . . " and ending " . . . men who fail at that." El Gato describes the Keeper and the Keeper's

father role, but respects what his own father did for him and the family by working as a logger.

5. Pages 112 to 116, beginning "He materialized from the tree shadows . . ." and ending with the chapter. The Keeper gives El Gato the message about change in soccer and life.

Booktalk

Ask how many people in the group have heard about the rainforest. Ask them what they know.

The rainforest is a resource that may disappear before we can figure out why it is important. Its cures are vital and often mysterious. But this story is not about medicine or science. This story is about soccer and ghosts, a kind of ghost known as the Waiting Dead. Who brings these worlds of forest and supernatural together? An ordinary, poor boy whose father's job is to cut down that forest. A boy whose awkward long legs and arms earn him the name "the Stork." Disgusted and ashamed, he quits soccer at thirteen and hides from his friends. Where does he go? The forest. What does he find there? A soccer field, of course. Then on to the field comes a figure, a shadow. Is it human or otherworld? The boy can't tell. But it speaks, and it tells him that he belongs right there—in the forest, on the soccer field. The boy thinks that these words are part of a dream. That he will soon wake up. But it is no dream. He is looking at one of the Waiting Dead, and the Waiting Dead make plans for those who are alive. This ghost plays soccer. He is determined that the boy will also play soccer, that this ordinary boy will become the greatest goalkeeper in the world. Impossible? The boy thinks so, but then he becomes a man and truly learns to be, like this ghost man, a *Keeper.*

Learning Opportunities

1. Discuss the title's meaning and application beyond soccer.
2. The Keeper's lessons apply to life as well as soccer. Discuss how. You might wish to compare his advice to Mia Hamm's. (Related Work 4)
3. Choose a sport in which you participate. List the life lessons you have learned from participating. Share your list with the group and discuss it.
4. Using your library's resources, continue to research the importance of the rainforest. Share your information with the group.
5. Using your library's resources, research the life of one major athlete who has used his sports experience to make a major contribution to society. Share your information in a written, oral, or visual display.

Related Works

1. Allende, Isabel. Margaret Sayers Peden (trans.). **City of the Beasts.** New York: HarperCollins Publishers, 2002. 406p. $21.89. ISBN 0 06 050917 1. [fiction] MJ (See full booktalk in *Teen Genre Connections*, 2005, pages 87 to 90.) Fifteen-year-old Alex Cold visits the rainforest with his journalist grandmother, discovers a plot to kill the native tribe, and enters the spiritual world of the Beasts to save them and their home.

2. Bloor, Edward. **Tangerine.** New York: Scholastic Press, 1997. 294p. $4.99pa. ISBN 0 590 43277 X. [fiction] MJ Legally blind, Paul transfers to poorer and tougher Tangerine Middle School so that he can play soccer and discovers his own strengths, new friends, the family dysfunction that harmed him, and a love of the environment.

3. Cameron, Ann. **Colibrí.** New York: Farrar, Straus and Giroux/ Frances Foster Books, 2003. 240p. $17.00. ISBN 0 374 31519 1. [fiction] MJS (See full booktalk in *Teen Genre Connections*, 2005, pages 269 to 271.) Kidnapped and traveling under an assumed name, Colibrí discovers, through the advice of a mystical Day-Keeper, that her "uncle" is lying to her. She escapes, and he dies trying to kill her.

4. Hamm, Mia, with Aaron Heifetz. **Go for the Goal: A Champion's Guide to Winning in Soccer and Life.** New York: HarperCollins Publishers, 1999. 222p. $21.00. ISBN 0 06 019342 5. [nonfiction] MJS (See full booktalk in *Booktalks and More*, 2003, pages 132 to 134.) Although Mia Hamm speaks primarily to girls interested in soccer, her advice in Part I about working hard and sacrificing for success, following a passion, improving, focusing, and maintaining physical fitness encourages all teens to help themselves and those around them.

5. Swanson, Julie A. **Going for the Record.** Grand Rapids, MI: Eerdmans Books for Young Readers, 2004. 217p. $8.00pa. ISBN 0 8028 5273 4. [fiction] JS (See full booktalk in *Teen Genre Connections*, 2005, pages 68 to 70.) A seventeen-year-old soccer star, qualifying for the World Cup and Olympic teams, rethinks her sports focus when her father develops cancer.

3

Adventure/Survival

"Adventure/Survival" looks at man's interaction with the world and what that interaction teaches him. "Land" includes the survival effort of both animal and man. *Sleep Rough Tonight* considers the urban environment. *How Angel Peterson Got His Name* introduces humor. "Sea" includes both adventure and romance as it carries each character far into the unknown. "Air," man's most recent challenge, considers the mastery of the skies. *The Race to Save the Lord God Bird* describes a creature thought so superior that men destroyed it trying to possess its power. The other selections explore man's desire to conquer the air and other peoples.

Land

Bone, Ian. Sleep Rough Tonight.

New York: Dutton/Penguin Putnam, 2004. 241p. $16.99.
ISBN 0 525 47373 4. [fiction] MJS

Themes/Topics: bullies, urban survival, friendship

Summary/Description

Craving attention, Alex Pimentino encourages the senior bullies, but truly fears the Jockey, a classmate whom he indirectly sent to reform school for a year. The Jockey, now protecting Alex from the seniors, proposes that he and Alex sleep rough in the city so that Alex can become a man. Church-centered Marta, Alex's best friend and next-door neighbor, tells him to refuse, but Alex accepts and is drawn into the con of the Jockey and his uncle. Alex and the Jockey begin the night in a cemetery where a man steals Alex's coat. The two then pursue the thief (the Jockey's uncle) for revenge, and Alex thinks that he accidentally kills the man. Terrified, he calls Marta who helps him unravel the hoax. The Jockey pursues them, and although they escape, Alex returns to discover the Jockey's motive. The uncle and the Jockey run a theft ring and are recruiting Alex to help rob the business of Alex's father. Alex refuses. They attack him. The police, alerted by Marta, arrive in time. The experience changes Alex and Marta, who become closer to each other and more balanced in their lives.

Read Aloud/Reader Response

1. Chapter 2, pages 10 to 18. Alex, the clown, ponders the jungle coming-of-age story.
2. Chapter 6, pages 52 to 53, beginning "The whole frigging city . . . " and ending with the chapter. The Jockey proposes Alex's survival test in the city.
3. Chapter 9, page 80, beginning "You didn't say . . . " and ending " . . . up bog creek, ain't ya?" The Jockey attacks Alex about his smart remarks.
4. Chapter 12, page 111, beginning "He's just a pathetic . . . " and ending " . . . hundred times over!" The Jockey advocates going for revenge against the thief.
5. Chapter 20, pages 179 to 180, beginning "He looked at her . . . " and ending " . . . dark night ahead of them?" Alex contemplates courage.

Booktalk

Alex Pimentino gets his head dunked in the toilet almost daily by the too-big, too-dumb senior Barry Pilsener. Most of the time, big Barry doesn't even notice him. Alex bugs him to get his attention. That's not too hard for Alex. His mouth can match Barry's muscle, pound for pound. But there is one senior that Alex doesn't want to notice him—the lean, mean Jockey. Nobody messes with the Jockey, and Alex messed with him big time. Alex's mouth put the Jockey in Barlow Road Juvenile Detention Center. Now the Jockey is back, and Alex is sure that he is after him. But the Jockey is full of surprises. He wants to be friends with Alex. He'll teach Alex to be tough and handle the seniors himself. The Jockey wants the two of them to rough it in the urban wilderness. Maybe the Jockey is the real friend Alex is looking for, but maybe the Jockey is making sure that Alex never bugs anyone again. Alex will find out when they *Sleep Rough Tonight*.

Learning Opportunities

1. What does the lion hunt add to the story?
2. What choices do Marta and the Jockey offer Alex? Which ones are healthy?
3. List the adults in the story. Explain the role each one plays.
4. In Chapter 8, Alex's father sees Alex in the middle of the night and thinks that he is a ghost. How is that scene important to the story?
5. Using your library's resources, research a coming-of-age rite of passage in another culture. Compare it to Alex's.

Related Works

1. Almond, David. **Secret Heart.** New York: Delacorte Press, 2001. 199p. $17.99. ISBN 0 385 90065 1. [fiction] MJ Joe Maloney, bullied by the local boys, finds a new perspective on life when he answers the vision of the tiger and rejects the brutal masculine stereotype.
2. Koja, Kathe. **The Blue Mirror.** New York: Farrar, Straus and Giroux/Frances Foster Books, 2004. 119p. $16.00. ISBN 0 374 30849 7 [fiction] JS Hanging out at a downtown café, seventeen-year-old Maggy is exploited by an abusive teenager.
3. Lekuton, Joseph Lemasolai. **Facing the Lion: Growing Up Maasai on the African Savanna.** [nonfiction] MJS (See full booktalk in "Multiple Cultures"/"Learning from Other Countries," pages 234 to 236.) A Maasai man describes his growing up as part of a tribe and as part of an education-minded nation.
4. Mahy, Margaret. **24 Hours.** New York: Margaret K. McElderry Books, 2000. 200p. $17.00. ISBN 0 689 83884 0.[fiction] JS Drawn into a dysfunctional fringe world, seventeen-year-old Ellis solves a kidnapping and redefines his life.
5. Wynne-Jones, Tim. **The Boy in the Burning House.** New York: Farrar, Straus and Giroux/Melanie Kroupa Books, 2000. 213p. $16.00. ISBN 0 374 30930 2. [fiction] JS Fourteen-year-old Jim Hawkins helps a community outcast apprehend her abusive, adopted father for murder.

❦❧

Martin, Ann M. A Dog's Life: The Autobiography of a Stray.

New York: Scholastic Press, 2005. 182p. $16.99. ISBN 0 439 71559 8. [fiction] MJ

Themes/Topics: family, companionship, responsibility, human/ animal relationships

Summary/Description

A female stray dog, one of two surviving puppies, begins life with her mother and brother, Bone, in a shed. She first depends on her mother, then her more aggressive brother, but finally faces hostile humans, dangerous roads, and the elements independently. She and her brother leave the farm when they hear gunshots. Picked up on the road, they are tossed out a car window when they don't behave. A passer-by rescues the male. The female begins her roaming life that leads to garbage cans, another dog companion, a temporary home, and a pattern of wintering on farms and wandering with the arrival of spring. Stiff with age, she wanders onto the farm of eighty-two-year-old Susan, who gives her a permanent home.

Read Aloud/Reader Response

1. "The Wheelbarrow," pages 11 to 16. The technique used to describe the shed community could be used to describe people.
2. "The Throwaways," pages 51 to 53, beginning with the chapter and ending with " . . . as they went." The man who picks up the narrator and her brother throws them out the window.
3. "Squirrel Alone," pages 61 to 67. This chapter relates Squirrel's life immediately after losing her brother, Bone.
4. "The Fight," pages 75 to 82. Squirrel describes fighting the desperate and starving dogs whose territory Squirrel and Moon invade.
5. "Summer Dog," pages 123 to 131. Squirrel describes her brief stay with a family who adopts a dog each summer, ignores the dog after the novelty wears off, and then deserts the dog at the end of the summer.
6. "Home" pages 181 and 182. Squirrel describes her final home with Susan, also elderly and lonely.

Booktalk

Read "Night," pages ix to x. Yes, she has been all of these dogs. Her life story, A Dog's Life, will make you think a little more seriously about the dogs that you see everyday and the lives that you might share with some of them along the way.

Learning Opportunities

1. After reading A Dog's Life: The Autobiography of a Stray, discuss how you would now interpret the phrase "a dog's life."
2. Describe, with your reactions, each person with whom Squirrel comes in contact.

3. Is this work about animal rights?
4. Using your local humane society and your library's resources, find out the rules and procedures in dealing with feral dogs.
5. Rewrite one of the experiences that Squirrel describes from the point of view of another character in the experience or encounter.

Related Works

1. Branford, Henrietta. **White Wolf.** Cambridge, MA: Candlewick Press, 1998. 96p. $16.99. ISBN 0 7636 0748 7. [fiction] MJ (See full booktalk in *Booktalks Plus,* 2001, pages 26 to28.) Captured by pioneers, a young wolf cub is stolen by Indians, escapes, heads his own pack, and finally saves the life of his original owner.
2. Hobbs, Valerie. **Sheep.** New York: Farrar, Straus and Giroux/ Frances Foster Books, 2006. 115p. $16.00. ISBN 0 374 36777 9. [fiction] MJ Jack, a runt sheepdog, tells about the events that connect him to both kind and sadistic owners, and, finally, the boy he calls his own.
3. Kochalka, James. **Peanut Butter & Jeremy's Best Book Ever.** Gainsville, FL: Alternative Comics, 2003. 273p. $14.95. ISBN 1 891867 46 6. [graphic] MJS/A A hat- and tie-wearing sensitive cat interacts with an obnoxious exploitive bird.
4. Koja, Kathe. **Straydog.** New York: Farrar, Straus and Giroux/Frances Foster Books, 2002. 106p. $16.00. ISBN 0 374 37278 0. [fiction] JS (See full booktalk in *Teen Genre Connections,* pages 8 to 10.) Rachel, an individualistic and rebellious high school student, volunteers at an animal shelter where she decides to save an injured feral dog.
5. Morpurgo, Michael. **The Amazing Story of Adolphus Tips.** New York: Scholastic Press, 2006. 128p. $16.99. ISBN 0 439 79661 X. [fiction] MJ Through her diary written during the American preparation for D-Day, a British grandmother explains to her grandson how an independent, survivalist cat helped her find her first love.

ℭℑℭℑ

McMullan, Kate. Adrienne Yorinks (illus.).
My Travels with Capts. Lewis and
Clark by George Shannon.
New York: Harper Collins/Joanna Cotler Books, 2004. 266p. $16.89.
ISBN 0 06 008100 7. [fiction] JS

Themes/Topics: Lewis and Clark Expedition, George Shannon, diaries, overland journeys

Summary/Description

Sixteen-year-old George meets Captain Meriwether Lewis, runs away from an abusive uncle to join the expedition, and records the journey in his diary. He describes the leaders' contrasting personalities, the tough terrain, new and fascinating wildlife, harsh discipline, and the remarkable assets that Clark's slave and the teenage Sacagawea contribute to the exploration. He emphasizes the journey's accomplishment and the paternal attitude that the explorers held for the Native American population. The "Author's Note" explains that Shannon, the author's ancestor, was the expedition's youngest explorer and became a member of the Kentucky House of Representatives and the Missouri Senate.

Read Aloud/Reader Response

1. "Aug. 22, '03" entry, pages 9 to 10. Shannon agonizes over supporting his family or joining the expedition.
2. "Oct. 14, '03" entry, pages 15 to 16. Shannon contrasts Lewis and Clark and comments on the abject position of Clark's slave who supposedly grew up like a "brother."
3. "Council Bluffs/Aug. 3, '04," pages 73 to 75. The expedition encounters the Otto Indians.
4. "Mandan campsite/Nov. 6, '04," pages 121 to 122. The company meets Sacagawea.
5. "Fort Rock Camp/Oct. 29, '05," page 249. Shannon encounters a Native American chief who displays dried fingers in his medicine pouch.

Booktalk

Sixteen-year-old George Shannon is the oldest son. His father is dead. To support the family, George works for his Uncle Liam in Pittsburgh, Pennsylvania. The sour boss and inside job are about to drive George crazy. Then opportunity knocks, or, more accurately, a big dog knocks George down. The dog belongs to Captain Meriwether Lewis. Anybody good enough for his dog is good enough for the Captain. Just like that, George has a chance to leave Pittsburgh. The year is 1803. At the request of President Thomas Jefferson, Captain Meriwether and Captain Clark are putting an expedition together. They are assessing what the United States of America bought when it made the Louisiana Purchase. The job sounds better than working in a store. George trades his city responsibilities for wilderness hardships. Is it a good trade? Read about the long walk that made history and expanded a country in *My Travels with Capts. Lewis and Clark by George Shannon*.

Learning Opportunities

1. Continue to research the Lewis and Clark Expedition. You may start by reading *The Saga of Lewis and Clark: Into the Uncharted West* (Related Work 5). Explain how the information you find contributes to your appreciation of the story.
2. Research President Thomas Jefferson's term. You may want to read *Thomas Jefferson: Architect of Democracy* (Related Work 4). Share the information with the group.
3. After reading Captain Lewis's speeches to the Native American populations, read speeches given by Native Americans recorded in *In a Sacred Manner I Live: Native American Wisdom* (Related Work 3). Describe the differences.
4. Describe a day from another expedition member's point of view.
5. What makes Sacagawea such an important and amazing member of the expedition? You may wish to read *Sacajawea* (Related Work 1).

Related Works

1. Bruchac, Joseph. **Sacajawea.** New York: Harcourt Brace and Company/Silver Whistle, 2000. 199p. $17.00. ISBN 0 15 202234 1. [fiction] JS Sacajawea's son relates the stories that his mother and William Clark told him about the Lewis and Clark Expedition.
2. Lasky, Kathryn. **The Journal of Augustus Pelletier: The Lewis and Clark Expedition.** New York: Scholastic Press, 2000. 176p. (My Name is America). $10.95. ISBN 0 590 68489 2. [fiction] MJ Half French and half Omaha Indian, fourteen-year-old Gus joins the expedition after his stepfather tries to cut off Gus's ear.
3. Philip, Neil. (ed.). **In a Sacred Manner I Live: Native American Wisdom.** New York: Clarion Books, 1997. 93p. $20.00. ISBN 0 395 84981 0. [nonfiction] JS (See full booktalk in *Booktalks and More*, 2003, pages 44 to 46.) This collection of Native American pictures, poems, songs, and speeches ranges from 1609 to 1995.
4. Severance, John B. **Thomas Jefferson: Architect of Democracy.** New York: Clarion Books, 1998. 192p. $18.00. ISBN 0 395 84513 0. [nonfiction] JS (See full booktalk in *Booktalks Plus*, 2001, pages 245 to 247.) Severance presents Thomas Jefferson as a man of contradictions, a major one being his shrewd negotiation of the Louisiana Purchase and the disaster of his own personal finances.
5. Schmidt, Thomas, and Jeremy Schmidt. **The Saga of Lewis and Clark: Into the Uncharted West.** New York: DK Publishing, Inc., 1999. 210p. (A Tehabi Book). $35.00. ISBN 0 7894 4638 3. [nonfiction] JS (See full booktalk in *Booktalks and More*, 2003, pages 235

to 237.) The multi-layered account of the exploration includes the hardships endured by the expedition.

ʕʒʕ̣ʔ

Paulsen, Gary. How Angel Peterson Got His Name: And Other Outrageous Tales About Extreme Sports.
New York: Wendy Lamb Books, 2003. 111p. $12.95.
ISBN 0 385 72949 9. [nonfiction] MJS

Themes/Topics: Paulsen's childhood, Minnesota, late 1940s and early 1950s

Summary/Description

Paulsen recalls five outrageous adventures of boys he knew in a small northern Minnesota town. The foreword explains his own adventures. "A Note of Caution" compares their attempts to today's extreme sports. "How Angel Peterson Got His Name" describes Angel's attempt at world record skiing. "The Miracle of Flight" is a frugal encounter with an Army surplus kite. "Orvis Orvisen and the Crash and Bash" recounts self-punishment and daring bike attempts. "Girls and the Circle of Death" focuses again on Orvis, this time in a daredevil match with a bear. "And Finally, Skateboards, Bungee Jumping and Other Failures" relates the first bungee jump, a disastrous confrontation with a wasp's nest, initiated to trump the bear fight.

Read Aloud/Reader Response

Each story can stand on its own or be read in relation to the other four. All are entertaining and appropriate for reading aloud or oral interpretation.

Booktalk

Ask how many people in the group are familiar with extreme sports. Ask them to share their favorite event and the reason why it is their favorite event.

If you have read any of the *Hatchet* books by Gary Paulsen, you know that he can make up a great adventure story. In fact, some people consider him the king of survival and adventure stories. But Paulsen lived some real adventures too. These hair-raising experiences took place in northern Minnesota. In the late 1940s and early 1950s, extreme sports were unheard of—sophisticated sports equipment was too, so thirteen-year-old Gary Paulsen and friends decided to make up the sports and the equipment to go with them. They wondered about things like—How can a person break a world skiing record? Fly into the air on an Army kite? Wrestle a bear? Hitch a skateboard to a car? Or bungee jump with some old tires? What could go wrong? Plenty. Paulsen tells all, and he starts it all off with the unbelievable, laugh-out-loud tale of *How Angel Peterson Got His Name.*

Learning Opportunities

1. Create a series of radio programs by reading each story out loud with sound effects.
2. Using your library's resources, research extreme sports. Share the information with the group. You may wish to begin your research with *Highs!* (Related Work 1).
3. Chapter 3 opens with a short commentary on boys' names, pages 55 to 56. Reread the section that begins "There are boys' names . . . " and " . . . tough row to hoe." Research names and their effects on their owners. Share your information with the class.
4. Select one memory involving your family and friends. Shape it into a story, and share it in either oral or written form.
5. Using your library's resources, research life in the late 1940s and 1950s. Create a visual display with the pictures and facts that you find.

Related Works

1. Packer, Alex. Jeff Tolbert (illus.). Pamela Espeland (ed.). **Highs!: Over 150 Ways to Feel Really, Really Good . . . Without Alcohol or Other Drugs.** Minneapolis, MN: Free Spirit Publishing, 2000. 251p. $14.95. ISBN 1 57542 074 0. [nonfiction] MJS Packer connects young adults to positive activities. "Physical and Sensuous Highs" includes sources for X-treme sports and cheap thrills.
2. Paulsen, Gary. **Alida's Song.** New York: Delacorte Press, 1999. 88p. $15.95. ISBN 0 385 32586 X. [biography] MJS Paulsen recalls the summer his grandmother invited him to work with her on a farm owned by two bachelor brothers. The experience pulls him away from his alcoholic parents and into a world of hard work, natural rhythms, and good food.
3. Paulsen, Gary. **The Beet Fields: Memories of a Sixteenth Summer.** New York: Delacorte Press, 2000. 160p. $15.95. ISBN 0 385 32647 5. [biography] JS Paulsen tells how, in 1955 at sixteen, he leaves an abusive home and learns to sort out the difficult choices of the world.

4. Paulsen, Gary. **The Glass Café.** New York: Wendy Lamb Books, 2003. 99p. $12.95. ISBN 0 385 90121 6. [fiction] MJ Also filled with humor, this story tells about twelve-year-old Tony Henson, a talented artist who decides to sketch the exotic dancers in the club where his mother, also an exotic dancer, works.

5. Paulsen, Gary. **My Life in Dog Years.** New York: Dell Publishing, 1998. 137p. $4.99pa. ISBN 0 440 41471 7. [biography] MJS With the same slapstick humor he used in *How Angel Peterson Got His Name*, Paulsen writes character sketches for eight significant dogs in his life.

Sea

ℭℑℭ

Blumberg, Rhoda. **Shipwrecked!: The True Adventures of a Japanese Boy.**
New York: HarperCollins Publishers, 2001. 80p. $17.89.
ISBN 0 06 029365 9. [nonfiction] MJ

Themes/Topics: nineteenth-century Japan, tradition vs. change, sea life, Hawaii, conduct of life

Summary/Description

When his father dies in 1836, nine-year-old Manjiro becomes the head and sole support of his family. According to Japanese tradition, Manjiro must be a fisherman like his father. A storm drives his boat three-hundred miles from Japan. This "Isolated Empire" forbids foreigners and any information from the outside world. If one leaves Japan, he or she is forbidden to return. Marooned on an island, Manjiro and his fellow fishermen fear they will not be allowed to go home. An American whaling ship rescues them and takes them to Honolulu. The captain becomes Manjiro's foster father, and Manjiro accompanies him to New England where Manjiro excels in the maritime academy, signs up for a whaling expedition, and after earning six-hundred dollars in the 1848 California Gold Rush, returns to Japan with his shipmates. Encountering hostility and imprisonment, Manjiro eventually is released in 1852, visits his family, helps Japan reenter the world, and becomes an honored Samurai.

Read Aloud/Reader Response

1. Page 7. The opening paragraph describes Manjiro's difficult personal situation.

2. Page 17, beginning "in this era, . . ." and ending with "The construction of large ships [capable of sailing long distances] is prohibited." The passage illustrates the restrictive Japanese government.
3. Page 39, read the three paragraphs on page 39 beginning with "Manjiro was the first Japanese . . ." and ending "Chairs and benches were not used." Manjiro might encounter these difficulties in his new life.
4. Page 41, beginning "Captain Whitfield's business trip . . ." and ending "carrying loads." The passage shows the contrast between the American and Japanese cultures.
5. Pages 43 to 45, beginning "Although grateful and loving . . ." and ending " . . . not matched in other countries." Manjiro comments on American customs.

Booktalk

Manjiro is nine years old when his father dies. Manjiro must support his family. The year is 1836. According to Japanese law, he will be a fisherman like his father. After five years of backbreaking work and starvation pay, Manjiro decides to try his luck in Usa, another coastal village ninety miles from his home. It is a long way from home and family, but Manjiro finds work with a small group of fishermen almost as needy as himself. They set sail. Their expedition promises success. Suddenly, a storm comes up. It lasts a week and maroons them on an island three-hundred miles from shore. With their boat smashed, they have little hope of sailing home, but even if someone finds them, these fishermen have a big problem. Japan is "An Isolated Empire." No foreigners can live freely in Japan. This picture shows how the Japanese see foreigners. (*Show picture on page 23.*) Any Japanese citizen who leaves and tries to return can be killed. The government fears that the person will bring back the evil foreign ways. Manjiro fears, even if he survives on the island, that he will never see his family again. But for Manjiro, the home he longs for proves to be many years and thousands of miles away. He will travel to new countries, learn new jobs, and open new worlds. And those worlds will change the *Shipwrecked!* Japanese teenager and man even more than he changes them.

Learning Opportunities

1. Using your library's resources, further research nineteenth-century Japan.
2. Using your library's resources, prepare a report on Commodore Perry. Explain how that information adds to your understanding of the account.

3. Continue to research the history of the whaling industry. You may
    wish to refer to *Gone A-Whaling: The Lure of the Sea and the
    Hunt for the Great Whale* (Related Work 4) and *Black Hands,
    White Sails: The Story of African-American Whalers* (Related
    Work 3)
4. Trace the events of Manjiro's life. Then discuss how his reaction to
    each event determined his success.
5. Explain the most important aspect of this account for you.

Related Works

1. Cain, Timothy. **The Book of Rule: How the World Is Governed.**
    New York: DK Publishing, 2004. 320p. $30.00. ISBN 0 7894 9354
    3. [reference] MJS This reference discusses the governments of 193
    countries and explains how power evolves in each. Japan is exam-
    ined on pages 66 to 75.
2. Linnéa, Sharon. **Princess Ka´iulani: Hope of a Nation, Heart
    of a People.** Grand Rapids, MI: Eerdmans Books for Young
    Readers, 1999. 234p. $18.00. ISBN 0 8028 5145 2. [nonfic-
    tion] MJS (See full booktalk in *Booktalks Plus,* 2001, pages 238
    to 241.) Through this ill-fated princess's life, the Hawaiian and
    Western worlds clash as she struggles to give her people peace and
    freedom.
3. McKissack, Patricia C., and Fredrick L. McKissack. **Black Hands,
    White Sails: The Story of African-American Whalers.** New
    York: Scholastic Press, 1999. 147p. $15.95pa. ISBN 0 590 48313
    7. [nonfiction] MJS (See full booktalk in *Booktalks Plus,* 2001,
    pages 103 to 105.) Tying the history of whaling to the history
    of the slave ship, this account illustrates why Manjiro would be
    accepted for his skill and determination rather than rejected
    because of his skin color.
4. Murphy, Jim. **Gone A-Whaling: The Lure of the Sea and the
    Hunt for the Great Whale.** New York: Clarion Books, 1998. 208p.
    $18.00. ISBN 0 395 69847 2. [nonfiction] MJS (See full booktalk
    in *Booktalks Plus,* 2001, pages 106 to 107.) This history of whaling
    spans the earliest times to present day and includes extensive infor-
    mation about whales, ship owners, living conditions at sea, maps,
    and historical documents.
5. Yep, Laurence. **The Journal of Wong Ming-Chung: A Chinese
    Miner.** New York: Scholastic Press, 2000. 224p. (A Dear America
    Book/My Name Is America). $10.95. ISBN 0 590 38607 7. [fiction]
    MJ A young Chinese boy comes to America, the Golden Mountain,
    to search for riches and encounters great prejudice.

රු රු

Martel, Yann. **Life of Pi.**

New York: Harcourt Brace and Company/A Harvest Book, 2001. 401p. $7.99pa.
ISBN 0 15 803020 5. [fiction] S/A

Themes/Topics: animal behavior, faith, religion, family

Summary/Description

Piscine (Pi) Molitor Patel lives in India where his father is a zoo-keeper. When Pi's father decides to immigrate to Canada, Pi and his family arrange to sell and deliver the zoo animals. The boat sinks. Pi, a young man who enthusiastically embraces all religions, and the animals in his lifeboat are the only survivors: a hyena, a zebra, a Borneo orang-utan, and a Bengal tiger. Eventually, only Pi and the Bengal tiger, Richard Parker, remain. Pi establishes social dominance, and the two co-exist under almost impossible conditions for 227 days. The only man Pi encounters in the middle of the Pacific tries to kill him. They reach Mexico. Pi is rescued, and Richard Parker slips into the jungle. When the Japanese authorities question Pi, they do not accept his fantastic story, so he offers them a version featuring human barbarity. Then he asks them to choose. They choose the animal version.

Read Aloud/Reader Response

1. Chapter 4, pages 17 and 18, beginning with "To me, . . . " and ending with the paragraph. The passage describes zoo life.
2. Chapter 11, pages 52 to 53. Animals want to stay away from man.
3. Chapter 32, page 107, beginning "We had our own case . . . " and ending with the paragraph. A mouse survives in a cage of vipers.
4. Chapter 42, pages 139 to 141. The orang-utan arrives.
5. Chapter 58, pages 209 to 211, beginning with "I pulled out the survival manual . . . " and ending with the list. Survival instructions are in the manual.

Booktalk

Pi grew up in a zoo. He is a man now, but he has a most unusual zoo story from his youth, a survival story that others should hear. Pi was always spiritual. Very early in life, he embraced all religious beliefs. He also learned that the animals that any god created are just animals. Their instincts tell them to kill and to eat flesh. Suddenly, all these life lessons come together. Pi and his family are transporting animals to Canada. The zoo transport boat sinks. Pi finds himself in a lifeboat, but he is not alone. His companions are a hyena, a zebra, an orang-utan, and a Bengal tiger. The hyena, zebra, and orang-utan die. That leaves just Pi and Richard Parker, the Bengal tiger. Pi's animal lessons tell him that he too will soon die. But his spiritual beliefs tell him all things are possible. He combines this knowledge and lives. How? It is all a part of the beautiful life mystery, the miraculous *Life of Pi*.

Learning Opportunities

1. Identify the chapters that prepare us for Pi's survival to be believable.
2. Research the habits of a Bengal tiger. Share your research with the group. Discuss what this knowledge adds to the story.
3. Which story, the animals or the people, do you believe? Explain your answer.
4. Martel introduces another human survivor into the story. Why?
5. List each religious reference that Pi makes: Hindu, Christian, Muslim. Ask each person in the group to research a reference. Share the information and discuss how it relates to the story.

Related Works

1. Calabro, Marian. **The Perilous Journey of the Donner Party.** New York: Clarion Books, 1999. 192p. $20.00. ISBN 0 395 86610 3. [nonfiction] MJS Calabro describes the trip's hopeful and confident beginning, its procrastination, and its final deterioration of morale and health that resulted in cannibalism as well as the rescue and the effect on the survivor's descendents.
2. Fama, Elizabeth. **Overboard.** Chicago, IL: Cricket Books, 2002. 158p. $15.95. ISBN 0 8126 2652 4. [fiction] MJS (See full booktalk in *Teen Genre Connections*, 2005, pages 109 to 111.) Fourteen-year-old Emily spends seventeen hours struggling for survival, reflecting on her priorities, and bonding with a nine-year-old Muslim boy after her boat, filled with Muslim pilgrims, sinks.
3. Fraustino, Lisa Rowe (ed.). **Soul Searching: Thirteen Stories about Faith and Belief.** New York: Simon & Schuster Books for Young Readers, 2002. 267p. $17.95. ISBN 0 689 83484 5. [fiction] MJS The stories talk about the great faith required in all cultures to face life's problems and responsibilities.
4. Rylant, Cynthia. **God Went to Beauty School.** New York: Harper Tempest, 2003. 56p. $14.99. ISBN 06 009434 6. [poetry] JS (See full booktalk in *Teen Genre Connections*, 2005, pages 84 to 85.) In twenty-three poems, Rylant describes God's trip to the world during which he learns to appreciate simple things.

5. Watterson, Bill. **The Calvin and Hobbes Tenth Anniversary Book.** Kansas City, MO: Universal Press Syndicate, 1995. 208p. $14.95. ISBN 0 8362 0438 7. [graphic, cartoon strips] MJS/A In another story about a boy and a tiger, Calvin and Hobbes strive for dominance but work together to survive physically and emotionally in a puzzling universe.

ॐ ॐ

Philbrick, Rodman. The Young Man and the Sea.

New York: The Blue Sky Press, 2004. 142p. $16.95. ISBN 0 439 36829 4. [fiction] MJ

Themes/Topics: alcoholism, bullies, coming-of-age, death, family, beating the odds

Summary/Description

Twelve-year-old Skiff Beaman wants to keep the family boat, the *Mary Rose,* and his family afloat. After the death of Skiff's mother, Skiff's father drinks and ignores his son and livelihood. Skiff, harassed by the local bullies, turns to ninety-four-year-old Mr. Woodwell, who believes in Skiff's father and helps Skiff repair the boat, which needs a rebuilt motor, at a cost of five-thousand dollars. Skiff plans to earn the money by trapping lobster, but Tyler Croft, son of one of the town's wealthiest families, sabotages him. A fish story inspires Skiff to pursue the blue fin tuna with his father's perfectly balanced harpoon. The motor stalls, and the mist rolls in. The fish pulls Skiff into the water and drags the boat after Skiff manages to climb back in. He rows toward shore until the Crofts' boat, with Skiff's father aboard, finds him. Father and son bond. Skiff achieves fame. His father renews his friendships with Mr. Jack Croft and Mr. Woodwell. He takes care of the house, and agrees to attend AA meetings.

Read Aloud/Reader Response

1. Chapter 1, page 13. "When your whole life is sunk, . . . make it worse." Skiff thinks his life is completely finished.
2. Chapter 4, page 28. "They say a thing that's broke . . . if you work at it." Skiff resolves to fix his problems.
3. Chapter 6, pages 42 to 47. The chapter describes Mr. Woodwell and his boat shed.
4. Chapter 12, page 84. "You're a loser. . . . losing!" Tyler taunts Skiff.
5. Chapter 17, page 121, beginning "Mom's Three Rules." and ending "Yes, Mom. I promise." Skiff recalls his mother's guiding advice.

Booktalk

Twelve-year-old Skiff Beaman doesn't have much to look forward to. His mother is dead. His dad stays on the couch "like a sack of nothing," "sucks on his beer and stares at the cobwebs." The *Mary Rose,* their boat, just sunk. His dad won't do anything about it, so no home improvement is in sight. That wouldn't be so bad if the whole town didn't know about the Beamans being "swampers," or "white trash," or if rich boy, Tyler Croft, didn't spend his days harassing Skiff about his dead mother and drunken father. Skiff isn't doing too well on land, so he decides to make a change. He will fix that boat and go after a giant blue fin tuna, "The king of fish! The queen of the Seven Seas!"—a fish that could make the Beamans rich. Skiff Beaman gets his head beat in by bullies on land. Can he do any better when it's just *The Young Man and the Sea?*

Learning Opportunities

1. Discuss how the mother affects the story.
2. Identify each father/son relationship in the story. Discuss what Skiff and the reader might learn from each.
3. Using your library's resources, research the blue fin tuna. Share your information with the group.
4. Discuss the harpoon's importance to the story.
5. Compare how the settings of land and sea affect the story.

Related Works

1. Giff, Patricia Reilly. **All the Way Home.** New York: Dell Yearling, 2001. 169p. $5.99pa. ISBN 0 440 41182 3. [fiction] MJ When eleven-year-old Mariel runs away from her "almost mother" to find her biological mother, she discovers that her adopted mother is the one that she really loves.
2. Hemingway, Ernest. **The Old Man and the Sea.** New York: Scribner, 1995. 128p. $12.00pa. ISBN 0 684 80122 1. [fiction] S/A Inspired by the faith of a young boy, Santiago, an old fisherman, meets the sea's moral and physical challenges. The book first appeared in 1952 and won the Pulitzer Prize in 1953.
3. Hite, Sid. **The King of Slippery Falls.** New York: Scholastic Press, 2004. 217p. $15.95. ISBN 0 439 34257 0 [fiction] MJS (See full booktalk in *Teen Genre Connections,* 2005, pages 77 to 79.) In his sixteenth year, Lewis Hinton vows to catch a monster trout living in back of Slippery Falls, and his almost mystical pursuit turns into a personal journey.
4. Jennings, Patrick. **Outstanding in My Field.** New York: Scholastic Press, 2005. 176p. $16.95. ISBN 0 439 46581 8. [fiction] M Dominated

by his alcoholic father, eleven-year-old Ty decides to stand up and free himself from emotional turmoil.

5. Klise, Kate. **Deliver Us from Normal.** New York: Scholastic Press, 2005. 240p. $16.95. ISBN 0 439 52322 2. [fiction] MJ Eleven-year-old Charles Harrisong discovers that he is a positive and important part of his poor and off-beat family's happiness and success when the family sails away to free themselves from the bullying in Normal, Illinois.

⚞⚟

Rees, Celia. **Pirates!**
New York: Bloomsbury, 2003. 380p. $16.95. ISBN 1 58234 816 2. [fiction] MJS

Themes/Topics: eighteenth century, gender roles, slavery, family, England, Jamaica

Summary/Description

For an English girl of the early eighteenth century, fifteen-year-old Nancy has a rather masculine upbringing. When her father, a slave trader and sugar merchant dies, Nancy inherits the family's Jamaican plantation. Her degenerate brother accompanies her to Jamaica where she discovers two female house slaves to whom she is immediately drawn, an abusive overseer, and a plan for her marriage that is an economic alliance with a diabolical Brazilian plantation owner. Nancy, however, pledged her love to William, her lifelong friend whom she helped secure a ranking position in the British Navy. Nancy kills the overseer to prevent his raping Minerva, the younger house slave. Phillis, Minerva's mother, arranges for the three to join the maroons, runaway slaves and criminals hiding on the island. Knowing that the Brazilian will pursue his bride, Nancy and Minerva join pirates who visit the community. Throughout their journeys, Nancy's dreams tell her that the Brazilian is after her, but she refuses to throw away his gift, a ruby necklace and earrings, that draws him mystically to her. Nancy learns that Minerva is her half-sister. Minerva kills the Brazilian to save Nancy and the rest of the crew. Minerva, now pregnant, settles down with the ex-pirate she loves, and Nancy leaves to search for William.

Read Aloud/Reader Response

1. Chapter 8, pages 85 to 86, beginning "Don't it feel . . . " and ending " . . . half pirate already." Broom is described as kind, romantic, and handsome.

2. Chapter 10, page 109, beginning "She stood looking . . ." and ending " . . . burnt sienna." Nancy's description of Minerva anticipates that they are sisters.
3. Chapter 13, pages 128 to 140. Nancy faces a horrible marriage.
4. Chapter 20, pages 190 to 192, beginning "These were the Articles . . ." and ending " . . . *suffer present death.*" The Articles and Broom's ability to amend them reveal the ship's values and governing organization.
5. Chapter 37, pages 316 to 320. The description of the equatorial line crossing shows how quickly the ship's government can dissolve.

Booktalk

Instead of my introducing this story to you, let Nancy, one of the *Pirates!*, do the job. (*Read the "Preface," page 13.*)

Learning Opportunities

1. Using your library's resources, research the history of pirating. Share your findings with the group. Discuss how that information affects your understanding of the story.
2. Nancy, William, and Minerva face evil that seems out of control. Name the evil and list the events and decisions that help them obtain control of their fates.
3. List each parent. Describe why each is important to the story.
4. How does Rees communicate the Brazilian's overwhelming evil?
5. Discuss the importance and magical powers of the ruby necklace and earrings.

Related Works

1. Jaques, Brian. David Elliot (illus.). **The Angel's Command: A Tale from the Castaways of The Flying Dutchman.** New York: Philomel Books, 2003. 374p. $23.99. ISBN 0 399 23999 5. [fiction] MJ Set in 1628, this story sees Ben and Ned confronting pirates, privateers, and gypsy bandits in two action adventures.
2. McCaughrean, Geraldine. **The Pirate's Son.** New York: Scholastic Press, 1998. American ed. 294p. $16.95. ISBN 0 590 20344 4. [fiction] MJ (See full booktalk in *Booktalks Plus*, 2001, pages 74 to 77.) Three eighteenth-century teenagers leave traditional English roles and embrace the pirate world.
3. Meyer, L. A. **Bloody Jack: Being an Account of the Curious Adventures of Mary "Jacky" Faber, Ship's Boy.** New York: Harcourt Brace and Company, 2002. 278p. $17.00. ISBN 0 15 216721 5. [fiction] JS Within her thirteenth and fifteenth years,

orphaned Mary ("Jacky") Faber masquerades as a ship's boy and helps the Royal Navy defeat pirates.

4. Meyer, L. A. **Under the Jolly Roger: Being an Account of the Further Nautical Adventures of Jacky Faber.** New York: Harcourt Brace and Company, 2005. 318p. $17.00. ISBN 0 15 205345 X. [fiction] JS Now about fifteen or sixteen, Jacky becomes a British privateer but almost hangs for stealing her ship in this third Jacky Faber adventure.

5. Lee, Tanith. **Piratica: Being a Daring Tale of a Singular Girl's Adventure upon the High Seas.** New York: Dutton Children's Books, 2003. 288p. $17.99. ISBN 0 525 47324 6. [fiction] MJS Sixteen-year-old Art receives a bump on the head that launches her into the romantic pirating adventure that makes her a folk hero.

ॐॐ

Reuter, Bjarne. Tiina Nunnally (trans.).
The Ring of the Slave Prince.
New York: Dutton Children's Books, 2003. 373p. $22.99.
ISBN 0 525 47146 4. [fiction] MJ

Themes/Topics: Caribbean, seventeenth century, slavery, Inquisition, gender roles, coming-of-age, family, friendship

Summary/Description

In the 1639 world of the Caribbean, fourteen-year-old Tom O'Connor hopes to save his mother and half-sister from drudgery and abuse. Looking for treasure in a wrecked ship, Tom finds Ramón the Pious and a slave boy. Ramón claims the boy is an African prince whose father will reward his return. Tom receives half ownership for saving their lives. When Ramón disappears with the slave, Tom pursues them. His arduous journey follows the prophecies of the island's ancient healer and fortune-teller and makes him more compassionate. He acknowledges slaves as human beings, and frees the prince. Returning home, he finds his mother dead and his sister betrothed to a former Inquisition officer. When his sister and her fiancé sail for Spain, Tom and the prince join the crew, partly to stop the marriage. A notorious pirate captures the ship. Tom becomes a pirate to survive. A hurricane destroys the pirate ship and kills the fiancé. Eventually, Tom, with the help of his sister and the pirate, returns the prince, who is actually a fisherman's son, to his home and realizes the true meaning of riches.

Read Aloud/Reader Response

1. Chapter 1, pages 10 to 14, beginning "Put your hand on the table, Tom . . ." and ending with the chapter. Zamora cryptically outlines Tom's life. Throughout the book, Tom recalls her words. The selection is suitable for a dramatic presentation with two readers.

2. Chapter 2, page 16, beginning "Will was the most . . ." and ending " . . . I have the will." Tom describes how his determination gives him an advantage.

3. Chapter 5, pages 52 to 53, beginning " . . . he had always dreamed . . ." and ending "Then she'd be gone." Tom reflects on freedom and how difficult it is to achieve in adulthood.

4. Chapter 13, page 161, beginning with the chapter and ending " . . . resides the plague." Tom describes the rat and explains why he dislikes rats.

5. Chapter 19, pages 236 to 239, beginning "When night fell, . . ." and ending " . . . mix the yams with cooked bananas." Tom shifts from a master to a human being truly concerned about Nyo Boto.

6. Chapter 22, pages 287 to 290, beginning "On the upper deck . . ." and ending " . . . the presence of C. W. Bull." Tom encounters the notorious pirate, C. W. Bull.

7. Chapter 24, pages 326 to 327, beginning "At that second . . ." and ending " . . . for as long as we can." Tom knows that Orion's Belt is a bad omen for him, but acts.

Booktalk

Fourteen-year-old Tom O'Connor lives on a Caribbean island in the year 1639. That sounds like paradise, but his mother, sister, and Tom serve the stingy and cruel Señor López, who owns a rundown inn on the island of Nevis. Tom wants something better—for all of them. He decides to take advantage of another's misfortune. That's how the successful people he knows get ahead. Tom listens for news of shipwrecks. Then he searches the waters for their treasure. Surely, he will find gold. Instead he finds the golden-tongued Ramón the Pious and a small, almost dead black slave whom Ramón calls a prince. And Ramón has the prince's ring to prove his story. If Tom saves their lives, Ramón will give him half the slave, and, someday, half the reward from the prince's grateful father. Tom drags them into the boat and pulls in a new world with them. His destiny begins to follow the prophecy of the island fortune-teller, a prophecy that leads him to lies, treachery, crime, plantations, pirates, royalty, and possibly death as he follows *The Ring of the Slave Prince*.

Learning Opportunities

1. Using your library's resources, research the period's pirates. Share your information with the group.
2. Reuter resurrects several characters, but never tells the fate of Ramón. Discuss why.
3. Using your library's resources, research the Inquisition. Share the information with the group.
4. Using your library's resources, research the role of slavery in the New World.
5. Reuter presents several pictures of evil and abuse. Choose one. Explain the why and how of the evil. Discuss how each situation affects Tom.
6. Explain the roles of Feo and Nyo Boto in the story.
7. Choose one lie or story and explain its impact on the novel.

Related Works

1. Coelho, Paulo. Alan R. Clarke (trans.). **The Alchemist.** San Francisco, CA: HarperSanFrancisco, 1998. 174p. $13.00pa. ISBN 0 06 250218 2. [fiction] JS/A In this fairy tale–like novel, Santiago, a young shepherd, seeks his personal calling, learns about the world and himself, finds love, and discovers his riches and treasure at home.
2. Lawrence, Iain. **Ghost Boy.** New York: Delacorte Press, 2000. 326p. $15.95. ISBN 0 385 32739 0 [fiction] MJS Fourteen-year-old Harold Kline, an albino, seeks a new life in the circus, but discovers that a new life will come at home when he is the one who changes.
3. Lawrence, Iain. **The Wreckers.** New York: Delacorte Press, 1998. 196p. $15.95. ISBN 0 385 32535 5. [fiction] MJ (See full booktalk in *Teen Genre Connections,* 2005, pages 111 to 112.) In this high seas mystery, fourteen-year-old John Spencer saves his father's life and learns about the wreckers, people who lure ships close to the shore so that they will crash and lose their cargo.
4. Meltzer, Milton. **Witches and Witch-hunts: A History of Persecution.** New York: The Blue Sky Press, 1998. 128p. $16.95. ISBN 0 590 48517 2. [nonfiction] JS (See full booktalk in *Booktalks and More,* 2003, pages 187 to 189.) Meltzer explains how witch-hunts become a search for the why of bad events.
5. Meyer, L. A. **Under the Jolly Roger: Being an Account of the Further Nautical Adventures of Jacky Faber.** New York: Harcourt Brace and Company, 2005. 318p. $17.00. ISBN 0 15

205345 X. [fiction] JS Now about fifteen or sixteen, Jacky becomes a British privateer but almost hangs for stealing her ship in this third Jacky Faber adventure.

Air

CC

Hoose, Phillip. The Race to Save the Lord God Bird.

New York: Farrar, Straus and Giroux/Melanie Kroupa Books, 2004. 196p. $20.00. ISBN 0 374 36173 8. [nonfiction] JS

Themes/Topics: conservation, wildlife

Summary/Description

This history of sighting, destroying, and saving the Lord God Bird begins in Wilmington, North Carolina, 1809, with Alexander Wilson, who wants to paint and describe every U.S. species of bird. Like other specimen hunters, including John James Audubon, he shoots birds to study them. The bird's power and size make it a fascinating target for both Native Americans and white men. Southeastern expansion decreases habitat. Hat fashions encourage hunting. In the 1930s, Cornell Professor Arthur Augustus Allen, supported by the Audubon Society, tries to photograph the bird and record its song. The Singer Sewing Machine Company establishes the Singer Refuge in Louisiana, which protects the Lord God Bird, but does not produce its food. With the reduction of the Singer tract and the coming of World War II, the bird disappears. In 1985 to 1987, the Cuban Ivory Bill, the bird's closest relative, is spotted.

Chapters begin with a map showing the Lord God Bird's habitat. "The Collapsing Forest: Mapping the Loss of Ivory-Bill Habitat" appears on pages 156 and 157. Sidebars contain supplementary information. Photographs and illustrations provide images of the bird, its times, and pursuers. Extensive chapter notes provide background information and additional sources.

Read Aloud/Reader Response

1. Introduction, pages 3 to 5. This passage explains extinction.
2. Prologue, pages 8 to 10, beginning "Wilson preferred to sketch . . ." and ending with the prologue. The passage describes Wilson capturing an Ivory-billed Woodpecker.

3. Chapter 5, "Feathered Gold," pages 48 to 49, beginning "For
    centuries . . . " and ending " . . . as much as an ounce of gold." This
    passage explains the fashion threat.
4. Chapter 8, pages 79 to 81, beginning with the chapter and ending
    " . . . an ornithologist's work." The description illustrates the ardu-
    ous bird watching.
5. Chapter 10, pages 106 to 109. This section describes the sighting of
    and interaction with an Ivory-billed Woodpecker.

Booktalk

It's just a woodpecker, right? Ornithologists think this bird is a big deal.
The Ivory-billed Woodpecker is huge and loud. In a few hours, it can turn
a tree, table, or wall into sawdust. It makes Woody Woodpecker look calm.
Once it ruled the American South and Cuba. U.S. presidents watched its
progress. Native Americans sought its magic. Collectors wanted to stuff it
and display it in their living rooms. Ladies displayed its plumage on their
hats. Where is it now? Ornithologists would like to know. Why? Because
it is the poster child for conservationists. It is the bird that disappears,
hides, and appears again, in spite of mankind. It may be one of the few
species surviving the sixth wave of extinction, mankind's almost unstop-
pable destruction of the environment. Scientists think that the race to
save the environment is also *The Race to Save the Lord God Bird.*

Learning Opportunities

1. In the chapter notes, Hoose cites several of his sources. Choose
    one, examine it, and share what you find with the group.
2. Using your library's resources, follow the search for *The Lord God
    Bird.* Periodically report your information to others in the group.
3. Using your library's resources, locate a reliable bird reference. One
    day per week, watch birds. Keep a journal of sightings. Share them
    with the group.
4. Contact the Audubon Society. Ask for information about its mission.
    Use the information in a visual display.
5. Related Works 1 through 4 recount fiction and nonfiction struggles
    to save birds. Discuss how these works compare with *The Race to
    Save the Lord God Bird.*

Related Works

1. Burgess, Melvin. **Kite.** New York: Farrar, Straus and Giroux, 2000.
    182p. $16.00. ISBN 0 274 34228 8. [fiction] MJ After trying to rob a
    kite nest, Taylor Mase commits himself to saving one surviving kite
    in spite of the landowner's pressure to kill the bird.

2. Hiaasen, Carl. **Hoot.** New York: Alfred A. Knopf, 2002. 292p. $15.95. ISBN 0 375 828181 3. [fiction] MJ (See full booktalk in *Teen Genre Connections,* 2005, pages 37 to 39.) Roy Eberhardt pursues a barefoot boy and becomes entangled in an environmental struggle to save owls.

3. Myers, Anna. **Flying Blind.** New York: Walker & Company, 2003. 192p. $16.95. ISBN 0 8027 8879 3. [fiction] MJ Murphy, a seer macaw, inspires thirteen-year-old Ben to embrace his destiny of saving wild birds.

4. Osborn, Elinor. **Project UltraSwan.** Boston, MA: Houghton Mifflin Company, 2002. 64p. $16.00. ISBN 0 618 14528 1. [nonfiction] MJS Researchers are teaching the nearly extinct trumpeter swans migration routes to reintroduce them to the eastern United States.

5. Schmidt, Thomas, and Jeremy Schmidt. **The Saga of Lewis and Clark: Into the Uncharted West.** New York: DK Publishing, Inc., 1999. 210p. (A Tehabi Book). $35.00. ISBN 0 7894 4638 3. [nonfiction] JS (See full booktalk in *Booktalks and More,* 2003, pages 235 to 237.) The multi-layered volume tells about the Lewis and Clark expedition that included recording the wildlife the explorers encountered.

Lawrence, Iain. **B for Buster.**

New York: Laurel-Leaf, 2004. 317p. $5.99pa. ISBN 0 440 23810 2. [fiction] MJS

Themes/Topics: World War II, courage, pigeons, Air Force, alcoholism

Summary/Description

Sixteen-year-old Kak enlists in the Canadian Air Force during World War II and becomes the wireless operator on *B for Buster,* a bomber. The fear that develops after his first flight isolates him from his crew members and pushes him to reveal his age and stop flying. Bert, the caretaker of homing pigeons that accompany every flight, befriends him. Humiliated and punished for refusing to bomb houses, Bert helps Kak meet his duty and control his fear. The pigeons that Bert teaches him to love save Kak's life. A map of Europe with enlarged maps of the United Kingdom and Germany introduce the novel. An "Author's Note" explains the factual base and the important role of pigeons during World War II. A "Glossary" defines unfamiliar terms.

Read Aloud/Reader Response

1. Chapter 3, pages 36 to 38, beginning "There's Lofty!" and ending with the chapter. After Lofty lands with an engine out, he changes.
2. Chapter 7, pages 76 to 80, beginning "Allo, . . . " and ending "I needed sleep." Bert gives Kak comfort after his first flight but also shows rage and inspires fear.
3. Chapter 10, pages 111 to 115, beginning "Fly home!" and ending with the chapter. Bert and Kak discuss fear and courage in relation to birds and men.
4. Chapter 22, pages 250 to 252, beginning "Wheezy jeezy, . . . " and ending with the chapter. The padre visits the crew as Buzz hunts for a four leaf clover.
5. Chapter 27, pages 297 to 301, beginning "Lofty started weaving . . . " and ending with the chapter. The crew falls into chaos, the plane blows up, and Percy saves Kak.

Booktalk

Kak is sixteen. His dad drinks all the time, and his mother is content to be a punching bag. Kak wants out of his small Canadian town and loser life. And he has a big out, World War II. He lies about his age, tells everyone he is an orphan, enlists in the Canadian Air Force, and sooner than he thinks, he is in England. His job is wireless operator. His plane is *B for Buster*. Just like the cartoon heroes he loves—"Shazam!"—he is ready for action. He gets it: search lights, ground artillery, and night fighters. He learns fast that there is a hit out there that can knock them out of the sky. He knows that Buster is so old that it could just fall on its own. Kak wants out of that plane. If he tells that he is underage, the Air Force has to take him off even faster than they put him on. Then he meets Bert, the pigeon man. The others make fun of the homing pigeons that accompany every flight. The birds are just a substitute for something they don't have— modern radio equipment. The fliers make even more fun of Bert, the dirty, apologizing man who makes the dirty birds his friends and family. But Bert seems to know things that the crew won't talk about. Things like fear, and shame, and duty. Just like flying, these feelings require a man to find a delicate balance, a balance that even the birds seem to understand. Kak is trying to learn the ABCs of that balance and stay alive. He starts his course on life and death with *B for Buster*.

Learning Opportunities

1. Using your library's resources, continue to research animals used in wartime. Share the information that you find with the group.

2. List the father figures that Kak finds in the story. Explain what each man teaches him.
3. Using your library's resources, research the weapon technology used and developed in World War II. Share the information with the group.
4. Using your library's resources, research the targets assigned to *B for Buster*. Share the importance of each with the group.
5. Poetry and poetic expression are important in the story. Find the full poem whose first two lines are quoted on page 22. Discuss how it applies to the story.
6. Find additional war poetry. Discuss how it deals with the feelings Kak experiences.

Related Works

1. Chan, Gillian. **A Foreign Field.** Toronto, ON: Kids Can Press, 2002. 192p. $16.95. ISBN 1 55337 349 9. [fiction] J Combining narrative, letters, and a flyer's nightmares about crashing, Chan builds the romantic war story of a sixteen-year-old pilot training for the Royal Air Force and the fourteen-year-old girl who loves him.
2. Fiscus, James W. (ed.). **Critical Perspectives on World War II.** New York: The Rosen Publishing Group, 2005. 176p. (Critical Anthologies of Nonfiction Writing). $30.60. ISBN 1 4042 0065 7. [nonfiction] JS The fives chapters of articles explain the causes of, the world reaction to, the combination of hate and patriotism, and the theaters of World War II. "Last Train from Berlin" by Howard K. Smith, pages 19 to 27, describes the building of Hitler Youth. "The Last Enemy: The Memoir of a Spitfire Pilot" by Richard Hillary, pages 130 to 137, distinguishes between the jobs of the bomber and the fighter pilots.
3. Freedman, Russell. **Children of the Great Depression.** [nonfiction] MJS (See full booktalk in "History"/"Defining Leaders and Events," pages 221 to 223.) With narrative and pictures, Freedman depicts the meager and challenging life for children during the Great Depression. A picture of a Hooverville that includes cardboard box houses, described by Ratty, appears on pages 20 and 21. The hero rings like the one Kak treasures are described on page 90.
4. Levine, Ellen. **Darkness over Denmark: The Danish Resistance and the Rescue of the Jews.** New York: Holiday House, 2000. 164p. $14.95. ISBN 0 8234 1775 7. [nonfiction] MJS Combined with the factual description of the Nazi Occupation are the heroic stories of writers, clergy, policemen, students, doctors, and teachers

who prove that individuals can make a difference in the face of overwhelming evil.

5.   Magee, John G. "High Flight." Wikipedia: The Free Encyclopedia. Available: http://en.wikipedia.org/wiki/John_Gillespie_Magee,_Jr. (Accessed September 2006). John G. Magee, Jr. was a pilot officer in World War II. He died when he was nineteen. The poem is dated 1941. The lines quoted in *B for Buster* were used by President Reagan to mourn the Challenger disaster. The entry includes background of the family and the poem.

6.   Philip, Neil (ed.). Michael McCurdy (illus.). **War and the Pity of War.** New York: Houghton Mifflin Company, 1998. 94p. $20.00. ISBN 0 395 84982 9. [poetry] MJS (See full booktalk in *Booktalks Plus*, 2001, pages 44 to 46.) The collection includes poems from several wars, but "An Irish Airman Foresees His Death," a World War I poem by W. B. Yeats, aptly expresses Kak's situation and fears. A World War II poem, "Song of the Dying Gunner AA1" by Charles Causley, appears on page 57.

☙❧

McCaughrean, Geraldine. **The Kite Rider.**
New York: HarperCollins Publishers, 2001. 272p. $15.95.
ISBN 0 06 623874 9. [fiction] MJS

Themes/Topics: death, family, sacrifice, friendship, courage, thirteenth-century China, Yèän dynasty, Mongols, Kublai Khan, circus, kites

Summary/Description

Twelve-year-old Haoyou sees his father die when a ship's first mate ties the father to a kite to test the wind and predict the success of an ocean voyage. The mate then tries to marry Haoyou's mother. With the help of a cousin, supposedly a seer, Haoyou shanghais the first mate. Haoyou and the cousin leave town with a circus in which Haoyou attaches himself to a kite and flies over the crowds. His cousin translates messages the crowd receives from their ancestors. His lazy exploitive uncle catches up to the circus and demands all Haoyou's money. Kublai Khan comes to see the circus, and keeps Haoyou to spy and drop bombs on his enemies. A storm defeats the Khan and releases Haoyou, who returns home to discover that his uncle sold Haoyou's mother and sister to the liquor house. Haoyou saves them and defeats his enemies. The family sails off with the circus. Haoyou makes his living as a kitemaker.

Maps of thirteenth-century China and Haoyou's journey introduce the story. A concluding "Author's Note" explains its historical context.

Read Aloud/Reader Response

1. Chapter 1, pages 3 to 12. The chapter describes the death of Haoyou's father.
2. Chapter 3, pages 24 to 30, beginning "You!" and ending with the chapter. Mipeng, the medium, tells the mother not to marry and tells Haoyou to become a kitemaker.
3. Chapter 5, pages 49 to 51, beginning "Haoyou and his cousin . . . " and ending " . . . that he liked her so much." Mipeng explains her wedding and job as a medium.
4. Chapter 11, pages 127 to 131, beginning, "At the end of his bed . . . " and ending " . . . in their prayers?" Haoyou, the Phoenix, realizes he is part of a supportive community.
5. Chapter 12, pages 148 to 149, beginning "The yurt was dark . . . " and ending " . . . chaos and disorder." Mipeng challenges Haoyou's obedience.

Booktalk

Ask how many people in the group have ever flown a kite. Then ask how many have experienced parasailing. You may wish to have a kite with you.

In thirteenth-century China, kites were serious technology. Beautiful and fascinating, they entertained children, but also helped men talk to the gods. One type of man/god communication was called "Testing the Winds." Before a boat set sail, the ship's captain predicted the success of the voyage by strapping a man to a kite and sending him into the sky. He usually chose someone who was very drunk or very stupid. When twelve-year-old Haoyou accompanies his sailor father to the docks, neither he nor his father realizes that the father, who is neither drunk nor stupid, will test the winds—and die. Nor do they know that the father's killer plans to marry Haoyou's beautiful mother. But Haoyou cannot dwell on the injustice of the event or why he did not prevent it. He must protect and support his family. How does he do it? He becomes, against all his fears and dreams, *The Kite Rider.*

Learning Opportunities

1. Using your library's resources, find ten facts about the rule of Kublai Khan that might enhance or support the narrative. Share those facts with the group.
2. Using your library's resources, research the history of kites. Share the information that you find with the group.

3. Conduct a kitemaking contest. You might want to refer to *The Magnificent Book of Kites: Explorations in Design, Construction, Enjoyment & Flight* (Related Work 2).
4. Discuss how McCaughrean uses Haoyou's circular journey for her purpose.
5. List each character in the story. Discuss what each teaches Haoyou about the balance of personal choice and obedience.
6. Discuss why the circus is an appropriate setting for *The Kite Rider.* Compare how the circus is used in *Ghost Boy* (Related Work 3) and *Secret Heart* (Related Work 1).

Related Works

1. Almond, David. **Secret Heart.** New York: Delacorte Press, 2001. 199p. $17.99. ISBN 0 385 90065 1. [fiction] JS Bullied Joe Maloney finds a new perspective on life when a circus, which sees him as its savior, comes to town.
2. Eden, Maxwell. **The Magnificent Book of Kites: Explorations in Design, Construction, Enjoyment & Flight.** New York: Sterling Publishing Co., Inc., 2002. 464p. $14.95pa. ISBN 1 57912 025 3. [nonfiction] JS/A This comprehensive reference teaches the reader how to design, build, and fly thirty different kites as well as understand the aerodynamics involved.
3. Lawrence, Iain. **Ghost Boy.** New York: Delacorte Press, 2000. 326p. $15.95. ISBN 0 385 32739 0 [fiction] MJS (See full booktalk in *Teen Genre Connections*, 2005, pages 11 to 13.) Fourteen-year-old Harold Kline discovers that the circus mirrors the real world.
4. Park, Linda Sue. **A Single Shard.** New York: Clarion Books, 2001. 152p. $15.00. ISBN 0 395 97827 0 [fiction] MJS (See full booktalk in *Teen Genre Connections*, 2005, pages 282 to 285.) A young Korean boy named Tree-ear learns the art of pottery and manhood.
5. Wilson, Diane Lee. **I Rode a Horse of Milk White Jade.** New York: Orchard Books, 1998. 232p. $17.95. ISBN 0 531 30024 2. [fiction] MJ (See full booktalk in *Booktalks Plus*, 2001, pages 8 to 10.) A twelve-year-old handicapped girl loses her family but discovers her talent to train horses for the great Kublai Khan.

Oppel, Kenneth. Airborn.

New York: EOS, 2004. 355p. $17.89. ISBN 0 06 053181 9. [fiction] MJS

Themes/Topics: airships, pirates, imaginary creatures, father/son relationships, friendship

Summary/Description

Fifteen-year-old Matt Cruse is a cabin boy on the *Aurora,* an airship on which his deceased father served. Unafraid of heights, he accomplishes a balloon rescue of dying Benjamin Molloy, who tells about beautiful, winged creatures. One year later, Molloy's granddaughter, Kate, is an *Aurora* passenger retracing her grandfather's journey. The ship, boarded by pirates, is robbed and damaged by the pirate ship and a sudden storm. It lands on an uncharted island for repairs. Kate believes it is the island described by her grandfather and persuades Matt to explore it with her. They discover a "grounded" winged creature and the pirate village. Masquerading as crash survivors, they try to protect the *Aurora* but eventually battle the pirates to save the ship, passengers, and crew. Kate becomes a famous lecturer who describes the creatures, and Matt uses his reward to enter the Airship Academy and care for his family. A diagram of the ship introduces the story.

Read Aloud/Reader Response

1. Chapter 1, page 9, beginning "Just then . . . " and ending with the paragraph. Matt describes Captain Walken.
2. Chapter 1, pages 12 to 17, beginning "I know you'll not . . . " and ending "Very good work, indeed." The balloon rescue communicates Matt's self-image and resourcefulness.
3. Chapter 2, pages 26 to 28, beginning "We ourselves were bound . . ." and ending " . . . having a meal six hundred feet in the air." Matt describes the ship's size and luxury.
4. Chapter 11, pages 178 to 181, beginning "The birds stopped singing, . . ." and ending " . . . the one that fell." Matt describes their first encounter with the injured cloud cat.
5. Chapter 21, pages 351 to 353, beginning "But you're happy here, . . ." and ending " . . . Isabel and Sylvia." Matt describes his academy adjustment and how it matured him.

Booktalk

Ask how many people in the group have seen an airship or a blimp. You might want to supplement the picture on the book's cover with additional pictures.

Fifteen-year-old Matt Cruse lives on an airship. He has a land home with his mother and sisters, but he feels really at home only in the sky. He was born on an airship, and he is sure that he is light enough to fly. In fact, he almost has a chance when the captain asks him to carry off a balloon rescue. A tattered balloon drifts dangerously near the ship. An old man lay at the bottom of the gondola. Matt is dangled toward the balloon, and surrounded by cut lines, flames, and smoke. He gets the man back to the ship alive. Matt is a hero, but his challenges and adventures are just beginning. The man has stories—tales about beautiful, mysterious, never-before-seen creatures. Is he raving in his delirium, or do these creatures exist? One year later the answers lead Matt to pirates, love, and a new world. A world where earth and sky crash against each other. A world where the only way he can survive is to stay *Airborn*.

Learning Opportunities

1. Discuss how the author uses father/son relationships in the novel.
2. Using your library's resources, research airships. Share the information with the group.
3. How does the author build Szirglas's evil?
4. Why is Bruce an important character?
5. Discuss the similarities and differences between Matt and Kate.
6. Matt Cruse is an exciting character. Is he a believable one?

Related Works

1. Colman, Penny. **Adventurous Women: Eight True Stories about Women Who Made a Difference.** New York: Henry Holt and Company, 2006. 186p. $18.95. ISBN 0 8050 7744 8. [nonfiction] JS Taking on the wilds, disease, war, and the system that held them back, these women exhibit the same daring and enthusiasm demonstrated by Kate.
2. Kesel, Barbara. **Flying Solo.** Olsmar, FL: CrossGeneration Comics, 2003. 164p. (Meridian). $9.95 (Traveler Edition). ISBN 1 931484 54 6. [graphic] MJS (See full booktalk in *Teen Genre Connections*, 2005, pages 182 to 185.) Having inherited the leadership of the sky city, Meridian, Sephie battles her evil uncle and cosmic forces as she struggles to keep her kingdom's balance between sky and land. This is the first book in the series.
3. Meyer, L. A. **Under the Jolly Roger: Being an Account of the Further Nautical Adventures of Jacky Faber.** New York: Harcourt Brace and Company, 2005. 318p. $17.00. ISBN 0 15 205345 X. [fiction] JS Jacky Faber becomes a British privateer, leads her own ship, seizes enemy cargo, reunites with friends and enemies, and almost hangs.
4. Oppel, Kenneth. **Skybreaker.** New York: HarperCollins Publishers, 2006. 369p. $17.89. ISBN 13: 978 0 06 053228 4. [fiction] MJS In

this *Airborn* sequel, Matt and Kate join the owner of the *Skybreaker* and a mysterious gypsy girl. The four battle pirates and fantastical creatures to salvage the valuables from a legendary ghost ship.

5. Updale, Eleanor. **Montmorency and the Assassins: Master, Criminal, Spy?** New York: Orchard Books, 2006. 416p. $16.99. ISBN 0 439 68343 2. [fiction] MJS Using collections of animal specimens and international intrigue, Updale gives Montmorency another opportunity to employ both his identities to battle terrorism.

Mystery/Suspense

"Mystery/Suspense" explores murder, mayhem, and the unknown in three contexts. "Contemporary" is closest to our experience. "Historical" connects us to the conditions of our past. "Paranormal" adds an unreal and fantastic layer to an already clouded world.

Contemporary

Abrahams, Peter. **Down the Rabbit Hole: An Echo Falls Mystery.**
New York: HarperCollins Publishers/Laura Geringer Books, 2005. 375p. $16.89.
ISBN 0 06 073702 6. [fiction] MJ

Themes/Topics: murder, acting, Sherlock Holmes, family, Alice in Wonderland

Summary/Description

Eighth-grader Ingrid Levin-Hill meets a local eccentric, Cracked-Up Katie, just before the woman is murdered. Trying to retrieve her shoes left at the crime scene, Ingrid gets involved in the case. Ingrid also wins the role of Alice in *Alice in Wonderland* being produced by the Prescott Players. Vincent Dunn, a new resident and fellow player, is trying to secure a key to Prescott Hall, home of the Players. Ingrid researches town history and discovers a love triangle involving Phillip Prescott, the wealthiest man in town, Cracked-Up Katie, and a young actor who died accidentally. Dunn becomes the production's director after a freak "accident" hospitalizes the original director. He throws Ingrid out of the play. Ingrid, curious about Dunn's demands for a key, discovers him digging up bones in the Prescott Hall basement. The bones belong to Phillip Prescott, who supposedly deserted Cracked-Up Katie. Dunn, who killed him and faked his own death, dies trying to kill Ingrid. Ingrid, recovering and explaining her involvement to the sheriff, returns to her lead role and routine life.

Read Aloud/Reader Response

1. Chapter 1, page 1, opening paragraph. Ingrid describes the teenage years as one long physical revision.
2. Chapter 5, pages 56 to 57, beginning "Coach Ringer concluded . . ." and ending " . . . a whole new way of seeing the game." Ingrid realizes that playing hard and playing to win are two different things.
3. Chapter 6, pages 70 to 73, beginning "What do you think . . ." and ending " . . . fear only hurts." Grampy leads Ingrid to believe only in herself and think about his assertion that a struggle to survive can make a person forget fear.
4. Chapter 21, page 251, beginning "You're rich . . ." and ending " . . . twenty-four seven." Ingrid defines rich to Stacey.
5. Chapter 25, page 311, beginning "Secrets had different . . ." and ending " . . . much heavier."

Booktalk

Murder? Mayhem? Not in a little town like Echo Falls. Ingrid Levin-Hill lives there. She has a pretty good eighth-grade life. She likes soccer, and acting. She is one of the best players on the soccer team, and she won the lead in *Alice in Wonderland.* Her father has her and her brother on the fast track to very good colleges, but math grades may derail his plan. She has some issues with her hot-shot athlete brother, but he is spending more time out of the house. She is one of her grandfather's favorite people, but that means she has to listen to lots of stories about the old days. Things aren't perfect between her parents, but no question, they'll stay together. Overall, Ingrid has a solid and predictable life. Then the town has a murder. Ingrid should let the police handle it. But Ingrid was at the murder scene minutes before the crime. She talked to the victim, a town eccentric called Cracked-Up Katie. And worst of all, Ingrid left her soccer shoes at the scene. Now she has to get them back before the police start asking questions. But getting them back isn't that easy. Someone else shows up at the same time she does. Ingrid is sure that it is the murderer. Her hero, Sherlock Holmes, would do something about that kind of a hunch, and so does Ingrid. She starts to ask questions. The answers might help her solve the case, but they could also take her life.

Can this possibly be the normal small town Echo Falls that Ingrid loves, or like Alice, is she just *Down the Rabbit Hole?*

Learning Opportunities

1. Inappropriate use of power, especially by adults, is a major issue in the novel. List the people who have power. Explain how each uses it and how each should use it.
2. Using your library's resources, continue to research the methods of Sherlock Holmes. Share these methods with the group. Then discuss parallels between Ingrid and Holmes.
3. Is Ty an important character in the novel? Defend your answer to the group. Be sure to use specifics from the text for support.
4. Shoes are central. Identify each pair mentioned. Explain why each pair is important.
5. Grampy is a major influence in Ingrid's life. Discuss that influence as both good and bad.

Related Works

1. Abrahams, Peter. **Behind the Curtain: An Echo Falls Mystery.** New York: HarperCollins Publishers/Laura Geringer Books, 2006. 346p. $16.89. ISBN 13: 978 0 06 073705 4. [fiction] MJ In this sequel to **Down the Rabbit Hole,** thirteen-year-old Ingrid foils an asteroid ring and a plot to force her grandfather to sell his land.
2. Harrison, Michael. **Facing the Dark.** New York: Holiday House, 2000. 128p. $15.95. ISBN 0 8234 1491 4. [fiction] MJS (See full booktalk in *Teen Genre Connections,* 2005, pages 135 to 137.) In this murder mystery, the accused murderer's son and the victim's daughter solve the murder but almost die in the effort.
3. konigsburg, e. l. **Silent to the Bone.** New York: Atheneum Books, 2000. 261p. $16.00. ISBN 0 689 83601 5. [fiction] MJS (See full booktalk in *Booktalks and More,* 2003, pages 151 to 152.) Thirteen-year-old Kane solves the crime when his best friend, who has stopped talking, is accused of dropping his six-month-old half-sister.
4. Mack, Tracy, and Michael Citrin. **Sherlock Holmes and the Baker Street Irregulars: The Fall of the Amazing Zalindas, Casebook No. 1.** New York: Orchard Books, 2006. 259p. $16.99. ISBN 0 439 82836 8. [fiction] M Ozzie, a brilliant Baker Street Irregular, helps Holmes solve the mystery of a death tied to a crime against the Crown and also to its mastermind Moriarity, Holmes's arch enemy. "The Science of Deduction: Sherlock Holmes's Mind at Work," pages 246 to 250, illustrates Holmes's deductive process.

5.   Reiss, Kathryn. **Blackthorn Winter.** New York: Harcourt Children's
     Books Division, 2006. 336p. $17.00. ISBN 0 15 205479 0. [fiction]
     MJ Fifteen-year-old Juliana pursues a man guilty of two murders
     and almost becomes his third victim.

ᘯ ᘰ

Brooks, Kevin. **Martyn Pig.**

New York: The Chicken House, 2002. 240p. $10.95. ISBN 0 439 29595 5. [fiction] JS

Themes/Topics: love, abuse, mysteries, murder, exploitation,
personal morality

Summary/Description

Fifteen-year-old Martyn Pig, fascinated with mystery stories, lives
in England. When Martyn's alcoholic, abusive father dies trying to
hurt him, Martyn fears that the police will either accuse him of murder
or send him to live with Aunty Jean, whom Martyn dislikes. Alex, an
older neighborhood girl Martyn loves, helps him hide the body and
collect an inheritance his father just received. Alex's boyfriend learns
about the plan and blackmails them. Martyn plants evidence implicating
the boyfriend. Alex kills the boyfriend, steals the inheritance, and leaves
town with her mother. Alex directs the evidence so that the police will
pick up Martyn, but believe that the dead boyfriend did the crime.
Martyn moves in with his aunt. Alex becomes a successful actress in the
United States. The novel depicts a world in which everyone personally
defines right and wrong. Alex's concluding letter rationalizes her actions
with the same logic that Martyn used when hiding the body.

Read Aloud/Reader Response

1.   "Wednesday," pages 1 to 3, beginning "It's hard to know . . . " and
     ending " . . . not very often." Martyn explains his name and how he
     deals with it.
2.   "Thursday," page 45, beginning "The thing about dreams . . . " and
     ending " . . . what that means." Martyn reflects on bad dreams.
3.   "Friday," pages 88 to 91, beginning "She gave me . . . " and ending
     " . . . bedroom door." Martyn describes the elaborate ruse to fool
     Aunty Jean.
4.   "Monday," pages 155 to 156, beginning "I killed a bird . . . " and
     ending "I didn't forget it." Martyn describes his regret, power,
     and indifference after killing a bird.

5. "Epilogue," page 230, beginning "You told me . . . " and ending "Love, A." Alex writes Martyn a letter and rationalizes her actions.

Booktalk

"Martyn Pig?"

"Yes. Martyn with a Y, Pig with an I and one G."

That's the routine fifteen-year-old Martyn goes through each time someone asks him his name. Then he has to deal with all the nicknames—"Porky, Piggy, Pigman, Oink, Bacon, Stinky, Snorter, Porker, Grunt. . . . " Will his dad consider changing their name? No. He's too busy drinking himself into a stupor and knocking Martyn around on his way. He's too busy living like a real pig. Can his mom help? No. She left the trough years ago. So one day Martyn kills his dad—by accident. Should he call the police? For sure, they'll think it's a murder and that makes him the murderer. If he doesn't go to jail, they won't let him live on his own. He'll have to live with ugly and mean Aunty Jean. That could be worse than a life sentence. Since Martyn knows how detectives—from Sherlock Holmes to Inspector Morse—work, he plans the foolproof cover-up that will get him out of this stinking life. But a body begins to smell after a while, and in real life, he can't close the book or change the channel. *Martyn* just may have more garbage than any *Pig* can handle.

Learning Opportunities

1. The opening of *Martyn Pig* is similar to the opening of *The Catcher in the Rye*. Discuss what each opening reveals about the character and how it hooks the reader.
2. Aunty Jean is a minor character with a major role. Explain her importance.
3. In the chapter titled "Monday," Martyn relates the shooting of a bird (Read Aloud/Reader Response 4). In the chapter "The Bird Hunter" from the *First French Kiss and Other Traumas* (Related Work 1), the main character also describes the shooting of a bird and how it made him feel. Compare the two incidents and how each relates to the larger work.
4. Alex sends Martyn a letter justifying her betrayal of him (Read Aloud 5). The novel does not end with the letter, however, but with Martyn's reaction to it and the line, "It was starting to snow." Discuss how this conclusion affects the novel.
5. Using your library's resources, research names and their connotations.

Related Works

1. Bagdasarian, Adam. **First French Kiss and Other Traumas.** New York: Farrar, Straus and Giroux, 2002. 134p. $16.00. ISBN 0 374 32338 0. [fiction] JS (See full booktalk in *Teen Genre Connections*, 2005, pages 73 and 74.) The narrator, Will, tells a series of stories that mark his entrance into adulthood.

2. Brooks, Kevin. **Candy.** New York: The Chicken House, 2005. 364p. $16.95. ISBN 0 439 68327 0. [fiction] JS A young man is willing to endanger his family for the love of his new girlfriend, a drug addict and prostitute.

3. Cormier, Robert. **The Rag and Bone Shop.** New York: Delacorte Press, 2001. 154p. $15.95. ISBN 0 385 72962 6. [fiction] MJ (See full booktalk in *Teen Genre Connections*, 2005, pages 129 to 131.) Under the pressure of a relentless interrogator, a twelve-year-old boy confesses to a murder he did not commit. Although he is proven innocent, he is haunted by the experience of being questioned and decides to kill the bully who torments him.

4. Cormier, Robert. **Tenderness.** New York: Bantam Doubleday Dell Publishing Group, Inc., 1997. 229p. $16.95. ISBN 0 385 32286 0. [fiction] JS (See full booktalk in *Booktalks Plus*, 2001, pages 64 to 66.) A serial killer gets away with murder but, ironically, is convicted of killing his girlfriend, a crime he did not commit.

5. Salinger, J. D. **The Catcher in the Rye.** Boston, MA: Little, Brown & Company, 1991. 224p. $6.99pa. ISBN 0316769487. [fiction] S/A Set in 1949 and first published in 1951, the book is about a young man who tells his psychiatrist about his alienation from the world.

ʚ̣ɞ

Cooney, Caroline B. **Code Orange.**

New York: Delacorte Press, 2005. 200p. $15.95. ISBN 0 385 90277 8. [fiction] MJS

Themes/Topics: terrorism, smallpox, high school

Summary/Description

When rich and smart high school student, Mitty Blake, chooses smallpox as his topic for a science class assignment, he encounters an envelope of smallpox scabs in an antique book. Researching the disease, he fears that he is infected and believes that he must die to save others. Posting messages on the Internet, he draws the attention of terrorists and government officials. The terrorists kidnap him and intend to harvest his disease. With materials he finds in his basement prison, he convinces them that he is infected, traps them, escapes, and lets them die of carbon monoxide poisoning before calling the authorities.

Read Aloud/Reader Response

1. Chapter 6, page 68, beginning "Olivia had left him . . . " and ending " . . . didn't include him." Mitty admires Olivia for her individuality, but knows he is the complete opposite.
2. Chapter 10, pages 108 to 112, beginning "He took out . . ." and ending "' . . . had never lived'?" Mitty reveals his slapdash approach to problems and his own self-disgust.
3. Chapter 10, pages 115 to 118, beginning "So—Mom, Dad . . . " and ending with the chapter. Mitty writes his "final" letter to his parents.
4. Chapter 11, page121, beginning "Mitty had not . . . " and ending " . . . could happen." Mitty reflects on the relative safety of America.
5. Chapter 18, page 190, beginning "Don't tell your children. . . . " and ending with the chapter. Derek, Olivia, and Mitty relate to the definition of a hero.

Booktalk

Ask how many people in the group have heard of smallpox. Ask them to share what they know. Then show pictures of victims.

Mitty Blake is rich, smart, and kind of lazy. He doesn't want to spend lots of time in a library researching some infectious disease for his science class term paper. He just browses through old books his mother has to find a good one, and he does. But his research methods give him another problem—smallpox. Someone, in 1902, saved smallpox scabs and hid them in a book. Mitty finds them, inhales them, and rubs them on his skin. In eight hours, he could be fully infected. In less than a month, he could be dead. But that really isn't what bothers Mitty the most. Mitty is a New Yorker. He saw his city attacked. He doesn't want it hurt again. He especially doesn't want to be the cause. And since Mitty talks to everyone, all the time, he could turn into a one-man plague. So Mitty gets on the Internet and asks for help. He gets a response, but not the kind he wanted. These people wear masks. They lock him in a basement. They plan to harvest his disease. Suddenly, Mitty's "no problem" life is over. Suddenly he is living *Code Orange.*

Learning Opportunities

1. Using your library's resources, continue to research smallpox and/ or biological weapons. You may wish to start with *Biological and Chemical Weapons* (Related Work 3) or *Smallpox* (Related Work 5).

2. Invite your librarian to speak to your group about research and source evaluation.
3. Complete Mr. Lynch's assignment from Chapter 1, page 2.
4. After completing the research assignment in Learning Opportunity 3, explore the suggestion of Mitty's English teacher and write an extended metaphor in which you compare the disease to a monster. You may wish to read Related Work 2.
5. Trace the changes that take place in Mitty from the beginning to the end of the novel.
6. Discuss what Olivia and Derek add to the novel.
7. Mitty contemplates taking his life or sacrificing his life. Discuss when these choices are cowardly and when they are heroic.

Related Works

1. Cooney, Caroline B. **The Terrorist.** New York: Scholastic Press, 1997. 198p. $15.95. ISBN 0 590 22853 6. [fiction] MJS Laura, living with her family in London for a year, tries to figure out who was responsible for the terrorist bomb that killed her brother and moves farther away from the friends and family who could help her, but closer to the killers.
2. Heaney, Seamus (ed.). **Beowulf:** A New Verse Translation. New York: W.W. Norton and Co, 2001. 215p. $13.95pa. ISBN 0 393 32097 9. [poetry] JS/A This translation, cited in the novel, emphasizes that Beowulf is a symbol for all time in the battle of what each man perceives as good and evil.
3. Kallen, Stuart A. (ed.). **Biological and Chemical Weapons.** New York: Greenhaven Press, 2006. 110p. (At Issue). $19.95. ISBN 0 7377 2699 7. [nonfiction] JS In a series of articles that present at least two sides of each issue, Kallen explores the dangers of biological and chemical weapons. Articles nine and ten, pages 71 to 88, specifically address smallpox.
4. Owen, Wilfred. "Dulce et Decorum est." First World War Poetry. Available: http://www.warpoetry.co.uk/owenl.html. (Accessed September 2006). Owen's poem is alluded to in the novel. (See Read Aloud/Reader Response 5.)
5. Ridgway, Tom. **Smallpox.** New York: The Rosen Publishing Group, 2001. 64p. (Epidemics: Deadly Diseases Throughout History). $26.60. ISBN 0 8239 3346 6. [nonfiction] JS Ridgeway describes smallpox, explains how it spreads, provides a timeline of its activity, and discusses its influence on history. Page 16 specifically explains the virus activity of smallpox scabs.

ᘓᘔ

Haddon, Mark. **The Curious Incident of the Dog in the Night-Time.**

New York: Vintage Contemporaries, 2003. 226p. $12.00.
ISBN 1 4000 3271 7. [fiction] S/A

Themes/Topics: autism, divorce, crime

Summary/Description

When Christopher John Francis Boone, a brilliant autistic teenager, discovers his neighbor's dead dog, he decides to find the murderer and keep track of the investigation by writing a murder mystery. Christopher discovers that his mother, whom the father told him died, lives in London with the former husband of Mrs. Shear, their next-door neighbor and the dog's owner. Christopher's father, after a lovers' quarrel with Mrs. Shear, killed the dog. Christopher fears that his father will kill him also and travels to London. His mother welcomes him, but his behavior ends her relationship with Mr. Shear. Christopher pressures her to move back home so that he can take his math exams. His parents do not reconcile, but better understand Christopher and their responsibilities toward him.

Read Aloud/Reader Response

1. Chapter 11, pages 6 to 8. The chapter describes Christopher's first encounter with the police after the murder.
2. Chapter 47, pages 24 to 26. The narrative illustrates Christopher's rigid behavior and academic brilliance.
3. Chapter 73, pages 46 and 47, beginning "These are some of my Behavioral Problems . . . " to the end of the list with footnotes. List and footnotes illustrate that Christopher is aware of his difficult-to-deal-with behavior.
4. Chapter 107, pages 69 to 74. The passage explains why *The Hound of the Baskervilles* is Christopher's favorite book and why Sherlock Holmes is one of his favorite detectives.
5. Chapter 229, pages 198 to 200. Christopher's favorite dream reveals what would make him happy.

Booktalk

(Read Chapter 1 aloud.)

This isn't your usual murder mystery. It *is* about the murder of a dog. That murder doesn't lead to another murder but to lots of other things that people thought Christopher, the detective, would never find out. The detective is unusual too. He is a teenager (not so unusual), and he is autistic (very unusual). He doesn't talk to people very well, and the so-called normal people don't know how to talk to him at all. This is the mystery story he wrote about an experience, all the details he noticed that no one else bothered with, and how those little details changed lives forever after *The Curious Incident of the Dog in the Night-Time.*

Learning Opportunities

1. Discuss how the chapter numbers impacted your reading.
2. How do the mother and father affect the story?
3. Using your library's resources, research autism. Share your information with the group. Discuss how your information supports or fails to support the story.
4. Is Christopher's school a necessary setting?
5. Discuss the ending. Would you have ended the novel the same way?

Related Works

1. Doyle, Sir Arthur Conan. "Adventure I—Silver Blaze." Page by Page Books. Available: http://www.pagebypagebooks.com/Arthur_Conan_ Doyle/Memoirs_of_Sherlock_Holmes/Adventure_I_Silver_Blaze_ pl.html. (Accessed September 2006). The short story about crime and death in horseracing contains the "curious incident" phrase, the central clue.
2. Edwards, Michele Engel. **Autism: Diseases and Disorders.** San Diego, CA: Lucent Books, 2001. 112p. $28.70. ISBN 1 56006 829 9. [nonfiction] MJS Edwards defines autism, specifies cause and treatment, presents social options, describes possibilities for autistic adults, and distinguishes between autistic savants and persons suffering from Asperger's Syndrome. Organization addresses and Web sites, source notes, further reading, and bibliography provide additional avenues for information.
3. Hautman, Pete. **Invisible.** New York: Simon & Schuster Books for Young Readers, 2005. 149p. $15.95. ISBN 0 689 86800 6. [fiction] JS Seventeen-year-old Douglas becomes immersed in a fantasy that covers the grief and guilt he feels for his best friend's death.
4. Hesser, Terry Spencer. **Kissing Doorknobs.** New York: Delacorte Press, 1998. 149p. $15.95. ISBN 0 385 32329 8. [fiction] JS (See full booktalk in *Booktalks Plus,* 2001, pages 148 to 150.) Tara Sullivan, who suffers obsessive-compulsive disorder, lives in constant conflict with friends and family.

5. Trueman, Terry. **Stuck in Neutral.** New York: HarperCollins Publishers, 2000. 116p. $14.95. ISBN 0 06 028519 2. [fiction] JS Fourteen-year-old Shawn McDaniel, who has cerebral palsy, cannot communicate or control his movements, but believes that his father plans to kill him.

ʊʓʮʊ

Hiaasen, Carl. **Flush.**
New York: Alfred A. Knopf, 2005. 263p. $16.95. ISBN 0 375 82182 1. [fiction] MJ

Themes/Topics: environment, bullies, river boats, fathers, brothers and sisters, Florida

Summary/Description

Noah Underwood and his younger sister, Abbey, live in Florida with their mother, who is a part-time legal secretary, and their father, who is in jail for sinking a gambling boat. The father wants Noah to help him convict the boat owner, Dusty Muleman, for pouring raw sewage directly into the water. While the father publicizes his cause and tries to control his temper, Noah and Abbey cooperate with Dusty's former fiancé to pour dye into the ship's toilets and expose the crime. The father's publicity gets the attention of his own father, an adventurer and emerald smuggler, who disappeared and was declared dead, ten years before. He returns and helps Noah and Abbey battle the owner, the owner's bullying son and friend, and the ship's bodyguards. The dye plan works, but Dusty is only fined ten-thousand dollars. When Dusty throws a reopening party, his own son and friend accidentally burn the ship, and prove that karma can be stronger than the law.

Read Aloud/Reader Response

1. Chapter 1, page 4, beginning "My mom and dad . . . " and ending " . . . in the scrapbook." The speeding ticket incident illustrates the difference in the parents' personalities.
2. Chapter 9, page 104, beginning "I bet there . . . " and ending " . . . trample it to death." The father reflects on how people abuse the environment.
3. Chapter 12, page 139, beginning "As disgusting . . . " and ending " . . . like it was radioactive." Noah shows his likeness to his father through his actions.
4. Chapter 13, page 157, beginning "Everything felt so good . . . " and ending with the chapter. Noah describes the beautiful sunset. The

green flash is first referred to in Chapter 6, pages 66 and 67, beginning "After lunch . . . " and ending " . . . unless you come along." The final reference occurs in the last chapter, pages 262 and 263, beginning "The sky . . . " and ending with the chapter.

5. Chapter 19, pages 234 to 241, beginning "Sometimes my parents . . ." and ending with the chapter. Noah reflects on and experiences the bonding and loss involved in nature and family as he fishes with his grandfather.

Booktalk

Noah knows all about the storms of nature. He lives with one, his father. Noah's father has a cause. He wants to keep Florida clean, no matter what it costs. Right now, the cause is costing the family quite a bit. Dad is in jail for sinking a gambling boat, and paychecks are on hold. Dad is focused on boat owner Dusty Muleman. Dusty pours raw sewage into the water and pollutes the beaches. Dusty isn't worried. He bribed and blackmailed his way this far, and he can do it again. Plus his hired goons and vicious son protect him. Noah's father has only two children and a wife on *his* side, and the wife is thinking divorce. But Noah's father keeps his eye on the goal. He has one small favor to ask Noah. He wants him to stop Dusty from turning the ocean into a giant toilet. All Noah has to do is convince the Coast Guard and police of Dusty's guilt while keeping himself, and maybe his little sister, from getting killed. Noah can rise to the occasion, no matter how insane. He has lots of guts, lots of practice, and he is putting together a plan, a plan that depends on one giant *Flush*.

Learning Opportunities

1. Using your library's resources, define *karma*. Explain how it applies to the story.
2. Using your library's resources, research one environmental challenge in your area. Explain how it is being managed. Present an oral or visual explanation to the group.
3. Compare Noah, his father, and grandfather. Discuss how they are alike and different.
4. What roles do Abbey and her mother play?
5. Right and wrong are major issues in the story. List each character and discuss what each one illustrates about those ideas.

Related Works

1. Bloor, Edward. **Tangerine.** New York: Scholastic Press, 1997. 294p. (An Apple Signature Edition). $4.99pa. ISBN 0 590 43277 X. [fiction]

MJ Moving to an upper-class housing development in Florida, a middle school student defends the land and solves a crime.

2. Hiaasen, Carl. **Hoot.** New York: Alfred A. Knopf, 2002. 292p. $15.95. ISBN 0 375 82181 3. [fiction] MJ (See full booktalk in *Teen Genre Connections*, 2005, pages 37 to 39.) Roy Eberhardt is drawn into an environmental fight to save the burrowing owl.

3. Hobbs, Will. **Jackie's Wild Seattle.** New York: HarperCollins Publishers, 2003. 200p. $16.99. ISBN 0 06 051631 3. [fiction] MJ A brother and sister accomplish a high risk rescue mission that generates money for an animal rescue mission.

4. Koja, Kathe. **Buddha Boy.** (See full booktalk in "Issues"/"Finding Inner Peace or Spiritual Clarification," pages 40 to 43.) [fiction] MJS A new boy in school teaches "what goes around comes around."

5. Larson, Gary. **There's a Hair in My Dirt: A Worm's Story.** New York: HarperCollins Publishers, 1998. 59p. $15.95. ISBN 0 06 019104 X. [fiction, illustrated fable] JS/A Hearing the story of a fair young maiden's romantic tour through the forest, a young worm appreciates the facts about the survival of the fittest in the natural world and the importance of his life within that world.

Historical

ଔଡ଼

Bradley, Kimberly Brubaker. **For Freedom: The Story of a French Spy.**
New York: Delacorte Press, 2003. 181p. $17.99. ISBN 0 385 90087 2. [fiction] MJ

Themes/Topics: World War II, German Occupation of France (1940–45), spies, singing

Summary/Description

In May 1940, thirteen-year-old Suzanne Good sees Germany invade France. German soldiers commandeer the Goods' house and sell the contents. During the occupation, Suzanne sees cruelty and prejudice, but the family attempts to live as normally as possible. At fifteen, Suzanne, who has studied voice, performs challenging operatic roles. Since she travels, the town doctor, and leader of the local resistance movement, asks her to deliver messages. In June 1944, she is betrayed. During interrogation, Suzanne tells nothing. In the middle of questioning, the German soldiers flee. She discovers that the Allies are invading the beaches of Normandy, and all but one of her fellow spies is dead. Her family, who thought she was just a confused, high-strung, and out-of-control teenager, hail her as a hero. An "Epilogue" explains each character's post-war fate.

Read Aloud/Reader Response

1. Chapter 1, page 1, beginning "*Always ...*" and ending "*... all right.*" Suzanne relates her father's advice to follow the rules and stay out of trouble.
2. Chapter 1, pages 5 to 9, beginning "Our friend Madame Montagne ..." and ending "... what was happening to Yvette." Suzanne and her friend see a young mother and her unborn baby blown up on the beach. This is their first look at war.
3. Chapter 6, page 46, beginning " 'No,' said Papa, ... " and ending " ... anything of value." In their new, much inferior apartment, the father responds to Suzanne's anger.
4. Chapter 7, pages 52 to 55, beginning "All around, ... " and ending " ... leave the armband off now." This incident illustrates small ways that the French resisted the Germans.
5. Chapter 22, page 163, beginning "I thought suddenly ... " and ending " ... would not change a thing." Suzanne reflects on the Germans telling her to trust them.
6. "Epilogue," page 181, beginning "For many years ... " and ending "Our own." Suzanne explains why she wants to tell the story of her Resistance experience.

Booktalk

In May 1940, Suzanne Good is thirteen. France and Germany have been at war for six months, but Cherbourg, Suzanne's small French town, is quiet. (*Using a map of France, show Cherbourg's location.*) Suzanne and her friend plan an afternoon by the water. The harbor is strangely empty. Only one other person walks on the beach, a woman. They hear buzzing noises that grow to a roar. Then explosions. Then silence. Then sirens. The woman lies dead on the beach. Her unborn daughter, dead before she is born, lies beside her. Now the war is real. But it is only the beginning. Soon German soldiers live in Cherbourg's houses. They take what they want and eliminate whom they want. But Suzanne can almost drown out the sounds and sights of that day at the beach. She is gifted with a lovely voice. At fifteen, she is beginning a glamorous and exciting life as an opera star. Then she receives an invitation to live a more private, dangerous life—the life of a spy. Should she face danger while others hide safely in the shadows? Can she play this role in life as well as she plays her roles on the stage? She will find out when she spies for the French Underground and acts her part *For Freedom.*

Learning Opportunities

1. Discuss why Bradley includes Yvette in the novel.
2. Using your library's resources, research the French Resistance during World War II. Share the information that you find with the group.
3. Using your library's resources, find out more information about Charles de Gaulle and his role in French history.
4. Using your library's resources, find out more information about spy techniques. Share your findings with the group. You may wish to start with Related Work 2.
5. List the changes in Suzanne from the beginning to the end of the book. Tie each change to a person or event in her life.

Related Works

1. Bennett, Cherie, and Jeff Gottesfeld. **Anne Frank and Me.** New York: G. P. Putnam's Sons, 2001. 288p. $19.99. ISBN 0 399 23329 6. [fiction] MJS (See full booktalk in *Booktalks Plus*, 2003, pages 192 to 194.) A freak accident transports a flighty teenager to a parallel world where she lives the life of a French Jew in 1942.
2. Janeczko, Paul B. Jenna LaReau (illus.). **Top Secret: A Handbook of Codes, Ciphers, and Secret Writing.** Cambridge, MA: Candlewick Press, 2004. 144p. $16.99. ISBN 0 7636 0971 4. [nonfiction] MJ The author explains the how to of code breaking plus some related historical impact.
3. Levine, Ellen. **Darkness over Denmark.** New York: Holiday House, 2000. 164p. $14.95. ISBN 0 8234 1755 7. [nonfiction] MJS The book relates the details of the Danish resistance.
4. Ungerer, Tomi. **Tomi: A Childhood under the Nazis.** Niwot, CO: The Roberts Rinehart Publishing Group, 1998. 175p. $29.95. ISBN 1 57098 163 9. [nonfiction] MJS/A (See full booktalk in *Booktalks Plus*, 2001, pages 164 to 166.) Tomi Ungerer, using his own childhood drawings, family pictures, poems, old copybooks, and examples of both French and German propaganda, explains how the Germans and French attempt to control the minds and fates of Alsace over a seven-year period.
5. Van Steenwyk, Elizabeth. **A Traitor among Us.** Grand Rapids, MI: Eerdmans Books for Young Readers, 1998. 133p. $15.00. ISBN 0 8028 5150 9. [fiction] MJ (See full booktalk in *Booktalks Plus*, 2001, pages 228 to 230.) Thirteen-year-old Pieter becomes a courier for the Dutch Resistance during the German occupation of Holland.

CRC

Ferris, Jean. **Much Ado about Grubstake.**

New York: Harcourt Children's Books, 2006. 272p. $17.00.
ISBN 0 15 205706 4. [fiction] MJ

Themes/Topics: nineteenth century, mining, orphans, swindles, friendship, blended family, love, Westerns

Summary/Description

In 1888, Arley, a sixteen-year-old orphan, mothers a group of dysfunctional, unsuccessful miners at her Grubstake, Colorado, boarding house. Two strangers arrive. One offers to buy up all the claims for a resort development. Arley suspects a scam and enlists the miners, the saloon owner, and the editor to uncover and thwart it. The second stranger, Morgan, stays at Arley's boarding house. A geologist working with the salesman, Morgan is an orphan who supports the orphanage where he grew up. He and Arley join forces and discover a valuable ore vein originating in her mine and running throughout the entire area. They stop the mine sales. The town is rich. Morgan becomes her manager and possible husband. Arley plans to move Morgan's orphanage to Grubstake and travel to the places around the world she only dreamed about.

Read Aloud/Reader Response

1. Chapter 3, page 39, beginning "Arley . . . " and ending " . . . with that?" Arley watches Charles Randall and Zeb talk about the mine and realizes that Zeb shows his feelings too much.
2. Chapter 4, pages 53 to 56, beginning "She clomped . . . " and ending with the chapter. Wing gives her perspective on the strangers entering town.
3. Chapter 8, pages 110 to 113, beginning "That which every . . . " and ending " . . . looking after her." Duncan reveals his method of getting a good story.
4. Chapter 12, pages 175 to 181, beginning "The first voice . . . " and ending " . . . some sleep." Morgan reveals his character and Arley starts to experience feelings for him.
5. Chapter 14, pages 206 to 212, beginning "You're as tough . . . " and ending " . . . pleased look." Everdene explains "strength of character."

Booktalk

Fair damsels, dastardly deeds, greed, and the Old West. In 1888, Grubstake, Colorado, has them all. Sixteen-year-old Arley, one of Grubstake's fair damsels, runs the local boarding house. Like her boarders who own tapped out mines, Arley doesn't have much hope for the future. When her dad blew himself up in his worthless mine two years ago, Arley substituted the exciting world of dime novels, her Penny Dreadfuls, for real life. But a stranger comes to town. He wants to buy all the mines and turn Grubstake into a winter resort—another unlikely prospect. Then a second stranger arrives. He has just one name—Morgan. He dresses all in black. He locks his room, doesn't talk much, and he loves doughnuts. Arley sees her life developing into a Penny Dreadfuls plot. She is convinced that (1) the two strangers are working together, (2) they found something valuable, and (3) they are willing to swindle the citizens of Grubstake to get it. Will Arley become just a damsel in distress and wait for her dashing hero to save the day? Not on your life. With the local newspaper, some fellow damsels, the miners, her Penny Dreadfuls library, and an endless doughnut supply, Arley is ready to take on the villains. Suddenly, life is real and full of surprises when there is *Much Ado about Grubstake*.

Learning Opportunities

1. Using your library's resources, continue to research each of the ores or rocks mentioned in the story. Share your information with the group.
2. Discuss how Ferris uses coincidence in the story.
3. Read both *Much Ado about Grubstake* and *Love among the Walnuts* (Related Work 1). Discuss the similarities and differences between the two stories.
4. How do the Penny Dreadfuls hurt and help Arley's view of her world?
5. List each character. Referring to details from the story, explain the situation of each character in ten years.
6. Write the fortunes that you think were contained in Wing's two dozen fortune cookies.

Related Works

1. Ferris, Jean. **Love among the Walnuts.** New York: Harcourt Brace and Company, 1998. 215p. $16.00. ISBN 0 15 201590 6. [fiction] MJ (See full booktalk in *Booktalks Plus*, 2001, pages 70 to 72.) In this humorous tale of love triumphs over evil, an unlikely group thwarts evil brothers trying to steal the family company.
2. Hardman, Ric Lynden. **Sunshine Rider: The First Vegetarian Western.** New York: Laurel-Leaf Books, 1998. 343p. $4.99pa. ISBN 0 440 22812 3. [fiction] MJS A comic cattalo and colorful

human characters force Wylie Jackson into manhood when he signs up for a cattle drive with a man he doesn't know is his father.

3. Hite, Sid. **Stick and Whittle.** New York: Scholastic Press, 2000. 208p. $16.95. ISBN 0 439 09828 9. [fiction] MJS In this 1872 setting, the least likely heroes save the day, get the girls, bag the money, and build true friendship.

4. Karr, Kathleen. **The Great Turkey Walk.** New York: Sunburst, 2000. 197p. $4.95pa. ISBN 0 374 42798 4. [fiction] MJ (See full booktalk in *Booktalks and More,* 2003, pages 77 to 80.) In 1860, fifteen-year-old orphan Simon Green drives a flock of turkeys to Denver, and, in this off-the-wall adventure, finds love and his own self-worth.

5. Kyi, Tanya Lloyd. **The Blue Jean Book: The Story behind the Seams.** Toronto, ON, Canada: Annick Press, 2005. 79p. $24.95. ISBN 1 55037 917 8. [nonfiction] JS Kyi chronicles the jeans story from gold rush to designer frenzy.

Lawrence, Iain. **The Convicts.**
New York: Delacorte Press, 2005. 198p. $17.99. ISBN 0 385 90109 7. [fiction] MJ

Themes/Topics: prisoners, nineteenth-century London, bullies, fathers/sons, loyalty

Summary/Description

Tom Tin leaves his near-insane mother when his father is marched off to debtor's prison at the direction of Mr. Goodfellow, a "pillar of the community," who is driving the family to ruin. Trying to raise money to free his father, Tom aids a "resurrection man" and unearths a corpse who is Tom's double. Tom, knocked unconscious when thrown from the grave robber's wagon, wakes up with child thieves who recognize him as Smasher, the boy Tom pulled from the grave. Tom must prove himself to be Smasher or die. Assigned to a robbery, he is arrested, tried, and sent to a prison ship ruled by a sadistic overseer and bullying fellow prisoners called "nobs." Tom befriends nine-year-old Midgely, who is eventually blinded by another boy, and conquers Weedle, who seeks revenge for the mutilation he suffered from Smasher. Tom and Midgely fail in an escape and are placed on a ship to Australia. On the ship, owned by Mr. Goodfellow, Tom reunites with his father, the captain, working off his debt. He tells Tom the story of his birth night when Tom's twin, who became Smasher, washed away in a storm. Knowing his son is alive, he vows to free himself of the Goodfellow brig, and with Tom, who maintains loyalty to Midgely, plan a new life.

Read Aloud/Reader Response

1. Chapter 1, pages 1 to 2, beginning with the chapter and ending " . . . for Camden Town." Tom describes the gruesome conditions and setting.
2. Chapter 8, pages 63 to 70. The chapter reveals the penal system's corruption and blindness as Tom is convicted and sentenced.
3. Chapter 9, page 74, beginning "I hadn't known it . . . " and ending " . . . with barred windows." Tom recounts why Mr. Goodfellow is after the family.
4. Chapter 10, pages 77 to 84. Tom describes the prison ship and the realization that the bully of his table is a boy disfigured by Smasher.
5. Chapter 18, pages 141 to 142, beginning "For the first time, . . . " and ending " . . . one and the same." Tom discovers the deep feelings he has for Midgely when Midgely is blinded.

Booktalk

Dead bodies. A slashed faced. Chains. A prison ship. All are part of fourteen-year-old Tom Tin's new life. Before this life began, Tom Tin was poor but sheltered. His mother constantly mourned his sister's death. His father was a sea captain without a ship. And Tom dreamed of a better life with a happy and successful family. But in nineteenth-century England, Tom didn't know that he was lucky to have any family and the life of a schoolboy besides. Then officers come at night. They drag his father off to debtor's prison. Tom turns to the streets to find money. Instead he finds a world filled with people more desperate than he—people willing to take money, clothes, or a life without a thought. He wins his first battle, almost kills a man, and finds what may be a fabulous diamond. Quick and easy success, or so he thinks. Tom and his family can survive. But his second battle is harder. He agrees to help a resurrection man dig for bodies. Tom looks in the grave, sees his own body, dead, with pennies on its eyes. The body belonged to a street boy named Smasher. The same people who feared and hated Smasher now hate Tom. The same people who killed him want to kill Tom. On the street, Tom has to be tougher and smarter than Smasher was, or Tom will be the next body in the grave. Now Tom begins another journey, the real journey of his life. He travels with a ghost by his side—a ghost who leads him into crime, family secrets, and prison, the even more dangerous world than the streets, the deadly world of *The Convicts*.

Learning Opportunities

1. Using your library's resources, research the penal laws of nineteenth-century England concerning juveniles. Share your information with the group.
2. Each boy that Tom encounters has a special personality and serves a particular function in the story. List each boy's character and explain how he aids the author's purpose.
3. After Tom leaves home, discuss what he learns about his father and himself.
4. List each setting and explain how each functions in the story.
5. Explain Mr. Goodfellow's importance in the story.
6. Outline a possible sequel to this story.

Related Works

1. Altman, Steven-Elliot, and Michael Reaves. Bong Dazo (illus.). **The Irregulars . . . in the Service of Sherlock Holmes.** Milwaukee, OR: Dark Horse Books, 2005. 126p. $12.95. ISBN 1 59307 303 8. [graphic] MJS A band of street children penetrate an underground other world as they help clear the name of falsely accused Mr. Watson.
2. Dickens, Charles. Don Freeman (illus.). **Oliver Twist.** New York: William Morrow and Company, 1994. 442p. $20.00. ISBN 0 688 12911 0. [fiction] MJS/A Published in the middle of the nineteenth century, this novel about a street urchin who lives in a child theft community criticizes the unfair labor and penal practices of the time.
3. Hausman, Gerald, and Loretta Hausman. **Escape from Botany Bay: The True Story of Mary Bryant.** New York: Orchard Books, 2003. 224p. $16.95. ISBN 0 439 40327 8. [fiction] JS Nineteen-year-old Mary Bryant, in 1786, is sentenced to hang for stealing a bonnet but is sent instead to pioneer in an Australian prison colony. Her arrest, journey, landing, colonization, escape, apprehension, return to England, and liberation all illustrate her integrity and bravery in the face of a cruel justice system.
4. Jaques, Brian. David Elliot (illus.). **The Angel's Command: A Tale from the Castaways of The Flying Dutchman.** New York: Philomel Books, 2003. 374p. $23.99. ISBN 0 399 23999 5. [fiction] MJ Set in 1628, this story sees Ben and Ned confronting pirates, privateers, and gypsy bandits in two adventures. It centers on Midgely's fantasy, the Flying Dutchman.
5. Meyer, L. A. **Under the Jolly Roger: Being an Account of the Further Nautical Adventures of Jacky Faber.** New York: Harcourt

Brace and Company, 2005. 518p. $17.00. ISBN 0 15 205345 X. [fiction] JS Jacky Faber returns to the sea as a pirate and takes her revenge on Muck, the grave robber.

ɕ˞ɕ

Updale, Eleanor. **Montmorency: Thief, Liar, Gentleman?**
New York: Orchard Books, 2003. 233p. $16.95. ISBN 0 439 58035 8. [fiction] MJS

Themes/Topics: Victorian England, crime, double life, identity

Summary/Description

In 1875, Montmorency, a petty thief, gravely injured in an escape, is apprehended. Robert Farcett, a young surgeon trying to distinguish himself, rebuilds Montmorency. In the process, Montmorency learns about himself and upper-class society. Hearing a lecture about the Victorian sewer system, Montmorency plans a double life. Scarper, his sewer identity, steals and hides the goods. Montmorency, his upper-class identity, fences the items. Montmorency saves the life of Lord Fox-Selwyn by chance. The Lord invites Montmorency to his private club, becomes his friend, suspects his true identity, and persuades him to become a government spy. With this new life and steady income, Montmorency makes reparation to his victims.

Read Aloud/Reader Response

1. Chapter 2, pages 6 to 11. Sir Joseph Bazalgette describes the sewer construction.
2. Chapter 16, page 81 and 82, paragraph beginning with "Some of them left because of Longman's daughter, Cissie, . . . " This description reveals Cissie's cartoon quality.
3. Chapter 18, pages 92 to 95, the beginning of the chapter to the sentence ending "gravy on her neck," at the bottom of page 95. Cissie demonstrates her character.
4. Chapter 27, pages 158 to 160, the paragraph beginning with the words "The water from the street foamed and spurted . . . " to the end of the chapter. The storm pulls Montmorency into the Thames. He manages almost miraculously to survive.
5. Chapter 32, pages 181 to 184. Fox-Selwyn invites Montmorency to "Bargles Club." The description reveals the members' lifestyle and Montmorency's adaptation.

Booktalk

A petty thief falls through a glass roof as he tries to escape the police. The fall should kill him. It doesn't. In fact, it gives him a whole new life—two lives. An ambitious doctor rebuilds the criminal's body. In the process, the prisoner learns about both science and the gentlemen's world that spawns the scientists. He rebuilds his mind. Healed and released, the ex-convict becomes—an aristocrat named *Montmorency*, from the life he learned, and Montmorency's despicable servant, Scarper, from the life he lived. These two personalities and the modern Victorian sewer system allow both identities to steal from the rich and keep the loot (if he is careful). Is there enough room in his world for two such different personalities? Or will one or both of them die—and soon? The answers all lie with the instant aristocrat, *Montmorency*.

Learning Opportunities

1. Cissie, a minor, comic character reveals a great deal about Montmorency. Contrast the two passages about her in Read Aloud/Reader Responses 2 and 3 with the scene described in the second half of Chapter 18. It begins on page 95 with the words "Montmorency's instinct was to ignore Cissie, . . . " and concludes with the chapter.
2. Acting and public persona are central issues. Explain their importance.
3. List the various settings in the novel. Explain the purpose of each.
4. The doctor and Fox-Selwyn begin as minor characters. After reading three of the episodes (See Related Works 3 and 4), explain their development and purpose.
5. Using your library's resources, find technical advances made during the Victorian period. Share them with the group and explain how these advances improved the quality of life.
6. Using your library's resources, research England's power during the Victorian period.

Related Works

1. Altman, Steven-Elliot, and Michael Reaves. Bong Dazo (illus.). **The Irregulars . . . in the Service of Sherlock Holmes.** Milwaukie, OR: Dark Horse Books, 2005. 126p. $12.95. ISBN 1 59307 303 8. [graphic] MJS A band of street children penetrate an underground other world to clear falsely accused Mr. Watson.
2. Geary, Rick. **The Beast of Chicago: An Account of the Life and Crimes of Herman W. Mudgett Known to the World as**

H. H. Holmes. New York: Nantier, Beall, Minoustchine, 2003. 80p. (A Treasury of Victorian Murder). $15.95. ISBN 1 56163 362 3. [graphic] MJS/A Including bibliographical references, Geary relates the crimes of the American Herman W. Mudgett, a trained doctor and the first apprehended serial killer.

3. Updale, Eleanor. **Montmorency and the Assassins: Master, Criminal, Spy?** New York: Orchard Books, 2006. 416p. $16.99. ISBN 0 439 68343 2. [fiction] MJS In this second sequel, the trio of Montmorency, Fox-Selwyn, and Farcett face a ring of anarchists.

4. Updale, Eleanor. **Montmorency on the Rocks: Doctor, Aristocrat, Murderer?** New York: Orchard Books, 2005. 368p. ISBN 0 439 60676 4. [fiction] MJS In this first sequel, Montmorency, with Fox-Selwyn and Farcett, battles drug addiction and Irish terrorists.

5. Waid, Mark. **Enter the Detective.** Oldsmar, FL: CrossGeneration Comics, 2003. 132p. (Ruse). $9.95. ISBN 1 59314012 6. [graphic] JS/A (See full booktalk and booktalks for a sequel in *Teen Genre Connections*, 2005, pages 166 to 170.) Simon Archard, master detective and favorite son, and Emma Bishop, his paranormally gifted assistant, battle a city-wide crime spree.

Paranormal

Gantos, Jack. **The Love Curse of the Rumbaughs.**
New York: Farrar, Straus and Giroux, 2006. 185p. $17.00.
ISBN 0 374 33690 3. [fiction] JS

Themes/Topics: Twins, mothers, secrets, taxidermy, fate vs. free will, horror stories

Summary/Description

Ivy, the narrator, at seven years old, is terrified by the stuffed body of a woman, the mother of the identical Rumbaugh twins who are close friends of hers and her own single mother. The novel recounts her discoveries from her seventh to seventeenth years: (1) one of the Rumbaughs is her father, (2) the family is cursed with an unhealthy love of mothers, and (3) she herself, trying to stop the curse by entering the religious life, must lose her own mother in an accident. During those years, with the brothers' instruction, Ivy masters taxidermy. She preserves her mother's hands, which she keeps in her pockets, and produces a replica of her mother's body. At the end of the novel, Ivy is planning how she will pass on the curse, possibly via the other Rumbaugh twin. Scenes from this gothic novel, filled with dark humor, may be controversial.

Read Aloud/Reader Response

1. "The Twins," pages 24 to 26, beginning "The doll . . . " and ending " . . . leapt toward me." Ivy discovers the stuffed Mrs. Rumbaugh.
2. "The Calling," pages 31 to 32, beginning "At T.P.C.C. parochial . . . " and ending " . . . not be turned off." Ivy discovers her "gift of focus."
3. "It Runs in the Family," pages 52 to 55, beginning "And then I waited . . . " and ending " . . . as my own mother." The description combines a view of the construction of the building and the human population.
4. "An Awakening," pages 144 to 148, beginning "Hide the truth . . . " and ending "Anger is a curse . . . " Ivy and the twins confront each other about her paternity and the curse.
5. "Birthdays," pages 153 and 154, beginning "I had to prove . . . " and ending "Yet I had my doubts."

Booktalk

Ask how many in the group know what taxidermy is. Ask one person to explain it.

Taxidermy, twins, mothers, and human limbs. They don't seem to be a likely combination, but for a girl named Ivy they make up a way of life. Ivy lives in the Kelly Hotel with her mother. Across the street is her second home, a pharmacy run by the Rumbaugh twins. The Rumbaughs look so much alike that neither she nor her mother can tell them apart. They never married because they devoted their lives to their mother. Since she died, they seem to give all their attention to each other, Ivy, her mother, and taxidermy. The Easter that Ivy is seven, she goes down to the pharmacy basement, not an unusual trip. She plays down there often. But this time she sees a doll. It's huge. Is it an Easter surprise from the doting twins? She examines it and knows that it is somehow familiar. It is old and dried. Then she remembers a picture in the twin's home. She realizes that the lady in the picture is the large stuffed doll—mother Rumbaugh, dead for eight years. Seven-year-old Ivy runs away screaming. But can she run far enough? Can she ever, in her life, get away from that sight, from that memory, or more important, from *The Love Curse of the Rumbaughs?*

Learning Opportunities

1. *The Love Curse of the Rumbaughs* is a gothic novel. Using your library's resources, continue to research the gothic novel. Explain the genre to the group. Illustrate your explanation with examples from *The Love Curse of the Rumbaughs.*
2. In the introduction, Ivy explains her story and alludes to three works. (See Related Works 2, 4, and 5.) Choose one of those works. Read it, and share your selection with the group via a booktalk. (The introduction itself would be an excellent booktalk for *The Love Curse of the Rumbaughs.*)
3. Ivy's introduction states that the story is not a "modern-day metaphor on the exploitation of human creation." Agree or disagree with that statement.
4. The cover includes four illustrations related to the novel. Choose another setting, character, or item from the novel and illustrate it.
5. Using your library's resources, continue to research the eugenics theory mentioned in Part 2, "Nine Years Later"/"The Rumbaughs." Ask others in the group to share your research project. Organize a debate about fate or DNA versus free will.

Related Works

1. Farmer, Nancy. **The House of the Scorpion.** New York: Atheneum Books for Young Readers/A Richard Jackson Book, 2002. 380p. $17.95. ISBN 0 689 85222 3. [fiction] JS (See full booktalk in *Teen Genre Connections,* 2005, pages 208 to 210.) A drug lord stays alive by farming parts from his clones, created by genetic engineering.
2. Hawthorne, Nathaniel. **The House of Seven Gables.** New York: Bantam Classics, 1981. 256p. $5.95pa. ISBN 0 553 21270 2. [fiction] S/A The Pyncheon family allows a curse on their ancestor to shape their lives for generations. First published in 1851, this work is believed to be a statement about Hawthorne's own family guilt.
3. Poe, Edgar Allan. Michael McCurdy (illus.). **Tales of Terror.** New York: Alfred A. Knopf, 2005. 89p. $15.95. ISBN 0 375 83305 6. [fiction] S/A This Poe collection, accompanied by a CD and illustrated with stark black-and-white pictures, includes "The Masque of the Red Death," "The Black Cat," "The Pit and the Pendulum," "The Tell-Tale Heart," "The Cask of Amontillado," and "The Fall of the House of Usher."
4. Poe, Edgar Allan. "William Wilson." Edgar Allan Poe. Available: http://bau2.uibk.ac.at/sg/poe/works/w_wilson.html (Accessed September 2006). Written in the first half of the nineteenth century by

Edgar Allen Poe, this short story focuses on a narrator overcome by the disposition inherited from his family.

5. Shelly, Mary. **Frankenstein.** New York: Pocket Books, 2004. 352p. $3.95pa. ISBN 0 7434 8758 3. [fiction] S/A Written in the first half of the nineteenth century, the novel traces a monster's creation and his fight for acceptance from his creator.

ᏆᏤ

Hearn, Julie. **The Minister's Daughter.**
New York: Atheneum Books for Young Readers, 2005. 263p. $16.95.
ISBN 0 689 87690 4. [fiction] JS

Themes/Topics: witchcraft, Puritans, seventeenth century, fairies, illegitimate babies, grandmother/granddaughter, father/daughters, Salem witch trials

Summary/Description

Raised by her grandmother, a midwife, Nell is learning her grandmother's wisdom. Nell is a Merrybegot, a child conceived in May Morning celebrations by a father and mother she never met. Both grandmother and granddaughter cooperate with the supernatural and human worlds. The new minister condemns the May Morning celebrations. Grace, his defiant elder daughter, is impregnated and deserted by the blacksmith's son. To hide her disgrace, Grace bullies her sister, Patience, into joining her claims of witchcraft against Nell and her grandmother. A mob "tests" the grandmother, and she dies. Nell, grieving, wanders away from the cabin and discovers a dying man whom she saves with a fairy charm. On All Hallow's Eve, she is arrested for witchcraft and sentenced to hang. Young Prince Charles, the man whose life Nell saved, rescues her. The minister's family immigrates to the New World, where Patience denounces Grace as a witch to defend herself from witchcraft charges in Salem, Massachusetts. The story is told in separate chapters through Patience's Salem confession and Nell's story in third-person narration.

Read Aloud/Reader Response

1. *"The Confession of Patience Madden:* The Year of Our Lord 1692," pages 1 and 2. Patience begins telling about Grace's pregnancy and false accusations against Nell and her grandmother.

2. "April 1645," "A Spell to Make Someone Like You," page 26, passage in bold print. The spell is good advice for anyone trying to make friends.

3. *"The Confession of Patience Madden:* The Year of Our Lord 1692," pages 102 to 107. Grace begins to have morning sickness and sets up the situation to accuse Nell of witchcraft.
4. "August 1645," pages 112 to 118, beginning "So Mistress Bramlow tells . . . " and ending " . . . *Aaaurgh!"* Nell learns about Grace's illness, decides to save the Merrybegot, and precipitates the witch-hunt against herself.
5. *"The Confession of Patience Madden:* The Year of Our Lord 1692," pages 189 to 191, beginning "The cunning woman's granddaughter . . . " and ending " . . . sticky and sweet." Patience relates how the inquisitor broke Nell.

Booktalk

Patience Madden lives in Salem, Massachusetts. The year is 1692. She is accused of witchcraft. Patience isn't a witch, but she knows about witch trials. In England, in 1645, she caused one. Not intentionally, but when her lie was born, it just grew and grew. The lie wasn't even her idea. It was her sister Grace's idea. Suddenly, Grace was sick, every morning. Patience thought Grace's sickness came from the night trips into the forest. Patience followed her and saw the devil. But Grace says that Nell is causing the sickness—Nell who is known for healing the sick and talking to fairies and piskies. So the sisters scream, speak in tongues, and spit pins to show how Nell bewitched and harmed them. The sisters are powerful and established. Their father is a min-ister. Nell is a Merrybegot, conceived during the wild May Morning celebrations. Her father is gone. She doesn't even know her mother. Her grandmother is old and forgetful. Who will listen to her? But fate listens. Suddenly, secrets and surprises create a collision course and a wild ride—perhaps with the devil—that can't be controlled even by *The Minister's Daughter.*

Learning Opportunities

1. Discuss why Hearn chooses to let Patience rather than Grace speak.
2. Using your library's resources, continue to research the history of witch trials. You may wish to begin with *Witches and Witch-hunts: A History of Persecution* (Related Work 3).
3. Discuss how the addition of fairies and piskies affects the story.
4. Note the number of times the fairy caul appears, and what it reveals about Nell each time.
5. Explain the importance of the minor character, Mistress Bramlow.

6. Choose one character and analyze that character in terms of good and evil.

Related Works

1. Aronson, Marc. **John Winthrop, Oliver Cromwell, and the Land of Promise.** New York: Clarion Books, 2004. 205p. $20.00. ISBN 0 618 18177 6. [nonfiction] JS (See full booktalk in *Teen Genre Connections*, 2005, pages 245 to 247.) Setting the stage for the clash between the worldly, Catholic, tolerant court of Charles I and religious extremists fueled by the Book of Revelations, *John Winthrop, Oliver Cromwell, and the Land of Promise* explains the seventeenth-century social context that produced John Winthrop and Oliver Cromwell. It gives valuable background on Puritan thought and the Salem colony.

2. Jordan, Sherryl. **The Raging Quiet.** New York: Simon & Schuster, 1999. 266p. $17.00. ISBN 0 689 82140 9. [fiction] JS (See full booktalk in *Booktalks and More*, 2003, pages 15 to 17.) When sixteen-year-old Marnie falls in love with and calms a deaf man, the village in which she lives forces her into a witchcraft trial.

3. Meltzer, Milton. **Witches and Witch-hunts: A History of Persecution.** New York: The Blue Sky Press, 1998. 128p. $16.95. ISBN 0 590 48517 2. [nonfiction] MJS (See full booktalk in *Booktalks and More*, 2003, pages 187 to 189.) Meltzer explains the history and why of witch-hunts.

4. Miller, Arthur. **The Crucible.** New York: Penguin Classics, 2003. 176p. $11.00pa. ISBN 0 14 243733 6. [drama] S/A Written in 1953, as an anti-McCarthyism statement, the play tells the story of the Salem witch trials of 1692.

5. Napoli, Donna Jo. **Breath.** New York: Atheneum Books for Young Readers, 2003. 260p. $16.95. ISBN 0 689 86174 5. [fiction] JS (See full booktalk in *Teen Genre Connections*, 2005, pages 173 to 174.) Twelve-year-old Salz (salt) suffers from cystic fibrosis. His symptoms and his membership in his grandmother's coven cause the 1284 village of Hamelin to distrust him.

※※

Horowitz, Anthony. **Raven's Gate.**
New York: Scholastic Press, 2005. 256p. (The Gatekeepers). $17.95.
ISBN 0 439 67995 8. [fiction] MJ

Themes/Topics: orphans, supernatural powers,
good vs. evil, bullies

Summary/Description

Orphaned fourteen-year-old Matt Freeman, apprehended during a robbery, is given two choices: jail or the home of Mrs. Deverill in remote Lesser Malling, a town of witches. Matt chooses Lesser Malling and tries to escape. Supernatural forces confound him, and people who help him end up dead. Gradually, he discovers his own supernatural powers. Because he is one of five children who once saved the world from the Old Ones in a previous life, his blood will allow the Old Ones to come into the world through *Raven's Gate.* To join ancient and nuclear powers, he is to be sacrificed. With a young reporter who finally believes his story, Matt summons his energy, escapes, and foils the attempt. When the reporter tries to sell the story, a member of the Nexus, a powerful group monitoring the supernatural/temporal battle between good and evil, arrives at the reporter's home, tells them that the organization squelched the story, and asks Matt and the reporter to come to the next confrontation in Peru.

Read Aloud/Reader Response

1. Chapter 4, pages 37 and 38, beginning with the chapter and ending "... forgotten him." Mrs. Deverill explains Matt's bleak situation to him.
2. Chapter 4, pages 44 and 45, beginning "And this is Asmodeus, ..." and ending with the chapter. Matt meets Mrs. Deverill's cat.
3. Chapter 5, pages 53 to 58, beginning "Mrs. Deverill had already ..." and ending with "You need to ..." Matt visits Lesser Malling for the first time.
4. Chapter 13, page 156, "You have...you are." Matt remembers his social worker saying that telling about himself meant taking responsibility for who he was.
5. Chapter 18, pages 220 to 222, beginning with the chapter and ending " ... time to pay." Matt sees the setting for his sacrifice, Omega One.

Booktalk

Fourteen-year-old Matt Freeman doesn't mean to rob anybody. He just goes along with his friend Kelvin, who protects him from the school bullies. He doesn't mean to stab anybody. He just watches Kelvin do it. He doesn't want to go to jail either, but a new crime program for teenagers gives him a choice: jail or life in a foster home. It seems like a no brainer at the time. Then he meets his foster mother. Jayne Deverill is old—and mean. If he doesn't do as he is told and eat what he is given, she tells him he will regret it. He believes her. The town she lives near gives him the creeps. Everyone seems glad to see him, but he doesn't get the idea that they have friendly intentions. He hears whispers and strange words, witch words. He plans to leave, but keeps coming back to the same place. Events, everywhere, seem out of his control. He is up against supernatural and super-powerful bullies this time, and they win. But he hears the phrase "One of five!" and learns that he is that one. No-backbone Matt Freeman is one of the five—children who lived hundreds of years ago, children who together saved the world. Who would believe it? Now, as he sees evil growing around him, he knows that he will have to save it again. He will have to find his own powers. He will have to win—against the big-time bully that can destroy the world, the power behind the *Raven's Gate*.

Learning Opportunities

1. How many bullies can you identify in the novel?
2. Using your library's resources, research the atom bomb and the power that its invention unleashed. You may wish to start with *The Atom Bomb: Creating and Exploding the First Nuclear Weapon* (Related Work 4).
3. If Matt is gifted with special powers, why isn't he stronger throughout the novel?
4. List each adult in the novel. Explain how each one affects Matt.
5. Discuss Horowitz's choice to represent the Old Ones as evil and the five children as good.

Related Works

1. Hersey, John. **Hiroshima.** New York: Vintage Books, 1985. 152p. $6.50pa. ISBN 0 679 72103 7. [nonfiction] JS/A Written in 1946, this journalistic account of the atom bomb compiles memories of the survivors. In the final chapter, written four decades after the original, Hersey tries to revisit the people he originally interviewed.
2. Horowitz, Anthony. **Evil Star.** New York: Scholastic Press, 2006. 320p. (Gatekeepers). $17.99. ISBN 0 439 67996 6. [fiction] MJ In this second adventure, Matt Freeman and Richard Cole travel to Peru where Matt meets Pedro, another of the chosen, and faces the evil Diego Salamanda, who releases the Old Ones.
3. Nix, Garth. **Mister Monday: Book One.** New York: Scholastic Press, 2003. 361p. (The Keys to the Kingdom). $5.99pa. ISBN 0 439 55123 4. [fiction] MJ In this first book of the series, twelve-year-old Arthur Panhaligon receives a magical key that pulls him into a parallel universe of monsters, mythical figures, and bizarre environments where he is expected to take on a hero's role and obtain all Seven Keys of the Kingdom.

4. Orr, Tamra. **The Atom Bomb: Creating and Exploding the First Nuclear Weapon.** New York: The Rosen Publishing Group, 2005. 64p. (The Library of Weapons of Mass Destruction). $26.50. ISBN 1 4042 0292 7. [nonfiction] MJS Orr's explanation is a basis for why the atom bomb might be tied to witchcraft. Page 25 shows the first nuclear reactor. Pages 55 and 56 quote Szilard's letter to Truman, which describes dropping the bomb on Japan as "opening the door to an era of devastation on an unimaginable scale."

5. Zindel, Paul. **The Gadget.** New York: HarperCollins Publishers, 2001. 184p. $15.99. ISBN 0 06 028255 X. [fiction] MJ (See full booktalk in *Teen Genre Connections,* 2005, pages 151 to 154.) Thirteen-year-old Stephen Orr, living in a new and strange Los Alamos home and frustrated by his father's distance and secrecy, unwittingly befriends a Russian spy who seeks information about the atom bomb project.

❧❦

Wooding, Chris. **The Haunting of Alaizabel Cray.**

New York: Orchard Books, 2004. 304p. $16.95. ISBN 0 439 54656 7. [fiction] MJS

Themes/Topics: murder, monsters, evil, London

Summary/Description

Seventeen-year-old Thaniel Fox, an orphaned wych hunter, discovers Alaizabel Cray, sick and alone. In his home, she exhibits the personality of an evil spirit, Thatch, whom The Fraternity is resurrecting to open the gates for other evil spirits to control the world. Thaniel and his guardian, Cathaline Bennett, join Alaizabel, the police, and the Beggar Lords to prevent the entry. Throughout the novel, Stitch-Face, a serial killer, preys on helpless women. He captures Alaizabel but releases her so that she can help her friends defeat The Fraternity, whom he knows will defeat him also. Thaniel stops the evil spirit entry, but does not destroy The Fraternity. At the end of the novel, Stitch-Face travels to The Fraternity leader's home to destroy him.

Read Aloud/Reader Response

1. Chapter 3, pages 28 to 30, beginning with "She had been standing there . . . " and ending with the chapter. The passage introduces Stitch-Face.

2. Chapter 4, pages 32 to 35, beginning with "Oh, . . . " and ending with "Who was Alaizabel Cray?" This description of Alaizabel, establishes her as a harmless and confused victim.

3.   Chapter 5, pages 56 to 58, beginning with "Maycraft made a faint . . . " and ending with the chapter. The scene illustrates Thaniel's skill in fighting the dangerous wych-kin.
4.   Chapter 6, pages 60 to 63, beginning "And yet Alaizabel . . . " and ending "You weren't." The passage shows Thatch's possession of Alaizabel.
5.   Chapter 22, pages 226 to 227, beginning "The Devil-boy's soulless . . . " and ending with the chapter. The Devil-boy introduces the idea of man's destiny.

Booktalk

Seventeen-year-old Thaniel Fox became a wych hunter at fourteen. He apprenticed for six years. His father was the most respected wych hunter in London. Now his father is dead. His great skill and magic did not save him. But Thaniel believes that he can protect himself. The British government pays well for hunting down the dangerous wych-kin that, since the last war, haunt London. One night, during an investigation in the Old Quarter, Thaniel is attacked. The attacker is furious and swift. Shrieking and howling, it hits him from the side. He is down, but swiftly back in control. He has it pinned to the floor. It doesn't look like any wych-kin he knows. It looks like a girl. She collapses. She looks sick now, weak and helpless. But in the Old Quarter things are not always what they seem. Should Thaniel help her? In spite of what he knows and what he does not, he says yes. He takes her home. She says her name is Alaizabel Cray. Like him, she lives in both the human and spirit worlds. But she doesn't understand how the combination pulls her in two different directions. Can he understand? And can either one of them survive *The Haunting of Alaizabel Cray*?

Learning Opportunities

1.   Many fantasies involve a battle between good and evil. How does that description apply and fail to apply to *The Haunting of Alaizabel Cray*? Be sure to consider Stitch-Face and Alaizabel Cray herself in the discussion.
2.   Draw a scene or character from the details that the author provides.
3.   Use several drawings and retell the story in a graphic novel format.
4.   The Devil-boy Jack is a strong, mysterious character. Discuss his function in the story. Be sure to consider that his eyes are sewn shut.
5.   Blindness in literature often indicates wisdom, the ability to perceive truths that others cannot. Using your library's resources, find other blind characters in literary works. Compare their importance to Devil-boy Jack's.

Related Works

1. Cabot, Meg. **Haunted: A Tale of the Mediator.** New York: HarperCollins Publishers, 2003. 246p. $15.99. ISBN 0 06 029471 X. [fiction] JS Susannah Simon becomes more entangled with the spirit world as she protects the one-hundred-fifty-year-old ghost who lives in her bedroom and the sinister Paul who pursues her.

2. Del Vecchio, Gene. **The Pearl of Anton.** Gretna, LA: Pelican Publishing Co., Inc., 2004. 256p. $16.95. ISBN 1 58980 172 5 [fiction] JS This story tells about the battle among the Chosen One, Pure Evil, and Evil Less than Pure.

3. Rowling, J. K. **Harry Potter and the Sorcerer's Stone.** New York: Arthur A. Levine Books, 1997. 509p. $17.95. ISBN 0 590 35340 3. [fiction] MJS (See full booktalk in *Booktalks Plus*, 2001, pages 181 to 182.) Harry discovers his wizard blood and his responsibility for fighting Voldemort.

4. Russell, Barbara Timberlake. **The Taker's Stone.** New York: DK Publishing, Inc., 1999. 231p. $16.95. ISBN 0 7894 2568 8.[fiction] MJ (See full booktalk in *Booktalks and More,* 2003, pages 159 to 161.) Fourteen-year-old Fischer steals three stones and becomes a Taker who sets in motion a battle between good and evil.

5. Waid, Mark. **Enter the Detective.** Oldsmar, FL: CrossGeneration Comics, 2003. 132p. (Ruse). $9.95. ISBN 1 59314 012 6. [graphic] S/A. (See full booktalk in *Teen Genre Connections*, 2005, pages 166 to 167.) In this first volume of the series, Simon Archard, master detective and favorite son, and Emma Bishop, his assistant gifted with supernatural powers, are stumped by a city-wide crime spree.

Zusak, Markus. **I Am the Messenger.**

New York: Alfred A. Knopf, 2002. 357p. $20.50. ISBN 0 375 93099 X. [fiction] S

Themes/Topics: self-esteem, heroes, taxicab driver, writer/character relationship

Summary/Description

Average nineteen-year-old Ed Kennedy, an underage cabdriver, drifts through life with his three friends until they witness a bank robbery. Ed pursues the robber, becomes a hero, and begins receiving Aces that direct him to help people. Responding to the ace of diamonds, Ed saves a wife routinely raped by her husband, befriends a lonely, elderly woman, and inspires a teenage runner to trust her barefoot style even though she habitually comes in second. The ace of clubs involves him in saving a parish, helping a single mother, and solidifying the relationship of two brothers. The ace of spades directs him to a lonely immigrant family, a confrontation with his own mother, and a lonely theater owner. The ace of hearts requires him to uncover and confront his friends' crippling secrets, and, finally, the joker challenges Ed to direct his own life. Tracking the origins of the messages, he discovers that a writer created his character to prove what an average person can achieve. The situations and language require a mature audience.

Read Aloud/Reader Response

1. Two of Diamonds, "sex should be like math: an introduction to my life," pages 19 to 21, beginning "I have . . . " and ending " . . . of a car door slamming." Ed describes his possessions, his family, and his person.
2. Jack of Diamonds, "another stupid human," page 74, beginning "I'm about . . . " and ending with the chapter. Sophie asks Ed if he is a saint.
3. Four of Clubs, "just ed," page 117, beginning "I dismiss the Ace of Clubs . . . " and ending " . . . not a card game." Ed reflects on his changing attitude toward cards.
4. Eight of Clubs, "juveniles," page 156, beginning "You know, . . . " and ending "The pleasure's mine." Ed accepts the priest calling him a saint.
5. Ace of Hearts, "the music of hearts," page 270, beginning "If I'm . . . " and ending " . . . earn it." Ed realizes he must control his life.
6. Two of Hearts, "the kiss, the grave, the fire," page 278, beginning "I want . . . " and ending " . . . life in your life." Ed reflects on what he needs to do to avoid ending like his father.
7. Joker, "the message," page 357, beginning "I'm not the messenger . . . " and ending "I'm the message." Ed realizes that his life is an example for others.

Booktalk

Ed Kennedy, a nineteen-year-old cab driver, decides to be a hero. Actually, he doesn't decide to be a hero. He is caught in the middle of a bank robbery and decides to go after the robber. Ed doesn't even know why he makes that decision. Suddenly, he is in the papers, and his whole world changes. The praise and recognition are great, but he starts getting messages. They are written on aces from a deck of cards. Someone thinks he should be a professional hero or something. They think he drives a do-good cab. Ed would like to say no. He wants to stop saving the day, but there are consequences—heavy issues like messengers in the night, and abusive evaluations. Before the bank robbery decision, Ed is just average. He earns a check, has a few friends, and tries to stay on the good side of his family. He isn't sure who he is, where he belongs, or if he should even worry about those things. But now he can say, now he is forced to say, *"I Am the Messenger."*

Learning Opportunities

1. Zusak uses a deck of cards to tell his story. Describe his organization, and then discuss how it supports his purpose.
2. Using your library's resources, research the meanings and uses of playing cards. Share any information that you feel enhances your understanding of the novel.
3. List each person Ed helps. Discuss what each adds to his life.
4. Describe the Doorman. Discuss why he is important to the story.
5. Is Ed independent, or is the author in control?
6. Ed says that he is the message. Explain what you think that message is. Compare your explanation with explanations of others in the group.

Related Works

1. Funke, Cornelia. Anthea Bell (trans.). **Inkspell.** [fiction] MJS (See full booktalk in "Fantasy/Science Fiction/Paranormal"/"Discovering Different Worlds," pages 164 to 166.) Writers in a fantasy world find that their characters are out of control.
2. Lester, Julius. **Time's Memory.** New York: Farrar, Straus and Giroux, 2006. 230p. $17.00. ISBN 0 374 37178 4. [fiction] JS Ekundayo, a messenger appointed by the African creator god Amma who is the master of life and death, is sent to the new world on a slave ship and directed to quiet the souls of slaves improperly buried.
3. Wooding, Chris. **Poison.** [fiction] JS (See full booktalk in "Fantasy/Science Fiction/Paranormal"/"Revisiting the World of Fairy Tale, Myth, and Legend," pages 176 to 178.) Sixteen-year-old Poison journeys to save her sister and becomes the master writer of her world.
4. Zusak, Markus. **Fighting Ruben Wolfe.** New York: Arthur A. Levine Books, 2000. 224p. $15.95. ISBN 0 439 24188 X. [fiction] S (See full booktalk in *Teen Genre Connections*, 2005, pages 70 to 72.) The working-class Ruben brothers decide to fight for money and discover that their brotherhood is more important than the crowd's cheers.

5.   Zusak, Markus. **Getting the Girl.** New York: Arthur A. Levine Books, 2003. 272p. $16.95. ISBN 0 439 38949 6. [fiction] S (See full booktalk in *Teen Genre Connections,* 2005, pages 56 to 58.) Cameron tries to define himself in relation to his physically and emotionally tougher brothers, but ultimately relies on his words, not his fists.

Fantasy/Science Fiction/ Paranormal

"Fantasy/Science Fiction/Paranormal" uses the unreal world to produce real insights. "Discovering Our Roots" is a supernatural version of "Finding Our Talents and Friends" in Chapter 2, "Contemporary." "Discovering Different Worlds" is a fantastical "what if" that forces us to think outside the box. "Revisiting the World of Fairy Tale, Myth, and Legend" develops a new perspective on the old and familiar. All three prepare us for dealing with "Meeting the Challenges of the Future," where we will face universal problems in new contexts.

Discovering Our Roots

ඌ ඍ

Bass, L. G. **Sign of the Qin: Book One.**
New York: Hyperion Books for Children, 2004. 383p. (Outlaws of the Moonshadow Marsh). $17.99. ISBN 0 78681918 9. [fiction] MJS

Themes/Topics: good vs. evil, Chinese legend, outlaws, corrupt rule, kung fu, mythology

Summary/Description

When the Emperor's wife gives birth to a son marked with the outlaw sign of the Qin, the Emperor banishes her and plots to kill the son. He fears that the son is the new Starlord and will return justice to the land. A tattooed monk blocks the assassination and befriends the banished wife, the daughter of his mentor. In addition to earthly opponents, the developing Starlord confronts a hoard of newly released demons from the dark kingdom of Yamu, Lord of the Dead. The Starlord's spiritual guardian, assigned by the good King of Heaven, is a re-incarnated trickster monkey who hopes that this assignment will guarantee him immortality. As the Starlord matures, he learns kung fu secrets of the Twelve Scrolls and prepares to save the earth from destruction, but first he joins the outlaws whose sign he shares. A "Cast of Characters" introduces the story. A "Key to Chinese Characters" at the end of the book explains the meaning of each Chinese character introducing each chapter. The "Author's Note" explains the story's combination of legend, history, and mythology.

Read Aloud/Reader Response

Vivid description and rapid action make the entire book an excellent read aloud, but the following passages are specifically suggested for discussion.

1. Chapter 1, pages 9 to 11, beginning with the chapter and ending with " . . . mark of the outlaw." The prince's birth indicates his supernatural powers.
2. Chapter 2, pages 16 to 21, beginning "The first and only offender . . ." and ending " . . . it was going to blow up?" Monkey defends himself in this passage, which could easily be used for a multiple-part dramatic reading.
3. Chapter 7, pages 52 and 53, beginning with the chapter and ending with " . . . opened his eyes." The Master Hand reads the moving and changing tattoos of General Calabash, the Tattooed Monk, and concludes that Monkey will be Starlord's guardian.
4. Chapter 8, pages 58 to 61, beginning with "The bunyip's lamentation . . ." and ending with the chapter. White Streak's encounter with the bunyip leads to a discussion of guilt, bravery, family support, and love.
5. Chapter 35, pages 272 to 275, beginning with "Mercy has many faces, . . ." and ending with the chapter. The Tattooed Monk tells his history. Silver Lotus expresses his desire to learn from him. Their tasks include providing the Starlord with the wisdom from the Temple of the Five Blessings and facing, once again, the power of Yamu.

Booktalk

An evil Emperor awaits the birth of his son, who will continue his powerful kingdom. Then he sees this new baby. The boy is beautiful, perfect, but the father notices a mark, the *Sign of the Qin,* a brand shared by the outlaws who rot in the Emperor's dungeons. This boy may be the new

Starlord who will overthrow the kingdom and return justice to the land. The Emperor vows to kill this usurper, but a monk with future-telling tattoos and a trickster monkey sent by the Master Hand, the King of Heaven, foil his plan. Others come into this boy's life, some with magical powers, and some with just good hearts. They keep him alive and help him to learn the kung fu secrets of the Twelve Scrolls. Some are the outlaws with whom he shares the sign. Each day he becomes stronger and more knowledgeable about the world of earth and spirit that one day will be his, but will he ever be powerful enough to defeat his greatest enemy—the Lord of Death? Will he ever be powerful enough to fulfill his fate dictated by the *Sign of the Qin?*

Learning Opportunities

1. The characters are classified. Choose a graphic organizer and try to depict their relationships that reach outside of those classifications.
2. Choose a favorite character or scene. Illustrate it.
3. The author's note states that the story combines mythologies. Research other mythologies for characters or figures representing death, heroism, the role of women, the trickster, or the father and son relationship. Share your information with the group.
4. List the many settings of the story. Discuss the purpose of each.
5. Research the history and role of kung fu in the Chinese culture. Share your information with the group.

Related Works

1. Constable, Kate. **The Singer of All Songs.** New York: Arthur A. Levine Books, 2004. 304p. $16.95. ISBN 0 439 55478 0. [fiction] MJS Sixteen-year-old Calwyn and an intruder oppose the powerful Samos, who wishes to be *The Singer of All Songs.*
2. Hearn, Lian. **Across the Nightingale Floor: The Sword of the Warrior, Episode 1.** New York: Firebird, 2002. 193p. (Tales of the Otori). $6.50pa. ISBN 0 14 240324 5. [fiction] S Sixteen-year-old Tomasu becomes the adopted son of the mysterious Lord Otori Shigeru, discovers his ties to skilled assassins, and begins his journey to his true self and revenge.
3. Pullman, Philip. **The Golden Compass: His Dark Materials Trilogy.** New York: Alfred A. Knopf, 1995. 299p. $20.00. ISBN 0 679 87924 2. [fiction] MJS (See full booktalk in *Booktalks and More*, 2003, pages 161 to 162.) Lyra, an orphan, learns her identity, her parents' identity, and the powers that attempt to control her.
4. Rowling, J. K. **Harry Potter and the Sorcerer's Stone.** New York: Arthur A. Levine Books, 1997. 509p. $17.95. ISBN 0 590 35342 X.

[fiction] MJS (See full booktalk in *Booktalks Plus*, 2001, pages 181 and 182.) Young Harry discovers he inherited exceptional powers.

5. Seto, Andy. (author). Wang Du Lu (story). Wayne Moyung and Stephen Ip (trans.). **Crouching Tiger, Hidden Dragon.** Fremont, CA: ComicsOne Corp., 2002. 89p. $13.95pa. ISBN 1 58899 999 8. [graphic] JS This volume establishes the relationships between two feuding families, highly trained in the art of kung fu, and the allies who will be drawn in to their conflict.

෴

Bell, Hilari. **The Goblin Wood.**
New York: HarperCollins Publishers, 2003. 294p. $17.99.
ISBN 0 06 051372 1. [fiction] MJS

Themes/Topics: prejudice, integrity, responsibility, magic, goblins, love

Summary/Description

Eleven-year-old Makenna, who lives in the Realm of the Bright Gods, sees her mother, a hedgewitch, killed by a village mob. She leaves the village and floods it in revenge. She befriends a goblin, Cogswhallop. Five years later she is the goblin general leading the fight against humans driving the goblins from the forest. Cogswhallop is second in command. Eighteen-year-old Tobin, who takes the blame and punishment for his brother's treason, will regain his property and status as a knight if he kills Makenna, rumored to be a sorceress. The goblins capture Tobin. Tobin and Makenna develop mutual respect and love. Tobin leads soldiers to the goblin camp but makes amends by rescuing Makenna and helping her guide the goblins to the safe Otherworld. Tobin and Makenna join them, but Cogswhallop and his family arrive too late to make the transition.

Read Aloud/Reader Response

1. Chapter 2, pages 23 to 27, beginning "It was a good . . . " and ending " . . . blueberries had joined it." Makenna and Cogswhallop meet. This passage is an appropriate dramatic reading for one to three people.
2. Chapter 8, pages 115 to 119, beginning "Tobin knelt . . . " and ending " . . . all goblins to the Otherworld." Tobin discovers the goblins and their intelligence and ability to fight.
3. Chapter 11, pages 157 to 164, beginning with the chapter opening and ending " . . . to think it over." Makenna interrogates Tobin,

but the lie detector spell reveals much about both characters. This passage is an appropriate dramatic reading for one to three people.

4. Chapter 11, pages 175 to 177, beginning "It started . . . " and ending " . . . approved." Makenna reveals her magical powers and compassion by saving a human child.

5. Chapter 14, pages 214 to 223, beginning with the chapter and ending " . . . .no answer to her words." Tobin is becoming close to the goblins.

Booktalk

Read aloud the italicized passage on pages 10 and 11.

Eleven-year-old Makenna witnesses her mother's death. She is so angry that she leaves her village under the cover of night and breaks the dike to flood the town. In five years, she is leading an army of goblins against the humans who killed her mother.

Eighteen-year-old Tobin, just convicted of treason for his brother's crime, loses his family, land, and good name. He can get it all back if he will do just one thing—help the priests kill the sorceress, the powerful Makenna, who bewitches the goblins. He agrees. But Tobin discovers that the battle between good and evil that was so clear in the human world becomes more confusing than he ever could imagine in *The Goblin Wood.*

Learning Opportunities

1. Using your library's resources, research goblin lore. Share your findings with the group.

2. Bell chooses to have Cogswhallop stay behind. Discuss her possible reasons.

3. Makenna decides that she is not a person her mother would approve of. Discuss why she says that. Discuss how her reasoning might apply to our modern world.

4. Is this book about good and evil? If you think it is, explain the elements or characters representing good and the elements or characters representing evil.

5. Discuss the role that prejudice plays in the novel and the factors overcoming it.

6. Discuss how balance functions in the novel, and in life.

Related Works

1. Jennings, Patrick. **The Wolving Time.** New York: Scholastic Press, 2003. 208p. $15.95. ISBN 0 439 39555 0. [fiction] MJS A young

werewolf and his parents save a young woman who is tortured to testify against them.

2. Jordan, Sherryl. **The Raging Quiet.** New York: Simon & Schuster, 1999. 266p. $17.00. ISBN 0 689 82140 9. [fiction] JS (See full booktalk in *Booktalks and More*, 2003, pages 15 to 17.) Sixteen-year-old Marnie and a young man who is an outcast because of his deafness fall in love and face accusations of witchcraft.

3. Landon, Dena. **Shapeshifter's Quest.** New York: Dutton Children's Books, 2005. 182p. $16.99. ISBN 0 525 47310 6. [fiction] JS Eighteen-year-old Syanthe leaves the forest imprisoning the shapeshifters to seek medicine for the sick, including her mother.

4. Spiegler, Louise. **The Amethyst Road.** New York: Clarion Books, 2005. 328p. $16.00. ISBN 0 618 48572 4. [fiction] MJ Suffering prejudice because of her ethnic heritage, Serena Wallace joins another outcast to form a new life.

5. Voigt, Cynthia. **Elske.** New York: Atheneum Books for Young Readers/Anne Schwartz, 1999. 245p. $18.00. ISBN 0 689 82472 6. [fiction] JS (See full booktalk in *Booktalks and More*, 2003, pages 111 to 113.) In a Viking-type society, two young women overcome the oppression of their communities and become national heroes.

෴

Hearn, Julie. **Sign of the Raven.**

New York: Atheneum Books for Young Readers/Ginee Seo Books, 2005. 336p. $16.95. ISBN 0 689 85734 9. [fiction] JS

Themes/Topics: mother/daughter relationships, mother/son relationships, eighteenth-century England, breast cancer, freaks or monsters, grave robbers

Summary/Description

When twelve-year-old Tom accompanies his mother, suffering from breast cancer, on a visit to his estranged grandmother, he rediscovers a gap in the basement that catapults him to eighteenth-century London. He encounters the tiny Astra, who is imprisoned by her owner and forced into prostitution. Astra persuades Tom to help the dying Giant, who fears his body will be sold to grave robbers. Tom discovers that the owner plans to kill Astra also, and sell her body with the Giant's. Saving the Giant's corpse and Astra's life, he works through mother/grandmother conflicts, the repulsion he feels for his mother's mastectomy, and his fear of her death. The eighteenth-century family who owns Astra parallels his modern one. In both centuries, the grandfather is the villain. The eighteenth-century mother and daughter sell the grandfather's body for dissection. The modern mother and daughter discover that the man, who deserted them both, dies alone.

Read Aloud/Reader Response

1. Chapter 2, page 14, "Friends are the relatives we choose for ourselves." This statement on the fob of his mother's key ring indicates her mixed feelings about trusting family.
2. Chapter 3, pages 31 to 33, beginning "Down the stairs . . . " and ending with the chapter. The passage describes the time travel gap in the grandmother's basement.
3. Chapter 8, pages 75 to 78, beginning "Malachi Twist . . . " and ending " . . . the benefactor's veins?" Malachi tells about the monster's fear of dissection. Tom reflects on the mystery of death and explains organ transplants.
4. Chapter 11, pages 104 and 105, beginning "I don't want . . . " and ending "Right?" In the science museum, Tom broaches the topic of life after death with his mother.
5. Chapter 12, pages 114 to 115, beginning "He put the cards back . . . " and ending "Time to go . . . " Tom finds three pictures in which the grandfather's face is blocked.
6. Chapter 28, page 281, beginning "Have faith, . . . " and ending " . . . cannot see and comprehend." Twist encourages Tom to trust what he can't see.

Booktalk

Twelve-year-old Tom is going to his grandmother's house. He hasn't been there since he was two. Mom and Grandma aren't very close, but his mom is recovering from cancer and wants to mend the family as well as her body. The holiday seems to be a bad idea. Then he goes down to his grandmother's basement and sees the gap. *Read the passage on pages 31 to 32, beginning "No definition, . . ." and ending ". . . all the while."* A voice says, *"Get yerself over."* He does. Suddenly, Tom is in the eighteenth century, and in the company of circus "freaks" or monsters. The voice was from Astra, "A Changeling Child." Listen to how her promoter describes her. *Read the Notice describing "A Changeling Child" at the beginning of the novel.* She and her friends are prime targets for grave snatchers. Doctors pay high prices for their unusual bodies. Tom is her only hope, but Tom's trip unearths a terrible secret in his own family history. It may close the gap forever. It might destroy his whole family, right in his grandmother's house, right next door to the *Sign of the Raven.*

Learning Opportunities

1. Describe each monster or freak. Explain the significance of each one.
2. Death is a central topic. What do you think Hearn is saying about it?
3. Using your library's resources, research grave robbers and their role in medicine.
4. Reread the opening chapter. How does it set up the events, tones, and themes?
5. In Chapter 9, Hearn alludes to Psalm 23 in the Bible. Read the psalm. Discuss how it applies to the story.
6. Discuss why time travel is central to Tom's problems of faith.

Related Works

1. Almond, David. **Secret Heart.** New York: Delacorte Press, 2001. 199p. $17.99. ISBN 0 385 90065 1. [fiction] JS Bullied Joe Maloney finds a new perspective on life when a circus, which sees him as its savior, comes to town.
2. Farmer, Nancy. **The House of the Scorpion.** New York: Atheneum Books for Young Readers/A Richard Jackson Book, 2002. 380p. $17.95. ISBN 0 689 85222 3. [fiction] JS (See full booktalk in *Teen Genre Connections*, 2005, pages 208 to 210.) Matteo Alacrán, the seventh clone of a one-hundred-forty-year-old drug lord, rises above his original purpose, providing body parts for the drug lord.
3. Heneghan, James. **The Grave.** New York: Farrar, Straus and Giroux/Frances Foster Books, 2000. 245p. $17.00. ISBN 0 374 32765 3. [fiction] JS (See full booktalk in *Booktalks and More*, 2003, pages 65 to 67.) Tom Mullen, abandoned as a baby in a toy department, is reunited with his true father through time travel.
4. Lawrence, Iain. **Ghost Boy.** New York: Delacorte Press, 2000. 326p. $15.95. ISBN 0 385 32739 0. [fiction] MJS (See full booktalk in *Teen Genre Connections*, 2005, pages 11 to 13.) Fourteen-year-old albino, Harold Kline, discovers his true self through his friendships with circus freaks he sees as like himself.
5. Yancey, Philip, and Tim Stafford (notes). **Student Bible: New International Version.** Grand Rapids, MI: Zondervan, 2002. 1440p. $32.99. ISBN 0 310 92784 6. [religious] JS This uses-friendly version includes "Insights" (background information), "Guided Tour" (essays providing a "bird's eye view"), and "100 People You Should Get to Know." A "Guided Tour" essay on page 586 explains the significance of Psalm 23 (page 585) and discusses its relationship to Psalm 22.

CACD

Rowling, J. K. Harry Potter and the Half-Blood Prince.

New York: Arthur A. Levine Books, 2005. 652p. $29.99.
ISBN 0 439 78454 9. [fiction] MJS

Themes/Topics: friendship, betrayal, self-sacrifice, love, loyalty, personal choice

Summary/Description

Impressed with Harry's status, Horace Slughorn returns to Hogwarts as the potions teacher, allows Harry to enter the class, and loans him a textbook belonging to the Half-Blood Prince. With the margin notes, Harry excels. Dumbledore tutors Harry in Dark Arts and takes him on memory travels revealing Voldemort's history. Dumbledore directs Harry to retrieve a memory from Slughorn involving a conversation with Voldemort, but Harry is distracted by Malfoy, whom Harry believes is conspiring with Snape. Harry tricks Slughorn into giving him the memory that reveals how Horcruxes produce immortality. Murder splits a person's soul. That soul piece is stored in an object, a Horcrux, outside the body. Harry and Dumbledore destroyed two of Voldemort's. They pursue a third, but Dumbledore weakens. Against Harry's warnings, he seeks help from Snape. Death Eaters, aided by Draco Malfoy, invade Hogwarts. Although Snape directs Malfoy to kill Dumbledore, Malfoy falters, and the murder falls to Snape, a double agent for Voldemort. Dumbledore dies. Harry leads the battle against the dark powers, confronts Snape who is forbidden to kill him, and learns that Snape is the Half-Blood Prince. Harry resolves to destroy the remaining Horcruxes. In the battle between good and evil, Ron discovers his feelings for Hermione, and Harry falls in love with Ginny Weasley. Harry, however, fears this relationship because people close to him die.

Read Aloud/Reader Response

1. Chapter 2, pages 36 to 37, beginning "Certainly Narcissa, I shall . . ." and ending with the chapter. Snape hesitates in promising Narcissa that he will watch over Draco.
2. Chapter 4, pages 64 to 74, beginning "Good evening, Horace, . . ." and ending "I'll want a pay rise, . . ." Slughorn reveals his character.
3. Chapter 9, pages 192 to 193, beginning "Once they were secured . . ." and ending with the chapter. Harry reveals the special notes in his potions book to Ron, Hermione, and Ginny.

4.   Chapter 23, pages 508 to 512, beginning "Harry sat in thought . . ." and ending with the chapter. Harry and Dumbledore discuss Voldemort and the prophecy.
5.   Chapter 28, pages 608 to 610, beginning "Harry heard . . ." and ending with the chapter. Harry concludes that Dumbledore's death was in vain.

Booktalk

Voldemort's evil is spilling into the Muggle world. Dumbledore makes a special trip to Harry's house. The wizard's hand is black and shriveled, but he won't talk about that now. He needs Harry to persuade an old colleague, Horace Slughorn, to return to Hogwarts. Slughorn will be the new potions teacher, but he is needed beyond the classroom. Slughorn holds memories, memories that could save two worlds—magic and human. What does that have to do with Harry? Slughorn loves to work with important people. Harry is as important as another former Slughorn student, Voldemort. Slughorn might share those memories with a Harry Potter, but will Harry be able to control them? Or will opening the door to those dark secrets bring more destructive magic than either world can handle? And will the evil that singed Dumbledore's hand burn an unsuspecting world as well? Slughorn shares something and someone else with Harry, too, a development no one anticipated. And so starts another battle between good and evil, a battle in which forces fight and blend at every turn. Will Harry and those who love him survive this next confrontation between *Harry Potter and the Half-Blood Prince?*

Learning Opportunities

1.   List all the teachers at Hogwarts and how each affects Harry Potter.
2.   How does Rowling carry out the love theme? Consider Harry's separation from Ginny.
3.   Do you think Rowling was right in choosing Dumbledore to die?
4.   Are Snape and Malfoy evil, or, as Dumbledore believes, do they have redeeming good?
5.   Discuss what you think will happen to each of the characters in the next novel.
6.   Mudblood continues to be a serious issue in the stories. Using your library's resources, continue to research societies and groups that believe in the importance of a pure blood community. You may wish to start your research with Nazi Germany.

Related Works

1. Rowling, J. K. **Harry Potter and the Chamber of Secrets.** New York: Arthur A. Levine Books, 1998. 341p. $17.95. ISBN 0 439 06486 4. [fiction] MJS (See full booktalk in *Booktalks Plus,* 2001, page 182.) Harry's personal choices, more than his abilities, ally him with good cosmic powers and demonstrate who he really is.
2. Rowling, J. K. **Harry Potter and the Goblet of Fire.** New York: Arthur A. Levine Books, 2000. 734p. $25.95. ISBN 0 439 13959 7. [fiction] MJS (See full booktalk in *Booktalks Plus,* 2001, pages 184 to 187.) Harry discovers that magic and insight require time and patience.
3. Rowling, J. K. **Harry Potter and the Order of the Phoenix.** New York: Arthur A. Levine Books, 2003. 870p. $29.99. ISBN 0 439 35806 X. [fiction] MJS. (See full booktalk in *Teen Genre Connections,* 2005, pages 190 to 192.) Harry's godfather, Sirius Black, dies.
4. Rowling, J. K. **Harry Potter and the Prisoner of Azkaban.** New York: Arthur A. Levine Books, 1999. 431p. $19.95. ISBN 0 439 13635 0. [fiction] MJS (See full booktalk in *Booktalks Plus,* 2001, page 183.) Harry learns his godfather is the notorious Sirius Black, and Harry's own father will always be with him.
5. Rowling, J. K. **Harry Potter and the Sorcerer's Stone.** New York: Arthur A. Levine Books, 1997. 509p. $17.95. ISBN 0 590 35342 X. [fiction] MJS (See full booktalk in *Booktalks Plus,* 2001, pages 181 to 182.) Harry discovers his powers.

Discovering Different Worlds

Bray, Libba. **A Great and Terrible Beauty.**
New York: Delacorte Press, 2003. 405p. $18.99. ISBN 0 385 90161 5. [fiction] S

Themes/Topics: supernatural, boarding schools, England, family relationships, forgiveness, nineteenth-century England

Summary/Description

Living in 1895 Bombay, India, sixteen-year-old Gemma, during a vision, sees her mother's suicide and the murder of one of two mysterious caped men. After her mother's real death, she is sent to an

English boarding school where she makes friends with three girls. The four form an occult society. Gemma discovers that her mother, who attended the same school, also entered the supernatural world under the influence of a girl called Circe. The four friends tap into power and freedom in the supernatural world. They attempt to use it in the real world, although Gemma's mother, from the spirit world, and the other caped man, Kartik, warn them not to. One girl dies. The mother's link to evil makes Gemma vulnerable to Circe. When Gemma forgives her mother, Circe loses the grip on the mother's spirit and Gemma. Gemma leaves magic, resolves to live her life in truth, and develops affection for Kartik. Behavior, which could be considered controversial, requires a mature audience.

Read Aloud/Reader Response

1. Chapter 3, page 27, beginning "A man wants . . . " and ending with the sentence. Gemma's stuffy older brother outlines the period's expectations for women.
2. Chapter 4, pages 40 to 43, beginning "I am Mrs. Nightwing, . . . " and ending " . . . dress for prayers." Mrs. Nightwing first meets Gemma.
3. Chapter 8, pages 86 and 87, beginning *"What frightens you?"* and ending *"Will you know the truth?"* Mary Dowd's diary sets the tone for the novel and Gemma's final decision to live in truth.
4. Chapter 16, page 191, beginning "Things aren't good . . . " and ending " . . . that makes them so." Miss Moore emphasizes the idea of personal control.
5. Chapter 21, pages 236 to 239, beginning " . . . I'm already running . . . " and ending "She is gone." Gemma, with her own powers, connects with her mother in the spirit world.

Booktalk

Read the passage on page 15 beginning "There's something coiled, . . . " and ending "No!"

Gemma is sixteen today. She will remember that scene for the rest of her life. The date is June 21, 1895. The place is Bombay, India. Gemma and her mother fought about England that day. Gemma wanted to live there, where she thought that life was cool and civilized. Her mother did not. With her mother's death, Gemma gets her wish. She goes to England and lives in a boarding school. She meets some "civilized" English girls who are ready to scratch her eyes out on a whim. But then Gemma discovers she has something extra—supernatural powers, the same powers that led her to the vision of her mother's suicide. Powers that can change lives and the world. What will she do with these new powers? Does one girl have the strength to control *A Great and Terrible Beauty?*

Learning Opportunities

1. Discuss Kartik's role in the novel.
2. What do Felicity, Pippa, and Ann reveal about an English girl's life in that time period?
3. Miss Moore plays a minor but significant role. Discuss her influence in the novel.
4. "The Lady of Shalott" is a central allusion in the novel. Read the entire poem and research the character. Then discuss the poem's relationship to the novel. You may wish to start with Related Work 5.
5. Chapter 28 ends with Gemma saying, "We're all damaged somehow." How does her statement relate to the novel? Discuss it, particularly in relation to Chapter 29.

Related Works

1. Divakaruni, Chitra Banerjee. **The Conch Bearer.** Brookfield, CT: Roaring Brook Press/A Neal Porter Book, 2003. 263p. $18.75. ISBN 0 7613 2793 2. [fiction] MJ Twelve-year-old Anand, of India, joins the supernatural Brotherhood of Healers and leaves his earthly home forever.
2. Galloway, Priscilla. **Snake Dreamer.** New York: Delacorte Press, 1998. 231p. $14.95. ISBN 0 385 32264 X. [fiction] MJ (See full booktalk in *Booktalks and More,* 2003, pages 95 to 97.) Sixteen-year-old Dusa Thrashman discovers her connection to the mythical Gorgons through snake dreams.
3. Lawrence, Michael. **A Crack in the Line: Volume I.** New York: Greenwillow Books, 2003. 323p. (Withern Rise). $16.99. ISBN 0 06 072478 1. [fiction] JS Sixteen-year-old Alaric and Naia both live in Withern Rise but in alternative realities.
4. Springer, Nancy. **I Am Mordred: Tales from Camelot.** New York: Philomel Books, 1998. 184p. $14.15. ISBN 0 399 23143 9. [fiction] MJ Mordred, whose life hovers between the natural and supernatural worlds, loves his father in spite of his fate to battle and kill him.
5. Tennyson, Lord Alfred. "The Lady of Shalott." Poets.org. Available: http://poets.org/viewmedia.php/prmMID/16080. (Accessed September 2006). The site provides the full text of "The Lady of Shalott."

ᑕᔐᑐ

Farmer, Nancy. The Sea of Trolls.

New York: Atheneum Books for Young Readers/A Richard Jackson Book, 2004. 459p.
$17.95. ISBN 0 689 86744 1. [fiction] MJ

Themes/Topics: Norse mythology, druids, Vikings, bards, trolls, brothers/sisters

Summary/Description

Eleven-year-old Jack, overworked and underappreciated by his father, apprentices to the local Bard, also known as Dragon Tongue. In 793 A.D., Beserkers raid the Saxon village and capture Jack and his spoiled sister, five-year-old Lucy. Olaf One-Brow claims Jack. A fierce female shipmate, Thorgil, owns Lucy. A mysterious crow, that Jack names Bold Heart, joins them. They arrive at the court of King Ivar the Boneless and his half-troll queen. A spell gone bad forces Jack, Olaf, and Thorgil to undertake a quest to Jotunheim, home of the trolls. They will learn how to reverse the spell before the queen kills Lucy. The journey teaches Jack his powers within the life force, and Thorgil the joy of life. Jack rescues Lucy, and the queen destroys herself. Returning to the Saxon village, Jack discovers the seemingly witless Bard who changes himself back into a man from the crow Bold Heart. Lucy is more mature and appreciative. Thorgil, back with her people, joins the life force. Jack learns that understanding good means acknowledging evil.

Read Aloud/Reader Response

1. Chapter 4, pages 28 to 37. The Bard discusses the danger and beauty of the life force.
2. Chapter 11, pages 100 to 101, beginning "The girl's a slave . . . " and ending " . . . said all the time." The monk echoes the negative beliefs Jack hears from his father.
3. Chapter 13, pages 124 to 127, beginning "What's wrong . . . " and ending " . . . until she gets there." Olaf explains Thorgil's unhappiness in relation to the afterlife.
4. Chapter 20, page 199, beginning "I have lived . . . " and ending " . . . a great crime." Rune shares that the secret of life is appreciating fleeting beauty and happiness.
5. Chapter 36, pages 362 to 373. The magic of Mimir's Well is self-realization. The importance of that realization is echoed by the Rune in Chapter 40, page 410, beginning "Your power . . . " and ending " . . . *spit* into Mimir's Well."

Booktalk

Nobody pays much attention to eleven-year-old Jack, unless they have some hard work they need done. His sister Lucy is the star, the little princess that her father adores. But the year is 793 A.D. Magic lives in the forests, and the Beserkers, fierce Northern fighters, sail the waves. A man who seems to know all about magic asks Jack to work for him. Jack's life gets better. Instead of breaking his back all day, he listens to stories and the sounds of nature. But men across the sea are building weapons and planning raids. Jack's Saxon village is a target, and his sister Lucy manages to put him right in the warriors' path. After a fierce raid on their village, both Jack and Lucy find themselves on a boat. They are surrounded by barbarians. They may live the rest of their lives as slaves, but Jack has magic. That magic brings opportunities even on the worst day. And that worst day comes in the kingdom of Ivar the Boneless and his half-troll queen. That day Jack makes a mistake in his magic. The queen wants him to correct it. If he doesn't, Lucy will die. He must journey again. He needs the help of the fierce Northerners to complete his quest. And they will all cast their sails again—this time to a land of magic that weaves good and evil into a tapestry of dragons, giant spiders, and troll bears. It is a voyage from which Jack may never return. It is the phenomenal journey on *The Sea of Trolls*.

Learning Opportunities

1. Using your library's resources, continue to research Norse culture. Identify information that supports the story. Build an annotated bibliography for other readers. You may wish to start with Related Works 3 and 5 or Farmer's own bibliography.
2. Discuss what lessons this novel might have for the United States post–9/11/2001.
3. Compare Jack and Thorgil. Discuss how they are alike and different.
4. Is Lucy worth saving? Give your reasons.
5. List any life lessons that you identified in the quest, and give an example for each.

Related Works

1. Branford, Henrietta. **The Fated Sky.** Cambridge, MA: Candlewick Press, 1999. 156p. $16.99. ISBN 0 7636 0775 4. [fiction] JS (See full booktalk in *Booktalks Plus*, 2001, pages 48 to 50.) The harsh and magical Viking world is perceived through one woman's eyes. Sixteen-year-old Ran, accused of her mother's death, avoids execution and lives to see her children grow to adulthood.

2. Heaney, Seamus (ed.). **Beowulf: A New Verse Translation.** New York: W. W. Norton and Co., 2001. 215p. $13.95. ISBN 0 393 32097 9. [epic poetry] S/A The full story includes the formidable monsters and the young and old Beowulf who confronts them.

3. Jovinelly, Joann, and Jason Netelkos. **The Crafts and Culture of the Vikings.** New York: Rosen Central, 2002. 48p. (Crafts of the Ancient World). $29.25. ISBN 0 8239 3514 0. [nonfiction] MJ Explaining and illustrating the Viking culture, the book also details how to construct the following: Viking Longboat, Helmet, Shield, Trading Scale, Coins, Jewelry (Thor's Hammer), Jelling Stone, and Game Board.

4. Newth, Mette. **The Transformation.** New York: Farrar, Straus and Giroux, 2000. 195p. $16.00. ISBN 0 374 37752 9. [fiction] S (See full booktalk in *Booktalks and More*, 2003, pages 224 to 226.) Set in fifteenth-century Greenland, the story relates the love of Navarana, raised as a shaman, and Brendan, an orphan schooled in the harsh and guilt-ridden monastic life.

5. Richardson, Hazel. **Life of the Ancient Vikings.** New York: Crabtree Publishing Company, 2005. 32p. (Peoples of the Ancient World). $8.95pa. ISBN 0 7787 2074 8. [nonfiction] MJ This book explains and illustrates the Viking culture and its influence on the modern world.

୯ঽৄৄ

Funke, Cornelia. Inkheart.

New York: Scholastic Press/The Chicken House, 2003. 544p. $19.95.
ISBN 0 439 53164 0. [fiction] MJS

Themes/Topics: reality vs. fiction, loyalty, family, relationships, heroism, trust

Summary/Description

When Dustfinger, a mysterious and sinister stranger, arrives, twelve-year-old Meggie and her father Mo, whom Dustfinger calls Silvertongue, enter Mo's secret world. Mo read the fictional characters from *Inkheart* into existence, the same year Meggie's mother left. Capricorn, the novel's arch villain, wants to destroy all *Inkheart* copies and stay in the real world. He thinks that Mo has the last copy. The three flee to the home of Aunt Elinor, an avid book collector, but

Capricorn's men kidnap Mo. Dustfinger takes Meggie and Elinor to Capricorn's village. The two join Mo in prison. Meggie discovers that she shares her father's power. With the help of Farid, a character from another story, and Fenoglio, the author of *Inkheart,* Meggie, Mo, and Elinor defeat Capricorn and find Meggie's mother whose life tangled with Capricorn's during Mo's initial reading. Dustfinger and the other characters still seek a return to fiction worlds. Meggie and her parents live with Elinor, and Meggie decides to be a writer who creates "another kind of magic."

Read Aloud/Reader Response

1. Chapter 2, page 15, the paragraph beginning with "Mo had painted the box poppy-red." Meggie's book chest reveals the family's love of books.
2. Chapter 3, page 25 to 26, the paragraph beginning with "Capricorn can't bind books like your father, . . ." Capricorn is described as a terrorist.
3. Chapter 14, page 123 and 124, the beginning of the chapter to the sentence ending " . . . but as bright as silver coins." Capricorn is much different than Meggie imagined.
4. Chapter 40, page 379, the passage in italics beginning "But one being was feared even more than Capricorn's men . . ." The Shadow's description reveals that Capricorn creates more evil.
5. Chapters 58 and 59, pages 520 to 534. The concluding chapters complete the plot and character development.

Booktalk

The mysterious Dustfinger, a stranger in the night, appears. Suddenly, twelve-year-old Meggie and her father Mo, a man Dustfinger calls Silvertongue, pack and leave their home. They are running from evil, an evil Mo unleashed years ago with his silver tongue. But the scarred and twisted Dustfinger pursues them. He is evil's messenger. Does he seek knives, guns, bombs of destruction? No. He seeks something more sinister—powerful words. In the world of once upon a time, one man's imagination created fantastic characters. Mo read them into reality. These characters destroy the weak and unsuspecting. They bribe the cruel and corrupt. They know that Mo can help them expand their power. Meggie is the key to forcing his cooperation. If this father and daughter can expand evil, do they have the power to destroy it? If they have such magical powers, do they have the courage to tangle their lives again into the terrifying world of *Inkheart?*

ርሯ ౪౨

Funke, Cornelia. Anthea Bell (trans.). Inkspell.

New York: Scholastic Press/The Chicken House, 2005. 672p. $19.99.
ISBN 0 439 55400 4. [fiction] MJS

Summary/Description

Dustfinger finds a path to the *Inkheart* world through Orpheus, who both reads and writes characters into different worlds. Fifteen-year-old Farid and thirteen-year-old Meggie, against the wishes of Dustfinger and Mo, join Dustfinger and discover that Fenoglio has lost control of his characters. Mortola and Basta, seeking revenge for Capricorn's death, cross over with Mo and Resa. All become embroiled in a conflict between the kingdoms of Adderhead and the Prince of Sighs. Mo, critically wounded by Mortola, is further endangered because he is identified as The Bluejay, a folk hero character Fenoglio patterned after Mo. To solve all the conflicts, to "write his wrongs," Fenoglio decides to create a new version of Cosimo, the Prince of Sigh's dead son, but his new character's description triggers a war in which Farid, now loved by Meggie, dies. Dustfinger exchanges his own life for Farid's, and Fenolglio and Meggie summon Orpheus to accomplish the impossible and bring Dustfinger back.

Read Aloud/Reader Response

1. Chapter 5, pages 46 to 47, beginning "But her old friends, . . . " and ending " . . . strange and familiar." Meggie realizes that books grow fatter when read.
2. Chapter 7, page 77, beginning "I know you think . . . " and ending " . . . not by justice." Mo warns Meggie that when the romantic world of books becomes reality, danger grows.
3. Chapter 17, pages 164 to 165, beginning "Why are you staring . . . " and ending " . . . and the Shadow!" Mortola believes the book world is the real world where her son still lives.
4. Chapter 28, page 264, beginning with "The wrong words . . . " and ending with the paragraph. Dustfinger reflects on the limits of words to explain.
5. Chapter 72, pages 601 to 602, beginning with "There's a story . . . " and ending " . . . kneeled down beside her." Dustfinger gives his life for Farid.

Booktalk

(*Hold up the book.*) *Inkheart* is a story about stories and magical readers who can transport characters from one world to another. But the story doesn't end with the last page. Dustfinger has to find his way back into his story. Basta, with all his evil, is still on the loose in the real world. And although Mo, Meggie, and Resa were reunited, they ponder those other worlds that still claim their lives. Their story, just like our stories, continues. In this sequel, (*Hold up Inkspell.*) Dustfinger finds his way back into the heart of *Inkheart*'s evil, and Farid wants to follow him. Meggie thinks about all her mother's stories from *Inkheart* and longs to explore them. But how? How can anyone risk opening a door that might dangerously tangle fiction and reality again? Meggie and Farid can and do. They follow Dustfinger into his world where they don't belong. And then discover that Fenoglio, the writer, has lost control of the story. The characters have taken over. Meggie and Farid may need a new world to fit them both. They surely will need an *Inkspell* to create it.

Learning Opportunities

1. Using your library's resources, find a great villain from literature. Read the work in which the character appears. Then describe in a written or oral presentation what might happen if that character entered the real world.
2. Dustfinger is a puzzling character. Discuss why.
3. Discuss the importance of Meggie's mother in the stories.
4. An author, a bookbinder, readers, and a collector confront the characters now come to life. Discuss which real life person is the most powerful and why.
5. The author chooses several settings. Identify each and explain its importance.

Related Works

1. Divakaruni, Chitra Banerjee. **The Conch Bearer.** Brookfield, CT: Roaring Book Press/A Neal Porter Book, 2003. 263p. $18.75. ISBN 0 7613 2793 2. [fiction] MJ Twelve-year-old Anand and a girl street sweeper named Nisha fight evil forces to secure a sacred conch that will keep the world safe and heal his family. A night messenger begins the story.
2. Funke, Cornelia. **The Thief Lord.** New York: Scholastic Press/The Chicken House, 2001. 352p. $15.70. ISBN 0 439 40437 1. [fiction] MJ (See full booktalk in *Teen Genre Connections*, 2005, pages 154 to 156.) Able to change time, an unlikely group adjusts their world to find happiness.
3. Nix, Garth. **Mister Monday: Book One.** New York: Scholastic Press, 2003. 361p. (The Keys to the Kingdom). $5.99pa. ISBN 0 439 55123 4. [fiction] MJ Twelve-year-old Arthur Panhaligon is accosted by two men from another world, who pull him into

a parallel universe of monsters, mythical figures, and bizarre environments where he is expected to take on a hero's role and secure all Seven Keys to the Kingdom.

4. Roberts, Katherine. **Spellfall.** England: The Chicken House, 2000. New York: Scholastic Press, 2001. 256p. $15.95. ISBN 0 439 29653 6. [fiction] MJ (See full booktalk in *Booktalks and More*, 2003, pages 157 to 159.) Natalie Marlins finds herself between real and magic worlds, where she is the only one who can save the soultree and her mother's spirit.

5. Wooding, Chris. **Poison.** (See full booktalk in "Fantasy/Science Fiction/Paranormal"/"Revisiting the World of Fairy Tale, Myth, and Legend," pages 176 to 178.) [fiction] JS When the phaeries steal her baby sister, sixteen-year-old Poison decides to rescue her and discovers a fantasy/literary world in which she is to be the master author.

Revisiting the World of Fairy Tale, Myth, and Legend

ɕ϶ʄϩ

Crossley-Holland, Kevin. **The Arthur Trilogy.**
New York: Arthur A. Levine. [fiction] MJ

The Arthurian legend, the details of medieval life, and the universal theme of personal quest emphasize that positive character can overcome negative circumstances. Word lists define unfamiliar medieval terms. Character lists, grouped primarily by setting, identify each significant person and animal.

Themes/Topics: medieval times, family, quest, prejudice, magic, ideal/practical, duty, father/son relationships

The Seeing Stone: Book One.
2001. 368p. $17.95. ISBN 0 439 26326 3.

Summary/Description

Thirteen-year-old Arthur, at the dawn of the thirteenth century, prepares to become a squire and knight. Left-handed, he struggles with knightly skills. Compassionate, he helps his father's serfs. A deep thinker and wordsmith, he writes his own thoughts rather than those of his tutor,

Father Oliver. His jealous older brother, Serle, rejects Arthur. Father Oliver thinks he should be a scholar or monk. Magical Merlin, his father's advisor, encourages Arthur to develop all his talents, and gives him the *Seeing Stone* to guide his choices. The stone allows Arthur to see the past and future. His own life parallels King Arthur's. Like Arthur, he is a foster child. His real father is his crude and abusive "uncle," who wounds him in an unfair fight and who killed the husband of Arthur's biological mother. As a squire, he leaves, supported by Merlin and his foster father, to find himself.

Read Aloud/Reader Response

1. Chapter 16, page 50. Arthur sorts out his life.
2. Chapter 20, pages 54 to 56. Merlin gives Arthur the *Seeing Stone,* and explains the uncertainty of "between-places."
3. Chapter 26, pages 74 to 76. Arthur reflects on Merlin.
4. Chapter 31, pages 90 to 92. Arthur has his first *Seeing Stone* encounter.
5. Chapter 52, pages 162 to 164, beginning "When I pulled the saffron bundle . . . " and ending with the chapter. Arthur sees, in the stone, that he will discover himself through his quest.

Booktalk

Thirteen-year-old Arthur lives in 1199, long after the legendary King Arthur. He isn't the young nobleman he should be. Arthur befriends the family's serfs. He favors his left hand even when forced to fight with his right. He writes his own words instead of his tutor's. And so, defective and uncooperative, he may never serve a knight or be a knight. But the spirit world, a gift from the magical Merlin, is Arthur's world also. With Merlin's *Seeing Stone,* Arthur glimpses the past and future. Strange parallels between King Arthur's life and his own appear. The tragedy, treachery, and triumph surrounding this king begin to envelop Arthur. What powers does this misfit really have? Are they Merlin's or his? What mysteries of birth, like those of King Arthur, threaten to destroy him? He cannot find the answers in Caldicot. Only his father and Merlin can release him to search for the answers beyond the castle and into *The Seeing Stone.*

At the Crossing Places: Book Two.
2002. 416p. $17.95. ISBN 0 439 26598 3.

Summary/Description

Arthur leaves Caldicot to serve Lord Stephen on the Fourth Crusade. Arthur relies on the *Seeing Stone* and the guidance of Lord

Stephen, who maintains justice and dignity in his estate. Attracted to Winnie de Verdon, Arthur confronts the jealousy of his half-sister Grace and wrestles with his feelings for Gatty, the loyal peasant girl. He inherits an estate from his crude and abusive father, finds out that his mother is common and poor, witnesses a priest blackmailing and seducing a peasant girl, realizes that his brother's illegitimate child will be acknowledged but not accepted, discovers that the murder of Jacob the Jew is supported by fear and resentment, dedicates himself to the Crusade, receives a blessing from a Saracen, and gains knighthood through his own brave and impulsive action. Arthur now doubts the Holy War and dreams about his future estate, Catmole, becoming Camelot.

Read Aloud/Reader Response

1. Chapter 17, page 70. Arthur assesses his sorrows, fears, and joys.
2. Chapter 36, pages 128 to 131. Arthur meets his crude and abusive father.
3. Chapter 40, pages 141 to 144. Arthur questions the excused murder of the Jew. Chapter 43, pages 154 to 157, is a follow-up to Chapter 40.
4. Chapter 54, pages 203 to 206. Arthur and Merlin discuss the importance and excitement of Crossing Places.
5. Chapter 59, pages 220 and 221. Arthur contemplates the types and levels of magic.

Booktalk

Arthur is finally leaving home. He is on his way to the Holy War, a squire to Lord Stephen de Holt. On his first day, he encounters the fair Winnie de Verdon in distress. He rescues her, and eagerly anticipates battle, that other part of the knight's life. But his battles come as he clothes himself with armor, improves both his fighting and writing skills, puts up supplies, confronts his father, learns about his mother, and discovers himself. Simultaneously, the *Seeing Stone* draws him into the stories of King Arthur and the Round Table knights. Through Merlin's gift, young Arthur sees journeys more thrilling than arrivals, and people much different than they appear. And, more important, he sees, in both the stone and his own life, that the most dangerous conflicts of body, mind, and heart come *At the Crossing Places*.

King of the Middle March: Book Three.

2003. 432p. $17.95. ISBN 0 439 26600 9.

Summary/Description

Arthur, embarking on a Crusade with Lord Stephen, continues to understand his own life in relation to King Arthur's. As the Crusaders become mired in politics and finances, Arthur encounters Saracens, witnesses needless deaths, and ultimately questions the necessity of the Crusades. He wonders if knights, instead of fighting, should help the poor and eradicate injustice, conditions which the church accepts as natural. He develops a better relationship with his brother Serle and realizes that his poor relationship with his father is his mercurial father's responsibility. His father dies in a fight with Lord Stephen because Arthur intervenes. Arthur accompanies the seriously wounded Lord Stephen home and discovers that Winnie's affections have turned to Tom. He finds his mother and plans to manage his own inherited estate.

Read Aloud/Reader Response

1. Chapter 7, page 21. Arthur describes the Venetians in relation to their famous glass.
2. Chapter 11, pages 31 to 34. Arthur sorts through the Crusaders' motivation.
3. Chapter 21, pages 74 to 76. Arthur and Lord Stephen discuss Arthur's knighthood.
4. Chapter 30, pages 100 to 104. Young Arthur is fascinated by his knighthood. The *Seeing Stone* shows him King Arthur's vision of Lady Fortune.
5. Chapter 61, pages 207 to 209. Arthur describes Giff and Godard hurling a small boy over the city walls.

Booktalk

Arthur is leaving home. Finally, he will embark on a Crusade. Finally, he will realize knighthood. With Lord Stephen and his *Seeing Stone* by his side, he has the best models and teachers. Yet the lessons aren't as easy as they seem. Knights have to pay bills, play politics with greedy leaders, follow silly rules, and sometimes kill—not because the killing is right, but just because it is practical. Knights still have unreasonable families, friends they can't help, and "enemies" that may not be as evil as they are made out to be. In the middle of personal and Holy Wars, Arthur must choose—traditions, the king's orders, the pope's orders, or his own beliefs that spring from the king within him, the *King of the Middle March*.

Learning Opportunities

1. Arthur is not permitted to use his left hand. Look up the definitions and etymologies of dexterous and sinister. Discuss what those definitions and etymologies tell us about the culture's attitudes toward left and right.

2. Merlin is a magical and controversial figure. Research the character of Merlin in the Arthurian legends. You may wish to start with *King Arthur* (Related Work 1). Discuss why young Arthur fears that Merlin will be persecuted or burned.
3. Discuss how the good brother and evil brother theme develops in the relationship between the following: Arthur and Serle; Sir John de Caldicot and Sir William de Gortanore; King Richard and King John. Research the lives of Kings Richard and John.
4. Arthur has good friends among the serfs. Explain these relationships. Consider the situations and characters that encourage and discourage the relationships.
5. Discuss why Arthur has difficulty defining himself as a Caldicot and why Merlin believes that Arthur must have a quest. How is the importance of a name related to both issues? In your discussion, consider the closing chapter of *At the Crossing Places.*
6. With the *Seeing Stone,* Arthur learns about his personal powers and ponders his problems by studying the past, but believes that only his future will define him as a person. Does the time relationship apply only to Arthur, or can it apply to any individual?
7. Cite at least one historical event that might give us insight into a current event.
8. The chapter "Crossing-Places" in *The Seeing Stone* defines and illustrates the "between-places" of life. Discuss the crossing places examined and the characters' attitudes toward them. Identify other crossing places in the novel. Discuss why Crossley-Holland devoted the entire second book to crossing places.
9. List crossing-places in your own life. Comment on the factors that influenced or influence your own decisions at these junctures.
10. In *King of the Middle March,* Arthur leaves the Crusade and returns home. Is his quest finished?

Related Works

1. Kerven, Rosalind. **King Arthur.** New York: DK Publishing, 1998. 63p. (Eyewitness Classics). $14.95. ISBN 0 7894 2887 3. [nonfiction] MJS (See full booktalk in *Booktalks Plus,* 2001, pages 131 to 133.) Kerven explains the Arthurian legend and the themes of good and evil surrounding it.
2. Levitin, Sonia. **The Cure.** New York: Harcourt Brace and Company, 1999. 184p. $16.00. ISBN 0 15 201827 1. [fiction] JS Set in 1348, the story focuses on the persecution of the Jews and a boy's resolve to build a utopia.

3. Springer, Nancy. **I Am Mordred: A Tale from Camelot.** New York: Plilomel Books, 1998. 184p. $14.15. ISBN 0 399 23143 9. [fiction] JS Arthur's illegitimate son tells about his upbringing, fate, and the personal decisions he makes in the face of both.

4. Thomson, Sarah L. **The Dragon's Son.** New York: Orchard Books, 2001. 192p. $17.95. ISBN 0 531 30333 0. [fiction] JS Thomson tells the stories of four people whose personal decisions affect the legendary Arthur. The Uther story is more sinister than the version in *The Seeing Stone.*

5. Vande Velde, Vivian. **The Book of Mordred.** Boston, MA: Houghton Mifflin Company, 2005. 342p. $18.00. ISBN 0 618 50754 X. [fiction] JS Through the experiences of Alayna, Nimue, and Keira, the reader learns about the complicated and challenging Mordred, whose principles destroy him and Camelot.

෴

Gaiman, Neil (text). Andy Kubert (illus.). Marvel 1602: # 1–8.
New York: Marvel Comics, 2005. 248p. $19.99pa.
ISBN 0 7851 1073 9. JS/A [graphic, fiction]

Themes/Topics: partnership of generations, tyranny, political change, self-sacrifice, loyalty, classic Marvel characters, 1602 England, the New World.

Summary/Description

A collection of Marvel characters (Dr. Strange, Nick Fury, Spiderman, the Fantastic Four, Irish-American Matt Murdock, Thor, Hulk, Magneto, Professor Charles Xavier, the X-Men, Captain America, Doctor Victor von Doom, and Uatu the Watcher) interacts with historical characters (Queen Elizabeth I, James I of Scotland, Virginia Dare and the Roanoke colony) to produce a fantastical conflict of good versus evil. Elizabeth's death, James's repressive reign, and the Spanish Inquisition join with strange storms that seem to signal the end of the world. As the Marvel characters battle for a magic device that would allow the possessor to control the world, they discover that the end of the entire universe is imminent because of a time travel forerunner, Captain America, who passed from the twentieth century into the Roanoke colony and now protects the shapeshifter, Virginia Dare. Fury brings about the forerunner's return, and many of the heroes immigrate to America. The edition includes an introductory essay by Peter

Sanderson, and "Afterword" by Neil Gaiman, script, sketches, and description of research preparation.

Read Aloud/Reader Response

1. "Time after Time: From 1602 to 2004" by Peter Sanderson. Introductory essay. Sanderson explains the combination of the characters and themes in relation to *Marvel 1602*.
2. Part One, page 18, panel 1. Fury ponders the why of man's existence.
3. Part Two, page 2, panel 3. Fury reads the school's motto concerning change.
4. Part Four, page 19, panel 5. The Old Man of Knights Templar contemplates tool and weapons.
5. Part Six, page 8, panels 1 to 5. Ben Grimm/The Thing shows the effectiveness of one crack.

Booktalk

Superheroes and history—an unbeatable combination. The year is 1602. Queen Elizabeth I is dying. James I is ready to take over the throne and bring the Spanish Inquisition to England. People with paranormal powers, people with transformed bodies, any people with differences are in danger. Turbulent weather approaches the continent from the Roanoke colony along with a young shapeshifter and her bodyguard. A secret weapon emerges from the Holy Land. And a twentieth-century time traveler threatens to end the universe. Enter the superheroes of Marvel Comics fame, and you have a tale of adventure and intrigue that you can't put down and won't forget. Enter *Marvel 1602*.

Learning Opportunities

1. After reading Sanderson's introductory essay, discuss the ideas that surprised you.
2. In Read Aloud/Reader Response 2, Fury reads the mutant school motto. Discuss the multiple ways it applies to *Marvel 1602*.
3. Discuss how *Marvel 1602* applies to modern terrorism.
4. List each character, the character's power, and the power's modern-day application.
5. Using your library's resources, research the background of one of the historical references. Share your information with the group.

Related Works

1. Aronson, Marc. **Sir Walter Ralegh and the Quest for El Dorado.** New York: Clarion Books, 2000. 222p. $20.00. ISBN 0

395 84827 X. [nonfiction] JS (See full booktalk in *Booktalks and More*, 2003, pages 232 to 235.) Ralegh saw his life as a performance and his exploration as exploitation.

2. Blackwood, Gary. **The Year of the Hangman.** New York: Dutton Books, 2002. 261p. $16.99. ISBN 0 525 46921 4. [fiction] MJS (See full booktalk in *Teen Genre Connections*, 2005, pages 142 to 144.) Set in 1777, this alternate history novel speculates what America would have been like if the British won.

3. Munroe, Kevin. **Olympus Heights.** San Diego, CA: IDW Publishing, 2005. 149p. $19.99. ISBN 1 93238255 0. [graphic] JS/A Oliver Dobbs, working for a local museum in Olympus Heights, Indiana, discovers that his secretive next-door neighbor is actually Zeus, who requires Oliver's help in waging a battle against evil.

4. Schmidt, Gary D. **William Bradford: Plymouth's Faithful Pilgrim.** Grand Rapids, MI: Eerdmans Books for Young Readers, 1999. 200p. $18.00. ISBN 0 8028 5151 7. [nonfiction] JS (See full booktalk in *Booktalks and More*, 2003, pages 244 to 246.) Schmidt describes Bradford's pilgrimage to the New World in the context of Elizabeth's church and James's persecution.

5. Thomas, Jane Resh. **Behind the Mask: The Life of Queen Elizabeth I.** New York: Clarion Books, 1998. 196p. $19.00. ISBN 0 395 69120 6. [nonfiction] MJS (See full booktalk in *Booktalks and More*, 2003, pages 247 to 249.) Thomas explains how the monarch shaped and is shaped by her times.

༄༅

Ferris, Jean. **Once Upon a Marigold.**

New York: Harcourt Brace and Company, 2002. 275p. $5.95pa.
ISBN 0 15 205084 1. [fiction] MJS

Themes/Topics: princesses, kings, family life, trolls, humor, parentage, love

Summary/Description

Edric, a troll, finds six-year-old Christian, a self-described inventor who refuses to return home, in the woods. Eleven years later, Christian watches the Princess Marigold through his telescope and corresponds with her by p-mail (carrier pigeon). Finally, he takes a job in the castle and discovers that Marigold's mother, Queen Olympia, drugs the king, wants to marry off Marigold, and plans to murder both the king and princess to gain the throne. Christian tries to stop the wedding, but is sent to the dungeon. Marigold, refusing the marriage, and Ed, suspected of conspiring with Christian, join him. The king joins Marigold and her triplet sisters against the queen, but the queen dominates until Christian appears at the ceremony armed with a new invention. In the subsequent confrontation, an arrow wounds Christian, but Marigold's loving touch heals him. Christian is a prince thought dead, the older brother of two of the triplets' husbands. Since his father is dying, Christian will soon be king. A servant reveals that the queen is not the girls' mother. Marigold and Christian become a trend-setting royal couple who join the two kingdoms. Ed finds status and love. The queen still challenges the kingdom.

Read Aloud/Reader Response

1. Chapter 2, pages 14 and 15, beginning with the chapter and ending " . . . with Cate and Bub." Ed tries to find out Christian's identity, but Christian stands his ground.
2. Chapter 2, pages 18 and 19, beginning "I think people shouldn't have children . . . " and ending " . . . trailed by Christian and the dogs." Christian reveals his rules for living.
3. Chapter 10, pages 135 and 136, beginning "If you were queen, . . . " and ending " . . . before they did bad things." Marigold and Christian share how each one of them would rule.
4. Chapter 12, pages 150 and 151, beginning "I should have known it was you . . . " and ending " . . . and are still giving me." Marigold realizes that Christian is the boy from her p-mails and tells him that his common birth will never affect her feelings for him.
5. Chapter 14, page 169, beginning " . . . what good . . . " and ending " . . . way of thinking." This short quotation simply reflects on worry as a waste of time.
6. Chapter 22, pages 253 and 254, beginning "So you're not . . . " and ending " . . . might soon be the only one." The passage distinguishes between the biological and nurturing parent.

Booktalk

Once upon a time . . . What do those words suggest to you? A princess? This story has several. A prince? It has plenty of those too, plus a troll, an evil queen, a dungeon, a forest, and romance. But this isn't your usual fairy tale. The princess isn't beautiful. The prince doesn't want a kingdom, and the troll's main goal is breaking up the tooth fairy monopoly. It all adds up to an off-the-wall, down-in-the-dirt adventure romance that shakes up the traditional family and business as usual at the same time. It starts with a little boy who runs away to hide in the forest, a troll who collects whatever he finds in the forest, and a princess who doesn't even know the forest outside her castle. That very important princess is Marigold. That's why the story isn't *Once Upon a Time,* but *Once Upon a Marigold.*

Learning Opportunities

1. Discuss what makes this story humorous.
2. Using your library's resources, locate three traditional fairy tales that involve a prince and a princess. After reading them, list the elements they share. Then discuss how Ferris uses these traditional elements or expectations to accomplish her purpose.
3. How would you describe Ed's function in the story?
4. The responsibility of power is a major theme in the story. List each mention of power. Then describe how each instance reveals the character involved.
5. State what you feel is the story's message or messages. Explain your answer.

Related Works

1. Haddix, Margaret Peterson. **Just Ella.** New York: Simon & Schuster Books for Young Children, 1999. 185p. $17.00. ISBN 0 689 82186 7. [fiction] MJS In this feminist retelling of the Cinderella story, fifteen-year-old Ella, discovering that the court centers on appearances and empty ceremony, decides to control her own life.
2. Napoli, Donna Jo. **Beast.** New York: Atheneum Books for Young Readers, 2000. 260p. $17.00. ISBN 0 689 83589 2 [fiction] JS (See full booktalk in *Teen Genre Connections,* 2005, pages 171 to 173.) In this retelling of "The Beauty and the Beast," Orasmyn, a young Persian prince, who offends the gods, is turned into a lion and makes his way back to humanity through true love.
3. Napoli, Donna Jo. **Crazy Jack.** New York: Delacorte Press, 1999. 134p. $15.95. ISBN 0 385 32627 0. [fiction] MJS (See full booktalk in *Booktalks and More,* 2003, pages 107 to 109.) Jack, a visionary, lives by the advice for a full life that his father forgot.
4. November, Sharyn (ed.). **Firebirds: An Anthology of Original Fantasy and Science Fiction.** New York: Firebird/Penguin, 2003. 420p. $19.99. ISBN 0 14 250142 5. [short stories] JS These stories use fantasy and science fiction to explore universal feelings. "Cotillion," pages 5 to 41, "Beauty," pages 69 to 105, "Mariposa," pages 107 to 120, "Byndley," pages 180 to 197, and "The Lady of the Ice Garden," pages 199 to 225, are some that have a fairy tale flavor.
5. Schmidt, Gary D. **Straw into Gold.** New York: Clarion Books, 2001. 172p. $15.00. ISBN 0 618 05601 7. [fiction] MJS (See full

booktalk in *Teen Genre Connections,* 2005, pages 175 to 177.) In this fairy tale retelling, Rumpelstiltskin is a wise man who saves the prince from an evil king and teaches his own foster son that relationships are more important than gold.

⟮ℑ⟯⟮ℑ⟯

Wooding, Chris. **Poison.**

New York: Orchard Books, 2003. 273p. $16.99. ISBN 0 439 75570 0. [fiction] JS

Themes/Topics: fairy tale, power of writing, sisters, blended families, journey, faith, responsibility

Summary/Description

When the phaeries steal her baby sister, Azalia, sixteen-year-old Poison sets out to bring her back. The elderly Fleet, who taught Poison legends and lore, connects her with Bram, a wraith-catcher. Bram transports Poison to Shieldtown, befriends her, and stays to protect her. Passing through the House of the Bone Witch, Poison encounters Peppercorn and Andersen, a beautiful young girl and a clairvoyant cat, serving the witch. After Bram and Poison kill the witch, the girl and cat join them. They meet the Phaerie Lord, who proposes a task. Poison must steal a two-pronged dagger to exchange for Azalea. Poison completes the task, but the secretary to the Phaerie Lord steals the dagger, and Poison learns that the Phaerie Lord plans to kill them. They follow the phaeries to the Hierophant, the master writer, a human who controls all, and reunite with Fleet, who lives in the Hierophant castle and helps collect stories of the realm. The Phairie Lord plans to make the secretary the Hierophant, and wipe out mankind. Although the secretary murders the Hierophant, the supremacy plot fails. Both the Phaerie Lord and his secretary are killed. Poison becomes the Hierophant. Azalea was released before Poison reached the phaerie kingdom. Her kidnapping was merely a catalyst for Poison's journey.

Read Aloud/Reader Response

1. "Soulswatch Eve," pages 1 and 2, beginning with the chapter and ending " . . . which you built yourself." Describing Poison and her home, the passage also alludes to belief and responsibility.
2. "Soulswatch Eve," pages 13 to 15, beginning with "Fleet brought her . . . " and ending with the chapter. Poison and Fleet discuss the relationship between stories and life.

3. "Shieldtown," pages 52 to 55, beginning "It was late evening . . ." and ending with the chapter. Poison encounters her sister but does not recognize her.
4. "Skins and Bones," page100, beginning "But you came . . ." and ending " . . . positions were reversed." Poison realizes Bram's heroism and wonders if she can emulate him.
5. "Storytelling," page 178, beginning "Why didn't you . . ." and ending " . . . in the right direction." Poison wonders why Fleet could not have taken her to the phaerie world, but Fleet indicates that each person must make his own journey, or choices, independently.

Booktalk

Ask how many people would choose a different name for themselves. Briefly discuss what the names might be and the reasons for their choices.

At fourteen, each citizen in the Black Marshes can choose a new name. The girls usually choose the names of flowers and herbs. The boys usually focus on animals and features of the landscape. The people of the Black Marshes believe that each person directs his or her life with this personal choice. But Foxglove isn't usual, and she doesn't feel anyone living in the Black Marsh community of Gull has taken control over anything. *Read aloud the paragraph beginning "She envied the villagers . . ." on page 4.* Foxglove rebels against her culture the same way she fights her stepmother, and her father, and anyone else who would try to control her. And when the powerful phaerie nation steals her baby sister, Azalea, Poison decides to fight them too and bring her sister back. Foxglove will take on all the worlds of the realm if necessary, and they'd better beware. Foxglove's new name isn't a herb or a flower. Foxglove's new name is *Poison*.

Learning Opportunities

1. Using your library's resources, research fairy tales. Identify as many types or story patterns as possible. Share your findings with the group.
2. On the basis of the information that you find in Learning Opportunity 1, identify as many traditional fairy tale character types as you can in the story *Poison*.
3. By the end of the story, would you give Poison another opportunity to choose a name for herself? Explain your answer.
4. Choose one story from your own life or from the life of another person. After telling the story, be sure to explain why you told it.

5. Make three lists: forces of good, forces of evil, both. Place each of the characters in one of these three categories and explain your reasons for the placement. Compare your list with lists composed by others who have completed the same exercise.

Related Works

1. Gardner, John. **Grendel.** New York: Vintage Books, reissue edition, 1989. 192p. $10.95pa. ISBN 0 679 72311 0. [fiction] S/A The monster from *Beowulf,* whose life has been characterized by the "Shaper," tells his own story.

2. Hettinga, Donald R. **The Brothers Grimm: Two Lives, One Legacy.** New York: Clarion Books, 2001. 180p. $22.00. ISBN 0 618 05599 1. [nonfiction] JS Included in this story are lists of all the brothers' publications and gathered tales.

3. Lester, Julius. **Time's Memory.** New York: Farrar, Straus and Giroux, 2006. 230p. $17.00. ISBN 0 374 37178 4. [fiction] JS Ekundayo, sent by the creator god Amma to calm the spirits disrupted by slavery, accomplishes his task by recording their stories.

4. Warner, Marina. **No Go the Bogeyman: Scaring, Lulling, and Making Mock.** New York: Farrar, Straus and Giroux, 1998. 435p. $35.00. ISBN 0 374 22301 7. [professional reference] A Warner explores the role of monster and terror in human lives.

5. Wooding, Chris. **Storm Thief.** New York: Scholastic Press, 2006. 320p. $16.99. ISBN 0 439 86513 1. [fiction] MJS Two ghetto teens, who survive by stealing, discover an artifact that controls their isolated world and, along with a created monster, become the center of a battle between good and evil.

Meeting the Challenges of the Future

ଔଐ

Adlington, L. J. **The Diary of Pelly D.**
New York: Harper Collins/Greenwillow Books, 2005. 282p. $16.99.
ISBN 0 06 076616 6. [fiction] JS

Themes/Topics: holocaust, discrimination, brave new world, personal identity

Summary/Description

Fourteen-year-old Toni V is the runt on a work gang clearing land after a war. This new society on a non-earth planet values new over old and physical work over thinking. In the rubble, Toni V finds Pelly D's diary. Pelly D, part of the upper-class, has a crush on a boy who subscribes to Heritage Clan beliefs that maintain that his gene group, the Atsumis, is superior to either the Mazzini or Galrezi groups. As the Heritage movement grows in power, gene testing and labeling become routine. Pelly D, along with those who are different, find their internet communication, homes, and property removed. Her brother runs away when called up for a work project. Her father, who tests as Atsumis, the favored group, distances himself from the family. On the last diary pages, Pelly, her remaining family, and boyfriend are being relocated, and probably will be extinguished. Toni V sees his group's attitudes similar to the ones she records. He becomes attached to Pelly D. By the end of the novel, he asks questions and plans his future. Violating society's rules, he keeps the diary.

Read Aloud/Reader Response

1. Pages 50 and 51, beginning "You all right . . . " and ending with the chapter. Toni V learns that reading the diary is so emotionally upsetting that it physically exhausts him.
2. Pages 60 and 61, beginning with the chapter and ending " . . . hard as she'd thought." Toni V reflects on Pelly D's evaluation of dates and wonders about his own relationships.
3. Pages 86 to 88, beginning with the section and ending " . . . are we headed to first?" Toni V reflects on the power of reading and how it allows him to really get to know a person.
4. Section 11.9, pages 122 to 124. Pelly D and her brother talk about the dangerous situation they are in. The brother sees the destruction and why it will happen. Pelly D is in denial.
5. 3.10 Midnight, pages 167 to 170, beginning "Moma Peg's . . . " and ending with the section. Pelly D reflects on their move to another apartment because of the government's racist policy and realizes the implications of her father's desire to distance himself.
6. Pages 178 to 181, beginning, "Toni V wished . . . " and ending with the section. Toni V, influenced by Pelly D's diary, stands up for Kiw P, an outcast, but finds himself being influenced by the group leader and bully.
7. Section 31.10, pages 227 to 229. Pelly D tries to deny that the city is at war.

Booktalk

Toni V is fourteen. He works for the City Five demolition crew. His planet just had a big war—like earth. He's there to help clean up. He never thought too much about why there was a war in the first place. In his world, thinking is shirking, and shirking is losing. For Toni V, life is just about his muscles and power drill. Then his drill hits something, a book. He isn't supposed to look. Old stuff is a waste of time. He should throw it away, but he looks. Some spoiled upper-class, stupid girl wrote it. It's a diary. For some reason, Toni can't put it down. He gets so tired his head hurts. She tells him something about more than just her. She tells him about the war. Now, for Toni V, the war has a face and a voice. He really would like to see that face. The voice says things he doesn't want to hear—things about his own world, about himself, but he can't shut that book or throw it away. Life means more than the roar and thud of his hammer. Suddenly, Toni V is part of the past and wondering about the future—all because of the thoughts of some upper-class snob who probably wouldn't give him the time of day—all because of *The Diary of Pelly D.*

Learning Opportunities

1. Ethnic cleansing is the basis of the story. Using your library's resources, define ethnic cleansing and describe one example for the group. You may wish to begin by reading the selections in Related Works.
2. Pelly D, her brother, mother, and father represent very different reactions to the racist events affecting their lives. Characterize each reaction and its possible results.
3. What is the difference between Pelly D's feelings for Ant Li and Marek T?
4. Does Pelly D change Toni V's life? Explain.
5. Discuss the role of Moma Peg in the novel. What does she reveal about the society?
6. Pelly D refers many times to the differences between her planet and the violent planet earth. How does the author use Pelly D's comparisons?
7. List the slogans and the reasons that you think they are used.
8. Could Pelly D's directive, "Dig—dig everywhere," be considered a slogan for a new society?

Related Works

1. Bagdasarian, Adam. **Forgotten Fire: A Novel.** New York: DK Ink, 2000. 273p. $17.95. ISBN 0 7894 2627 7. [fiction] MJS (See full

booktalk in *Booktalks and More*, 2003, pages 49 to 54.) A young man tells how he survives the 1915 Turkish purge of the Armenians.

2. Frank, Anne. **The Diary of a Young Girl: The Definitive Edition.** Otto H. Frank and Mirjam Pressler (eds.). Susan Massotty (trans.). New York: Doubleday, 1991. 340p. $25.00. ISBN 0 385 47378 8. [nonfiction] JS This new edition contains approximately thirty percent more material and is based on the scholarship of *The Diary of Anne Frank: The Critical Edition.*

3. Mikaelsen, Ben. **Tree Girl.** New York: HarperCollins Children's Books, 2004. 240p. $16.99. ISBN 0 06 009004 9. [fiction] JS Fifteen-year-old Gabriela Flores loses her teacher, classmates, and most of her family when the U.S. trained troops in Guatemala begin a systematic Indian massacre.

4. Müller, Melissa. **Anne Frank: The Biography.** Rita Kimber and Robert Kimber (trans.). New York: Henry Holt and Company, 1998. 330p. $14.00pa. ISBN 0 8050 5997 0. [nonfiction] S/A This work places Anne Frank in a family, social, and political context.

5. Springer, Jane. **Genocide**. Toronto, Ontario: House of Anansi Press/ Groundwood Books, 2006. 144p.(Groundwork Guides). $15.95. ISBN 13: 978 0 88899 681 7. [nonfiction] S Using several historical examples, Springer defines genocide and explains how prejudice creates it.

6. Ung, Loung. **First They Killed My Father: A Daughter of Cambodia Remembers.** New York: HarperCollins Publishers, 2000. 239p. $23.00. ISBN 0 06 019332 8. [nonfiction] JS (See full booktalk in *Booktalks and More*, 2003, pages 54 to 56.) Loung describes the destruction of her family under the Khmer Rouge.

Patterson, James. Maximum Ride: The Angel Experiment.

New York: Warner Vision Books, 2005. 440p. $6.99pa.
ISBN 0 446 61779 2. [fiction] JS

Themes/Topics: genetic engineering, adventure, blended family, man/animal relationship

Summary/Description

Fourteen-year-old Maximum Ride (Max) leads a six-member "family" made up of children, who have been injected in a secret government experiment with bird DNA and raised in cages. Fang, four months younger than Max, is dark and silent. Iggy, six months younger than Max, is blind. Eleven-year-old Nudge talks incessantly. Eight-year-old Gasman is a skilled mimic with a digestive problem. Six-year-old Angel reads minds. Jeb Batchelder, one of the original scientists who developed them, took them from the "School" and brought them to an isolated house, their present home, to live "normally." They last saw him two years ago. The Erasers, another mutant group who can transform themselves into wolves, act as guards, policemen, and executioners. Ari, Jeb's son, is one of the strongest and fiercest. The Erasers kidnap Angel, and return her to the school. The group sets out to rescue her. Jeb is working at the school, but Angel says his brain is like a dead man's. When Max is also captured, Jeb tells her that everything has been a test for her destiny, to save the world. With the help of hawks, the avians escape and travel to New York to discover their identities, but the Erasers track and find them. In one battle, Max kills Ari, whom Jeb calls her brother. All, except Max, discover their parentage. An interactive Web site, www.maximumride.com, allows readers to ask questions and react to the book and characters in written and oral formats.

Read Aloud/Reader Response

1. "Prologue," pages 1 and 2. Max describes their bizarre situation and warns that it could possibly be anyone's in today's world.
2. Chapter 8, page 26, beginning "Ari's last . . ." and ending " . . . *good guys.*" Ari's words to Max are the first confusing statement in this battle between good and evil.
3. Chapter 45, pages 139 to 142. The actions and reactions of both Max and Jeb reveal their characters.
4. Chapter 61, pages 191 to 193. Jeb tells Max that she is to save the world.
5. Chapter 99, pages 304 to 306, beginning "We all felt . . ." and ending with the chapter. Max expresses her dread of being discovered. The inner voice comments.

Booktalk

Maximum Ride. That's her name. This is her story. Let her introduce you to it herself. *Read the "Prologue," pages 1 and 2.*

Learning Opportunities

1. Using your library's resources, find two specifics about genetic engineering that are new to you. Share the information that you find with the group.

2. Including details of the story, describe Jeb Batchelder.
3. Draw pictures of each of the characters as you might imagine them.
4. Log on to www.maximumride.com. Participate in one of the activities.
5. After reading *Maximum Ride: The Angel Experiment* and *Maximum Ride: School's Out—Forever*, explain the relationship between the avian group and the Erasers.

Related Works

1. Armstrong, Jennifer, and Nancy Butcher. **Fire Us Trilogy.** New York: HarperCollins Publishers. [fiction] MJS (See full booktalk in *Teen Genre Connections*, 2005, pages 204 to 208.) **The Kindling: Book One.** 2002. 224p. $15.89. ISBN 0 06 029411 6. After an adult killing virus (fire us) sweeps the United States, eight orphans band together to form a family and find the president. **The Keepers of the Flame: Book Two.** 2002. 231p. $17.89. ISBN 0 06 029412 4. The travelers from Book One discover a cult-like community, The Keepers, that attempts to control them. The group escapes with some of the residents and continues to Washington. **The Kiln: Book Three.** 2003. 193p. $15.99. ISBN 0 06 008050. The group discovers that the president used the virus to purify the country and that as they reach adulthood, they will be susceptible to it. One group member sacrifices her life to destroy the president and the virus forever, and the "family" journeys away from all adults to build a new home.
2. Card, Orson Scott. **Ender's Game.** New York: TOR, 1991. 234p. $6.99pa. (Ender). ISBN 0 812 55070 6. [fiction] JS/A In this first book of the series, six-year-old Ender trains to be a battle commander of brilliant children who will save their world from a hostile ant-like population from another planet.
3. Farmer, Nancy. **The House of the Scorpion.** New York: Atheneum Books for Young Readers/A Richard Jackson Book, 2002. 380p. $17.95. ISBN 0 689 85222 3. [fiction] JS (See full booktalk in *Teen Genre Connections*, 2005, pages 208 to 210.) A drug lord plans to farm parts from his clones and live forever.
4. Patterson, James. **Maximum Ride: School's Out—-Forever.** New York: Little, Brown and Company, 2006. 409p. $16.99. ISBN 0 316 15559 4. [fiction] JS In this first sequel, the group is fooled by the FBI boss in charge of their project, and with the help of a Max duplicate, are almost captured and destroyed by Itex, a conglomerate with the power to destroy the world.

cʃ ʅɔ

Rosoff, Meg. How I Live Now.

New York: Random House/Wendy Lamb Books, 2004. 194p. $18.95.
ISBN 0 385 90908 X. [fiction] JS

Themes/Topics: England, family life, farm life, love, eating disorders, incest, terrorism

Summary/Description

Fifteen-year-old anorexic and hostile Elizabeth (Daisy) moves from New York City where she lives with her father and controlling, pregnant stepmother to rural England where she joins her aunt's family: one adult, four kids, a goat, and two dogs. Daisy's aunt leaves the five young people to fend for themselves and works against an impending world-wide war. Daisy and Edmond, one of Daisy's cousins, fall in love. The government authorities commandeer the house and divide up the family. Daisy and eleven-year-old Piper live with Major McEvoy's family, but Daisy hears Edmond telepathically. As the war escalates, Daisy and Piper seek the three boys. On their search, starvation cures Daisy's anorexia. Arriving home, the girls discover a massacre but manage to survive. Daisy's influential father tracks her down and arranges for her to return to the states. She returns to England, eventually finds her cousins, and reunites with Edmond, who started cutting himself when he discovered that she left.

Read Aloud/Reader Response

1. Chapters 1 and 2, pages 1 to 4. Daisy introduces herself and describes her first meeting with Edmond.
2. Chapter 8, pages 35 to 37. Daisy describes Isaac's quiet surveillance and care.
3. Chapter 12, page 59, beginning "This leaves me . . . " and ending " . . . what to say." Dr. Jameson, looking for much-needed antibiotics, confronts Daisy about her anorexia.
4. Chapter 20, pages 103 to 105, beginning "One night . . . " and ending with the chapter. Daisy describes the incident that starts the shooting war.
5. Chapter 28, page 159, beginning "One funny thing . . . " and ending " . . . has its silver lining." Daisy explains how her anorexia has lost its point.

Booktalk

Fifteen-year-old Daisy lives in New York. She fights with her father and evil stepmother. She struggles with food. She is anorexic. And suddenly the entire world decides to capture her mood. It is on the brink of war. What do Daisy's parents do? They send her to the quiet English countryside. She will live with her dead mother's sister and the sister's four children. From them she might learn about her mother, the woman Daisy's father never talks about. Then the world explodes. Terrorists occupy London as part of their world-wide assault. Daisy's aunt leaves for Oslo to try and stop the destruction. Daisy and her four cousins are alone, a new family. Like most families they have a common job—survival. Food is low because supply routes are cut off. They lose their home, because the army needs it. Next they lose each other because no one wants five new people at once. Then the shooting really starts. The countryside isn't quiet anymore. The dead bodies are no longer strangers. And Daisy, struggling to eat, drink, and live, must say that her private wars in the middle of New York are very different from *How I Live Now.*

Learning Opportunities

1. Using your library's resources, research anorexia and its causes. Share your information with the group. You may wish to start with Related Work 4.
2. Using your library's resource, research self-mutilation and its causes. Share your information with the group. You may want to read *Cut* (Related Work 5).
3. Using your library's resources, research coping with terrorism today. Share the information with the group. You may wish to start with Related Work 2.
4. Daisy and Edmond share a forbidden relationship. Discuss why the family accepts it.
5. Reread the final chapter. Discuss how it joins Daisy's personal wars with the world war.

Related Works

1. Block, Francesca Lia. **Wasteland.** New York: Harper Collins/ Joanna Cotler Books, 2003. 150p. $16.89. ISBN 0 06 028645 8. [fiction] S. A brother and sister have an incestuous relationship. After the brother's suicide, the sister discovers that her brother was adopted.

2. Casil, Amy Sterling. **Coping with Terrorism.** New York: The
    Rosen Publishing Group, 2004. 96p. $27.95. ISBN 0 8239 4484 0.
    [nonfiction] MJS Casil lists terrorist strikes and explains how the
    private citizen might aid the government and cope emotionally.
3. Hoffman, Alice. **Green Angel.** New York: Scholastic Press, 2003.
    128p. $16.95. ISBN 0 439 44384 9. [fiction] JS Losing her family
    in an apocalyptic explosion, Green drinks, tattoos herself, and no
    longer looks to the future until she realizes that her family will
    always be with her and that she is the ink to tell the future's story.
4. Kalodner, Cynthia R. **Too Fat or Too Thin?: A Reference
    Guide to Eating Disorders.** Westport, CT: Greenwood Press,
    2003. 228p. $51.95. ISBN 0 313 31581 7. [nonfiction] S/A Medical
    and psychological issues related to eating disorders are discussed
    in the chapters, which include resource lists of fiction, nonfiction,
    movies, periodicals, and Web sites. Chapter 3 focuses on Anorexia
    Nervosa.
5. McCormick, Patricia. **Cut.** Asheville, NC: Front Street, 2000.
    168p. $16.95. ISBN 1 886910 61 8. [fiction] JS (See full booktalk
    in *Booktalks and More,* 2003, pages 169 to 171.) Fifteen-year-old
    Callie recovers from self-mutilation caused by her dysfunctional
    family.

ᘓᘔ

Sleator, William. **The Last Universe.**

New York: Amulet Books, 2005. 215p. $16.95. ISBN 0 8109 5858 9. [fiction] MJ

Themes/Topics: quantum theory, space and time, mazes,
brothers and sisters, diseases

Summary/Description

Fourteen-year-old Susan and her dying sixteen-year-old brother,
Gary, explore a mysterious maze created by her scientist uncle.
They discover, according to a theory of quantum physics, alternative
worlds. Some of the worlds allow her brother to become stronger. When
her brother Gary has a relapse, the gardener who warned them away
from the maze, gives Susan a note that instructs her how to navigate
the maze safely. She finds her uncle, and grandparents who live in an
alternative reality. Her grandfather helps her return to her family. She
discovers that now her brother is completely healthy, and she is the one
beginning to die.

Read Aloud/Reader Response

1. Chapter 3, page 40, beginning "In Cambodia, ..." and ending "...
    himself, too." Luke tells the story about the father bird and the lotus.
2. Chapter 4, pages 63 to 66, beginning "Hey, why didn't you ..." and
    ending with the chapter. Lisa and Susan talk about the mysterious
    maze that Lisa wants to explore.
3. Chapter 6, pages 83 to 84, beginning "That's how electrons ..."
    and ending "... happening *here*." Gary explains leaking atoms and
    electrons.
4. Chapter 7, pages 100 to 107, beginning "Well quantum physics ..."
    and ending "... any certain answers." Gary explains quantum phys-
    ics in terms of his illness, uncertainty, and the possibility of a parallel
    universe.
5. Chapter 11, pages 149 to 150, beginning "I hardly slept at all ..."
    and ending "... for the time being." Lisa is torn between her origi-
    nal home and Gary's welfare.

Booktalk

At sixteen, Gary doesn't have long to live. His fourteen-year-old sister,
Susan, pushes him in a wheelchair, and she isn't enjoying the experience any more than he is. Together they explore their family property,
property their father inherited from their uncle, an award-winning scientist. Gardens fill the grounds, strange and sad places that are suddenly
changing. Flowers bloom in one day. Paths change direction. Suddenly,
the gardener turns guarded and distant. Gary believes that all this
change has something to do with his illness and his scientific uncle. He
convinces Susan to explore even further into the garden. They will enter
the mysterious maze, the part that no one talks about or goes near. Gary
knows that it holds the key to his recovery. Susan fears it means their
destruction. But no one can anticipate the final destination, a world his
uncle never revealed, the world of *The Last Universe*.

Learning Opportunities

1. Using your library's resources, find one other principle of physics.
    Try to explain it to the group in either a visual or oral presenta-
    tion.
2. *The Last Universe* is described as a "gothic, sci-fi thriller." Using
    your library's resources, define gothic and science fiction.
3. Using the definitions from Learning Opportunity 2, identify the
    novel's gothic and science fiction elements.

4. How does the quantum physics theory affect Sleator's characterization?

5. Predict what will happen in the next trip to the maze.

Related Works

1. Lawrence, Michael. **A Crack in the Line: Volume I.** New York: Greenwillow Books, 2003. 323p. (Withern Rise). $16.99. ISBN 0 06 072478 1. [fiction] JS Sixteen-year-old Alaric and Naia, who have the same mother and father but live in alternative realities, eventually, by accident, trade worlds.

2. Paulsen, Gary. **The Transall Saga.** New York: Delacorte Press, 1998. 248p. $15.95. ISBN 0 385 32196 1. [fiction] MJ (See full booktalk in *Booktalks Plus*, 2001, pages 192 to 193.) A blue light transports thirteen-year-old Mark Harrison to another world in another time, where he is swept up into a war and becomes a man.

3. Pullman, Philip. **His Dark Materials Trilogy.** New York: Alfred A Knopf. [fiction] MJS (See full booktalk in *Booktalks and More*, 2003, pages 161 to 166.) **The Golden Compass.** 1995. 399p. $20.00. ISBN 0 679 87924 2. Lyra must distinguish the powers competing for her life and the lives of the stolen children of the North. **The Subtle Knife.** 1997. 326p. $20.00. ISBN 0 679 87925 0. Fleeing his father's enemies, twelve-year-old Will encounters Lyra in an alternative reality. **The Amber Spyglass.** 2000. 518p. $19.95. ISBN 0 679 87926 9. Guided by the physicist Mary Malone, Will and Lyra return to their own realities and decide to build productive lives.

4. Sleator, William. **The Boxes.** New York: Dutton, 1998. 196p. $15.99. ISBN 0 525 46012 8. [fiction] MJ (See full booktalk in *Booktalks Plus*, 2001, pages 189 to 192.) Annie Levi opens boxes left in her care and discovers a supernatural world and a new maturity and confidence.

ぴ〠

Zevin, Gabrielle. Elsewhere.
New York: Farrar, Straus and Giroux, 2005. 277p. $19.95.
ISBN 0 374 32091 8. [fiction] MJS

Themes/Topics: future life, death, relationships, love

Summary/Description

Liz dies in a traffic accident shortly before her sixteenth birthday. She begins her new life in Elsewhere, a world where she becomes younger each day and learns about her spirit, which will be born back into earth. In the process of accepting her death, weaning herself from her earthly life, and discovering her talents, she bonds with the grandmother she never met, falls in love with another Elsewhere citizen who also struggles to accept his death, and forgives her hit-and-run killer. Death allows her to experience and enjoy many lives instead of just one.

Read Aloud/Reader Response

1. "Prologue: In the End," pages 3 to 6. Lucy, Liz's dog, processes Liz's death and bonds with Alvy, Liz's seven-year-old brother.
2. "In Memory of Elizabeth Marie Hall," pages 27 to 31, beginning "Girl, you are in . . . " and ending "*Dead.*" Liz witnesses her funeral and accepts her death.
3. "A Circle and a Line," pages 68 to 70, beginning "The video begins . . . " and ending " . . . drifting off to sleep." Liz views the Elsewhere video.
4. "Lucky Cab," page 109, beginning "Maybe Earth's not . . . " and ending " . . . don't think about—." Esther explains the relationship between life and death with a tree metaphor.
5. "Restoration," pages 228 to 229, beginning with the chapter and ending with "Aldous agrees." Recovering from her attempted return to earth, Liz reflects on her insights into *A Midsummer Night's Dream* and *Hamlet*.
6. "What Liz Thinks," pages 274 to 275. Liz returns to earth as a baby.

Booktalk

Liz is almost sixteen, not quite old enough to drive a car. So she bikes it to the mall to meet her friend. Unfortunately, she doesn't wear a helmet, and she doesn't pay attention to where she is going. Wham! She gets hit by a car and dies. End of story? Not quite. Just the beginning? Oh yes. She wakes up on a boat sailing down the Nile. She has a very cranky roommate, and the captain seems to be about seven. Liz doesn't believe it. You could say she is in de-Nile. After all, Liz is too young to die. There must be a mix-up, a dream, a mistake. Liz is kind of right. This boat thing isn't permanent. She has a whole new world ahead of her, and then a whole new world after that. But Liz wants her old world. Can she go back or, no matter where she turns, will she be headed *Elsewhere?*

Learning Opportunities

1. Liz refers to several literary works in relation to death. Read one or all of the works and discuss their appropriateness.

2. Using your library's resources, find another literary work dealing with death. Compare its insights with those presented in *Elsewhere*.
3. Trace Liz's journey to acceptance. Explain the significance of each pivotal event.
4. Discuss the role of dogs in the novel.
5. Compare and discuss Liz's entrance to and exit from *Elsewhere*.
6. The title could have several meanings. Discuss its relationship to the novel.

Related Works

1. Albom, Mitch. **The Five People You Meet in Heaven.** [fiction] JS/A (See full booktalk in "Issues"/"Finding Inner Peace or Spiritual Clarification," pages 35 to 37.) After he dies saving a little girl's life, eighty-three-year-old Eddie meets five people who illustrate that there are no random acts, sacrifice brings reward, letting go allows one to move on, love lasts through memories, and responsibility brings redemption and salvation.
2. Haddix, Margaret Peterson. **Turnabout.** New York: Simon and Schuster, 2000. 223p. $17.00. ISBN 0 689 82187 5. [fiction] MJS After participating in a DNA experiment, Mell and Anny Beth live two lifetimes, and now must find someone to take care of them as they return to infancy.
3. Partridge, Elizabeth. **John Lennon: All I Want Is the Truth.** [nonfiction] JS (See full booktalk in "History"/"Defining Leaders and Events," pages 225 to 227.) The biography relates the success and upheaval of John Lennon's life. In *Elsewhere,* Lennon chooses to be a gardener.
4. Rylant, Cynthia. **The Heavenly Village.** New York: The Blue Sky Press, 1999. 95p. $15.95. ISBN 0 439 04096 5. [fiction] MJS (See full booktalk in *Booktalks Plus,* 2001, pages 52 to 54.) In this village between heaven and earth, souls who still have business on earth complete their tasks before moving on.
5. Shelley, Percy. "Ozymandias." Sonnet Central. Available: www.sonnets.org/shelley.htm. (Accessed July 2006). The poem, alluded to throughout the story, involves one man's attempt at immortality. It is a model for writing sonnets. The Web address links to "Sonnet Central," which encourages the writing of modern sonnets and links to sample sonnets from different periods.

History

"History" includes books about the past or set in the past. Although two divisions are peace and war, "Choosing in Peace" also addresses serious conflicts, and "Choosing in War" includes islands of cooperation and peace. "Defining Leaders and Events" acknowledges that larger-than-life individuals and shared experiences often influence how people think and react both then and now.

Choosing in Peace

Chotjewitz, David. Doris Orgel (trans.). **Daniel Half Human.**

New York: Simon Pulse, 2004. 325p. $5.99pa. ISBN 9 780689 857485. [fiction] JS

Themes/Topics: Germany, 1933–1945, Nazis, friendship, prejudice, Jews, mixed marriages

Summary/Description

As an interpreter for the U.S. Army in 1945, Daniel returns to now bombed out Hamburg, Germany, where he grew up. The city tour reminds him of his former life. His first-person flashbacks introduce and conclude five parts of the main story told in third person. Upper-class Daniel and lower-class Armin are best friends. Both, against their parents' wishes, want to join Hitler Youth. Daniel discovers that his mother is Jewish. His family is slowly marginalized, while Armin progresses in the party. Armin, attracted to Daniel's Jewish cousin, secretly meets her, is discovered, and is pressured to betray the entire family on *Kristallnacht,* "the Night of Broken Glass." He gives the family a cryptic warning, but beats the father under pressure from his superiors and then ignores the family. His priority is his SS career. Daniel confronts him when, as an American interrogator, Daniel interviews German soldiers. Doing his duty, as the German soldiers claimed, Daniel exposes Armin as an SS.

Read Aloud/Reader Response

1. "A Letter Not Sent," pages 132 to 135. Miriam reveals her fear, confusion, and self-hate.
2. "Painting," pages 158 to 160, beginning with the chapter and ending with " . . . half Jewish from him." The passage reviews the relationship between Daniel and Armin.
3. "Shots in the Dark," pages 165 to 166, beginning with the chapter and ending " . . . the instant he was shot." Armin tells about the target practice that kills a twelve-year-old.
4. "My Honor Means Loyalty, I (SS Motto)," pages 168 to 173, beginning with the chapter and ending "Good. Dismissed." After Armin protests the death described in Read Aloud/Reader Response 3, his superior explains SS thinking.
5. "'The Loreley,'" pages 208 to 214, beginning "Daniel thought back . . ." and ending with the chapter. Daniel discusses his identity with Miriam.

Booktalk

Ask what it means to be blood brothers.

Daniel and Armin are blood brothers. They fight together. They go to jail together—even though Daniel is rich and Armin is poor. In 1933 Germany, the gap between rich and poor is wide, but like many other rich and poor young men, these friends share a dream. They want to become part of the Nazi Youth. And someday they want to fulfill the dreams of Adolf Hitler, their hero. But Daniel's parents have disturbing news. His mother is Jewish—subhuman. That means that he is half Jewish. He believes that his German blood is stronger than Jewish blood. But the government "research" says that inferior blood dominates. He hides the disgrace, even from Armin, his blood brother. Soon persecuted Jewish relatives show up. Teachers pressure him for family bloodlines. Everyone finds out Daniel's secret, even Armin. It is a time for choices. It is a time to do one's duty. How can that duty be the same for Armin, all German, and *Daniel Half Human?*

Learning Opportunities

1. Using your library's resources, continue to research the life of Joseph Goebbels, who engineered Nazi propaganda. You may wish

to start with *Joseph Goebbels: Nazi Propaganda Minister* (Related Work 5).

2. Examine the journeys of both Armin and Daniel. Do you believe that if Daniel had been of full German blood, he would have taken the same path as Armin?

3. Define *duty*. Use examples that illustrate what duty is and what it is not.

4. Using your library's resources, explain how a Jew is defined. Share the information with the group. Discuss the problems and contradictions that arrive in definition.

5. Using your library information, continue to research Hitler's rise to power. You may wish to start with *The Life and Death of Adolf Hitler* (Related Work 4). Share your information with the group.

Related Works

1. Adlington, L. J. **The Diary of Pelly D.** [fiction] JS (See full booktalk in "Fantasy/Science Fiction/Paranormal"/"Meeting the Challenges of the Future," pages 178 to 181.) In a diary he finds in rubble, a young man learns about a girl of mixed blood who was marginalized and eventually exterminated because of her race.

2. Baer, Edith. **Walk the Dark Streets.** New York: Farrar, Straus and Giroux/ Frances Foster Books, 1998. 280p. $18.00. ISBN 0 374 38229 8. [fiction] JS (See full booktalk in *Booktalks Plus,* 2001, pages 153 to 155.) Telling Germany's story and Eva Bentheim's story during the Nazi rise to power, the novel opens in 1933 and ends in 1940, when Eva leaves Germany for America.

3. Byers, Ann. **The Holocaust Camps.** Berkeley Heights, NJ: Enslow Publishers, Inc., 1998. 128p. (The Holocaust Remembered Series). $20.95. ISBN 0 89490 995 9. [nonfiction] MJS Byers explains how the German camps, which began as prison and labor camps with torture and high death rates, ended as extermination camps.

4. Giblin, James Cross. **The Life and Death of Adolf Hitler.** New York: Clarion Books, 2002. 246p. $21.00. ISBN 0 395 90371 8. [nonfiction] MJS. (See full booktalk in *Teen Genre Connections,* 2005, pages 250 to 252.) Giblin portrays a disturbed and dedicated individual who, with an exceptional gift for politics and speech making, appealed to the prejudices and fears of the German people after World War I.

5. Roberts, Jeremy. **Joseph Goebbels: Nazi Propaganda Minister.** New York: The Rosen Publishing Group, 2000. 112p. (Holocaust Biographies). $19.95. ISBN 0 8239 3309 1. [nonfiction] MJS Described as one of the most hate-filled members of Hitler's staff,

Goebbels used half-truth, exaggeration, and omission rather than lies to push for Jewish extermination.

ᏽᏽ

Jurmain, Suzanne. **The Forbidden Schoolhouse: The True and Dramatic Story of Prudence Crandall and Her Students.**
Boston, MA: Houghton Mifflin Company, 2005. 150p. $18.00.
ISBN 0 618 47302 5. [nonfiction] JS

Themes/Topics: women educators, African-American women, Connecticut history

Summary/Description

In 1831, twenty-eight-year-old Prudence Crandall, a Quaker, opens a girls' school in Canterbury, Connecticut. The board and community protest her admitting two African-American girls, but Crandall, inspired by the girls' industry and *The Liberator,* published by William Lloyd Garrison, enlists Garrison's support in opening an all African-American girls' school. Although Crandall garners moral and financial aid from other abolitionists, violence, prejudice, and manipulation of the law end her project. Before closing the school, Crandall enters what proves to be an abusive marriage. The new family moves West, first to Illinois and then to Kansas. Crandall continues as an educator and a political activist for African-Americans, women, and the temperance movement. In 1885, Canterbury formally apologizes to Crandall, and Connecticut grants her a four-hundred-dollar-per-year pension. Extensive pictures and documents create a visual context for her story. In the Appendix, "Part I: The Students," information is provided about each of Crandall's African-American students. "Part II: Friends and Enemies" explains what happens to each person who supported and opposed Crandall. "Source Notes" and a "Bibliography" guide the reader to additional information, and the index makes specific information easily accessible.

Read Aloud/Reader Response

1. Chapter 1, page 9, beginning "There were . . ." and ending " . . . answer to Sarah's request." The passage reveals the Northern prejudices that Prudence faced.
2. Chapter 5, pages 33 and 34, beginning "Samuel May . . ." and ending " . . . what will." The passage reveals the prejudices toward women.

3. Chapter 7, pages 44 to 51. The chapter explains the opposition to Crandall's school, including the inspiration for the Connecticut Black Law.
4. Chapter 9, pages 62 to 65, beginning "Her trial . . . " and ending " . . . this be possible?" Crandall decides to go to jail to gain attention and support.
5. Chapter 11, pages 73 to 78, beginning "The session . . . " and ending with the chapter. Crandall's trial demonstrates prejudice toward both African-Americans and women.

Booktalk

Prudence Crandall was a spinster. The year was 1831. She decided to support herself by opening a school for girls. Her intent was to produce students who were refined and successful—an acceptable goal for a single woman. But Prudence Crandall wanted more than refinement for her students. She wanted their education to include an awareness of the world around them. The world around them was in turmoil. The great national battle over slavery was beginning. A black preacher named Nat Turner raised an army and murdered fifty-five white Virginians—men, women, and children. Abolitionists called for an end to slavery. Some of the country's richest and most prominent men supported a Back to Africa movement. Prudence Crandall pondered how she could help in this confusion. When two African-American girls requested admission to her school, she said yes. The town, afraid of the power that reading and writing would give African-Americans, said no and reinforced the refusal with threats, violence, and unjust laws. Crandall's answer was to find more African-American women who wanted to learn. She was neither wealthy nor important, but she believed that everyone should have the opportunity for success even if that opportunity lived in *The Forbidden Schoolhouse.*

Learning Opportunities

1. Read Part II of the Appendix. Choose one of the people listed. Using your library's resources, continue to research that person's life. Share the information with the group.
2. Using your library's resources, continue to research the abolitionist movement. Share your information with the group.
3. Using your library's resources, research the Back to Africa movement as interpreted by both white and African-American groups. Share your information with the group.
4. Using your library's resources, research school integration in the twentieth century. Share your information with the group.

5. Using your library's resources, research the women's suffrage movement. Share your information with the group.

Related Works

1. Coleman, Penny. **Adventurous Women: Eight True Stories about Women Who Made a Difference.** New York: Henry Holt and Company, 2006. 186p. $18.95. ISBN 0 8050 7744 8. [nonfiction] JS These extraordinary accounts of female daring include, in Chapter 5, the story of Mary McLeod Bethune, who fought for her own education and dedicated herself, in 1904, to opening a school for Negro girls.

2. Cooper, Michael L. **Slave Spirituals and the Jubilee Singers.** New York: Clarion Books, 2001. 86p. $16.00. ISBN 0 395 97829 7. [nonfiction] JS The famous singing group from Fisk University, founded in 1866 by the American Missionary Association to help educate freemen, was directed by George White, who once angered his white neighbors by organizing Sunday school for local black children.

3. Harper, Douglas. "Exclusion of Free Blacks." Slavery in the North, 2003. Available: http://www.slavenorth.com/exclusion.htm (Accessed August 2006). This Web site discusses the harassment of free blacks in the North, and places the prejudice of some Connecticut citizens in a larger context.

4. Oppenheim, Joanne. **Dear Miss Breed: True Stories of the Japanese American Incarceration during World War II and a Librarian Who Made a Difference.** New York: Scholastic Nonfiction, 2006. 288p. $22.99. ISBN 0 439 56992 3. [nonfiction] MJS Miss Breed, a librarian during World War II, supports her Japanese patrons even when they are imprisoned in camps because of wartime hysteria.

5. Reef, Catherine. **This Our Dark Country: The American Settlers of Liberia.** New York: Clarion Books, 2002. 136p. $17.00. ISBN 0 618 14785 3. [nonfiction] JS This account describes Liberia from its founding in the nineteenth century by a group of white Americans, the American Colonization Society, to its troubled present day.

℆ ℔

Kidd, Sue Monk. The Secret Life of Bees.

New York: Penguin Books, 2002. 302p. $14.00. ISBN 0 14 200174 0. [fiction] S/A

Themes/ Topics: mothers, love, bees, Civil Rights, 1964, inter-racial dating, conduct of life

Summary/Description

In 1964, fourteen-year-old Lily Owens, who is known for accidentally killing her mother, accompanies Rosaleen, her nanny, to voter registration. Poor whites beat Rosaleen. Both Rosaleen and Lily go to jail. Lily's abusive father frees her, but refuses to bail out Rosaleen, who is beaten again and hospitalized. Lily breaks into the hospital and releases Rosaleen. Both run away to Tiburon, South Carolina: the town name written on the back of a picture of a black Madonna that Lily finds among her mother's things. They discover August and her two sisters. August, who operates a bee farm, was nanny to Lily's mother for nine years. The black Madonna is the farm's trademark. Although the sisters recognize Lily, they wait for her to share her secret, and welcome both refugees into the house. With the support of these three women and their extended community, Lily learns about bee keeping, discovers her mother's history, falls in love with her fellow worker, and finds the strength to leave her father permanently.

Read Aloud/Reader Response

1. Chapter 5, page 92, beginning "I hadn't been out . . . " and ending " . . . wants to be loved." August gives Lily a lesson in "bee yard etiquette." Her advice applies to humans also.
2. Chapter 8, page 147, beginning "You know, some things . . . " and ending " . . . choosing what matters." August and Lily discuss the difficulty of choosing what matters.
3. Chapter 8, pages 161 to 163, beginning "*Dear T. Ray . . .* " and ending " . . . *my mother left me.*" Lily writes to her father and pours out her hurt and anger.
4. Chapter 9, page 170, beginning "If the heat goes over . . . " and ending " . . . just my opinion." Lily explains the importance of slowing down and having time to reflect.
5. Chapter 14, page 280, beginning "Regrets . . . " and ending " . . . know that." August talks about the uselessness of regret.
6. Chapter 14, pages 288 to 289, beginning "Our Lady . . . " and ending "We are enough." August explains the importance of internalizing the spirit of Our Lady.

Booktalk

Bees. They fascinate us. They give us food, but they threaten us. With their pollen, bees inspire myths about life and resurrection. Yet we don't want them buzzing in our houses, and they quickly warn us that we shouldn't get too close to theirs. One night lots of them swarm into fourteen-year-old Lily Owens's bedroom. She tries to tell her father, but he never listens to much of what Lily says. After all, when Lily was four she shot her mother, and he wasn't too fond of Lily before that. Lily is supposed to do what she is told—right away—and keep quiet. If she doesn't, she finds herself kneeling on piles of grits until her knees are red, blue, and bruised. She doesn't even call her father by the usual father, dad, or daddy labels. She just calls him T. Ray. She is pretty sure that she is going to spend her life as an ugly house servant to a man she'll never please. T. Ray isn't about to let Lily, his free help, get a pretty dress or go to a school game or dance. Then two things happen. The bees swarm into her bedroom, and America passes the Civil Rights Act. Those two things don't seem related, but in Lily's life they are—big time. Change is in the wind. The bees lead her to new people—people who fight those who want to keep them down, people who can make their voices heard. Lily is on the move, even if her move could get her more bruised and beaten than she has ever been. And it is all planned with an ancient road map—*The Secret Life of Bees*.

Learning Opportunities

1. Explain how the story emphasizes the importance of names, and consider how Lily's name is related to the story's purpose.
2. Using your library's resources, further research the Civil Rights Act and the effect it had on America. Share the information that you find with the group.
3. Using your library's resources or the books listed in the "Credits," further research the lives of bees. Share the information that you find with the group.
4. List every detail in the novel related to civil rights and explain its significance to Lily's personal journey.
5. Describe how Kidd uses religion in the story. Be sure to cite specifics from the novel.

Related Works

1. Hesse, Karen. **Out of the Dust.** New York: Scholastic Press, 1997. 227p. $4.99. ISBN 0 590 37125 8. [fiction] MJS (See full booktalk in *Booktalks Plus*, 2001, pages 30 to 32.) Fourteen-year-old Billie Joe shares with her father the guilt of a fire that kills her mother and unborn brother. The guilt and the hardships of the Dust Bowl separate them.
2. Hosler, Jay. **Clan Apis.** Columbus, OH: Active Synapse, 2000. 158p. $15.00. ISBN 1 4046 1367 6. [graphic] S/A (See full booktalk in *Teen Genre Connections*, 2005, pages 280 to 282.) In five chapters, Hosler describes the life cycle of the honeybee through the life journey of Nyuki, a worker bee.

3. Lee, Harper. **To Kill a Mockingbird.** New York: HarperCollins/ Perennial Classics, 2002. 323p. $11.95. ISBN 0 06 093546 4. [fiction] JS Set in the Depression, this story of racial conflict is told through the eyes of the child whose widower father defends an African-American accused of raping a white woman. The novel was written in 1960, received the Pulitzer Prize in 1961, and was made into a movie in 1962.

4. Martin, Ann M. **A Corner of the Universe.** New York: Scholastic Press, 2002. 208p. $15.95. ISBN 0 439 38880 5. [fiction] MJS In 1960, twelve-year-old Hattie, against her family's wishes and with disastrous results, helps her mentally challenged uncle gain independence.

5. Martin, Ann M. **Here Today.** New York: Scholastic Press, 2004. 320p. $16.95. ISBN 0 439 57944 9. [fiction] MJ In 1963, Eleanor Roosevelt Dingman concludes that her home is with her friends and family in Witch Tree Lane rather than with her self-centered, career-minded mother.

konigsburg, e. l. **The Outcasts of 19 Schuyler Place.**
New York: Atheneum Books for Young Readers, 2004. 296p. $16.95.
ISBN 0 689 86636 4. [fiction] MJS

Themes/Topics: social action, individuality, uncles, camp, art, change

Summary/Description

The adult Margaret recalls the summer of 1983 when she was twelve. Her parents, who usually take her with them, decide to go to Peru without her. Her two great uncles, whom she adores, do not want her to stay with them. Upset but determined, she chooses to stay in Camp Talequa. Assigned to a cabin of Alums, she is harassed and bullied. She refuses to cooperate. The camp director calls the uncles who agree with her resistance and take her home with them. She discovers that the uncles may lose three giant towers, works of art built from scraps of metal and glass that they have been building for forty-five years. Joining forces with the children of two former neighbors, the son of the camp director, and the girls who harassed her, Margaret saves the towers. When her parents return, they announce their divorce.

Read Aloud/Reader Response

1. Chapter 1, pages 5 to 13, beginning with the chapter opening and ending with "But they had not." These opening pages describe the uncles and their environment. The narration and description establish the uncles as Old World gentlemen and provide a brief glimpse of Mrs. Kaplan's lack of people skills.
2. Chapter 1, page 23, beginning "Time is not . . . " and ending with " . . . merely redistributed." Alex Rose's answer to Mrs. Kaplan's cliché, "Time is money. . . . " establishes the time theme of the novel.
3. Chapter 4, pages 44 to 45, beginning "We were . . . " and ending with " . . . loyal subject." Margaret and Alex discuss the use of *we* in relation to three different contexts.
4. Chapter 9, pages 87 to 88, beginning "My father . . . " and ending with " . . . lot less time." Margaret explains to Jake a basic difference between her mother and father, their perception of waste and time.
5. Chapter 10, page 100, beginning "A real tattoo?" and ending " . . . knows what else." Uncle Morris reflects on how the tattoo has changed from prisoner identification to decoration.
6. Chapter 11, page 119, beginning "There is no reason . . . " and ending " . . . really do." Jake reflects on the drive to create something or do work that has no practical purpose.

Booktalk

In 1983, the summer that Margaret is twelve, no one wants her around. Her parents are going to Peru, without her for the first time. Her uncles, whom she adores and whom she thought adored her, don't invite her to visit with them. "What to do with Margaret" seems to be a family problem. Margaret decides to solve that problem herself. She chooses a summer camp. *(Read the passage in italics on pages 26 and 27.)* What she finds instead is a dictatorship where she is an outcast. So her Uncle Alex does come to rescue her. She will stay with them at 19 Schuyler Place after all. Then she discovers that her uncles are fighting a war of their own, and they're losing. Forty-five years ago, they started to build three giant towers in their backyard. They used scrap metal and pieces of broken glass. Throwaways. And they are still building. Margaret thinks the towers are beautiful, but the neighbors, very practical people worried about their property values, think they are eyesores. They want them gone, now. And they definitely have the clout to make it happen. What can a twelve-year-old summer camp reject and two old men, *The Outcasts of 19 Schuyler Place*, do? Whatever they can. The battle is on. Once again in history, timing, talent, and tenacity come up against money, power, and rules. Will there be a winner, justice, or something else, something no one even thought about?

Learning Opportunities

1. Using your library's resources, research one of the events listed at the opening of the novel. Ask others in the group to do the same. Share the information with the group and discuss the relationship of the event to the novel.
2. Discuss the significance of the college and the town names.
3. Another important work of art is the rose. Why do you think it is included?
4. Read Melville's "Bartleby, the Scrivener" (Related Work 3). Discuss why it is a central allusion.
5. Cite instances in the novel that center on language and communication.
6. Cite the passages in which time is mentioned. Then discuss its significance.
7. Discuss why konigsburg included Chapter 30.
8. Discuss how konigsburg's divisions, in addition to the chapter divisions, affect the story.
9. Draw a picture or construct a model of the towers.
10. Choose the national events happening this year that you feel will affect you the most. Explain why.
11. Is this novel about winning and losing?
12. *Silent to the Bone* is cited as a companion story, even though it is about a much different subject. Discuss why it is considered a companion story.

Related Works

1. Hiaasen, Carl. **Hoot.** New York: Alfred A. Knopf, 2002. 292p. $15.95. ISBN 0 375 82181 3. [fiction] MJ (See full booktalk in *Teen Genre Connections*, 2005, pages 37 to 39.) A new middle school student makes friends with a boy trying to save the owls and takes on greedy companies and his own personal bullies.
2. konigsburg, e. l. **Silent to the Bone.** New York: Atheneum Books, 2000. 261p. $16.00. ISBN 0 689 83601 5. [fiction] MJS (See full booktalk in *Booktalks and More*, 2003, pages 151 to 152.) An extremely intelligent teenager, accused of hurting his baby sister, loses his power of speech.
3. Melville, Herman. **Bartleby and Benito Cereno.** Mineola, NY: Dover Publications, 1990. 112p. $2.00. ISBN 0 486 26473 4.

[fiction] S/A "Bartleby, the Scrivener" (pages 1 to 46) is the story of a Wall Street employee in the mid-1800s who rebels against the period's oppressive capitalism with his signature statement, "I would prefer not to."

4. Nye, Naomi Shihab. **Going Going.** New York: Harper Collins/ Greenwillow Books, 2005. 232p. $16.89. ISBN 0 06 029366 7. [fiction] JS A teenager leads a crusade to save old buildings and small businesses from commercial destruction.

5. Spinelli, Jerry. **Stargirl.** New York: Alfred A. Knopf, 2000. 186p. $15.95. ISBN 0 679 88637 0. [fiction] MJS (See full booktalk in *Booktalks and More*, 2003, pages 8 to 10.) Looking back on his junior year in high school, Leo Borlock recalls a mystical and mysterious tenth-grade girl who refused to be intimidated.

CƷₑD

Peck, Richard. The Teacher's Funeral: A Comedy in Three Parts.

New York: Dial Books, 2004. 190p. $16.99. ISBN 0 8037 2736 4. [fiction] JS

Themes/Topics: education, teachers, country life, Indiana, early twentieth century, family

Summary/Description

Fifteen-year-old Russell Culver and his ten-year-old brother, Lloyd, think that the one-room Hominy Ridge School will close down when the local teacher dies, but the school board hires their seventeen-year-old sister, Tansy. Two pupils, the minister's son and a backwoods neighbor, attend school to court her. The young representative of the Overland Automobile Company contributes school supplies to win her attentions. Russell recounts his confusion about their interest in his sister and his own brushes with education that include burning down the boys' outhouse, hidden snakes, a cantankerous widow, Tansy's teacher evaluation, and his thwarted plans to strike out for the Dakotas. Looking back on these 1904 events from an adult perspective, Russell concludes his memoir with the success of all school inhabitants in life and love.

Read Aloud/Reader Response

1. Chapter 1, pages 3 to 5. Russell reflects on how the death of Miss Myrt Arbuckle might impact education in Hominy Ridge School.

2. Chapter 5, pages 34 to 45. The funeral oration for Miss Arbuckle becomes a tirade against the younger generation.
3. Chapter 11, pages 117 to 123, beginning "A puff adder . . ." and ending " . . . working the same territory." Little Britches discovers the puff adder. Tansy settles the situation.
4. Chapter 12, pages 127 to 133, beginning "I thought . . . " and ending " . . . in a puff of smoke." Aunt Fanny Hamline comes to school to serve warning but falls through the boards and into a ditch.
5. Chapter 14, pages 154 to 155, beginning "It stopped us cold . . . " and ending " . . . ought to take steps?" Eugene Hammond raises his status to serious suitor.

Booktalk

For fifteen-year-old Russell Culver, August of 1904 is a miracle month—the only teacher in Hominy Ridge School dies. The school could close, and Russell would be free to break out to the Dakotas, join a team of harvesters, and work the new all-steel threshing machines. It seems a dream come true, but the dream becomes a nightmare when the school board hires a new teacher in record time—Russell's seventeen-year-old sister Tansy. All hope is not lost, however. The board stipulates that the school needs eight pupils to run. Russell relaxes for a while, but a new population is motivated to learn—the young men competing for Tansy's hand. The learning machine, just like the all-steel threshing machines and the new-fangled cars, is in motion, and Russell seems to be the central cog that his sister is willing to work until it breaks. Lightning hitting the outhouse, snakes in the most unexpected places, and the rival suitors might discourage some teachers, but Tansy is a determined and driving force. She has her vehicle on the road of education, and she's ready to take the bumps and turns in stride. It's quite a journey, all because of *The Teacher's Funeral*.

Learning Opportunities

1. Discuss how the title applies to the novel.
2. Using your library's resources, continue to research early inventions of the twentieth century.
3. The pupils of Hominy Ridge School demonstrate several types of intelligence. Discuss each pupil's gifts.
4. Discuss the theme of personal responsibility in the story.
5. Glenn Tarbox is the man that Tansy finally marries. Do you agree with her decision? Explain your answer by referring to specifics

from the text. Be sure to consider Eugene Hammond and Charlie in your explanation.

6.   Essentially, teenagers run the school. Discuss the significance of that situation.

Related Works

1.   Burns, Olive Ann. **Cold Sassy Tree.** New York: Dial Press, 1986. 400p. $14.95pa. ISBN 0 385 31258 X. [fiction] S/A Fourteen-year-old Will Tweedy, living in a turn-of-the-century Georgia town, finds himself driving the first cars in town and defending his grandfather's controversial marriage.

2.   Duncan, Dayton, and Ken Burns. **Horatio's Drive: America's First Road Trip.** New York: Alfred A. Knopf, 2003. 173p. $24.95. ISBN 0 375 41536 X. [nonfiction] JS/A Based on a PBS documentary film directed by Ken Burns, this book, with extensive pictures of the period, tells how the adventurous and optimistic thirty-one-year-old Horatio Nelson Jackson, in 1903, became the first person to travel by automobile from San Francisco to New York City.

3.   Gallo, Donald R. (ed.). **Time Capsule: Short Stories about Teenagers throughout the Twentieth Century.** New York: Delacorte Press, 1999. 221p. $16.95. ISBN 0 385 32675 0. [fiction] JS This collection includes a short story for each decade of the twentieth century. The first short story, set in the first decade of the twentieth century, is "The Electric Summer" by Richard Peck. It appears on pages 3 to 16. Fourteen-year-old Geneva and her mother go to the World's Fair. Both realize that the world will be moving much faster and probably will be pulling them apart.

4.   Gray, Dianne E. **Together Apart.** New York: Houghton Mifflin Company, 2002. 193p. $16.00. ISBN 0 618 18721 9. [fiction] MJ (See full booktalk in *Teen Genre Connections*, 2005, pages 35 to 37.) At the end of the nineteenth century, family conflicts and progressive thinking enter the relationship of fourteen-year-old Hannah Barnett and fifteen-year-old Isaac Richards.

5.   Peck, Robert Newton. **Cowboy Ghost.** New York: HarperCollins Children's Books, 1999. 200p. $15.95. ISBN 0 06 028168 5. [fiction] MJ (See full booktalk in *Booktalks Plus*, 2001, pages 15 to 16.) In 1924, sixteen-year-old Titus takes over the cattle drive when the brother, whom he worships, dies. As in *The Teacher's Funeral*, teenagers successfully take on responsibilities.

Choosing in War

൚

Crist-Evans, Craig. **Amaryllis.**

Cambridge, MA: Candlewick Press, 2003. 184p. $15.99.
ISBN 0 7636 1863 2. [fiction, mixed format] MJS

Themes/Topics: brothers, fathers/sons, Viet Nam War, drug abuse

Summary/Description

With letters from his brother and a narrative describing his own feelings, fifteen-year-old Jimmy tells about his home life, and his brother, Frank, fighting in Viet Nam and eventually being reported Missing in Action. Their alcoholic father is emotionally and physically abusive. Their mother denies the situation, so the brothers turn to each other. As surfers, they focus on the *Amaryllis*, a ship that runs aground on Singer Island, Florida, during a 1965 hurricane. The ship becomes a metaphor for Frank's life as the war and personal demons overwhelm Frank. His letters reveal his fear, state his views of the war, and describe his drug use. When the announcement of Frank's disappearance arrives, the father realizes that he drove Frank out of the house. Jimmy's girlfriend helps Jimmy achieve closure. Some language and situations may be considered controversial.

Read Aloud/Reader Response

1. "Prologue," pages 1 to 6. Jimmy establishes the relationships in the family.
2. Chapter 2, Frank's letter to Jimmy, pages 15 to 17. The letter shows the close relationship between the brothers and the problems that will eventually destroy Frank.
3. Chapter 4, page 43, beginning "I guess it . . ." and ending " . . . in both directions." Jimmy talks about starting over after a hurricane, but the passage could refer to starting up again after any disaster— including war.
4. Chapter 11, Frank's letter, pages 105 to 107. Frank writes about his drug addiction.
5. Chapter 23, Jimmy's letter to Frank, page 181 to 182. Jimmy writes to Frank after Frank dies. Jimmy still tries to figure out their relationship, now just Jimmy's relationship, with their father.

Booktalk

Fifteen-year-old Jimmy Staples lives in Florida. He and his older brother, Frank, love to surf—especially in the perfect waves created by the stranded *Amaryllis,* a ship that ran aground on Singer Island, Florida, during a 1965 hurricane. But the times as well as the ocean are turbulent, and their surfing days are numbered. The war in Vietnam is raging, and Frank decides to sign up. He'll do anything to get away from their father, who drinks himself into a stupor, and then tries to make life—especially Frank's life—miserable. Can Frank stay alive when so many of his friends come home in body bags? Is the enemy Frank can't see, the one in his head, more dangerous than the one he is trying to fight with a gun? And if Jimmy loses Frank, is there anyone in the world he can care about? The mysterious ship, the *Amaryllis,* may just hold the answers.

Learning Opportunities

1. Using your library's resources, research the category Missing in Action. Choose one person placed within that category. Research the circumstances of the disappearance and the results of any search. Share your findings with the group.
2. After sharing your findings, discuss why Missing in Action might be a more difficult message for a family than Killed in Action.
3. Frank describes their home life in military terms, "Dad drinks and the family sustains casualties." Read Frank's letter on pages 46 to 49 (Chapter 5) aloud. Then discuss how word choices affect Frank's life. Be sure to consider his use of the word *gooks.*
4. Describe the mother and father. Do they have responsibility for Frank's choices?
5. Locate each geographical location mentioned in the novel. Using your library's resources, find out as much as possible about each in relation to the time period. Share your information with the group. Discuss how it supports your understanding.
6. On page 130, in the paragraph beginning "I still can't quite . . . " and ending with " . . . gasoline and napalm." And on pages 150 to 152, beginning with "I had gotten to the point . . . " and ending with " . . . tossed in our paths," the *Amaryllis* is discussed as a central symbol. Restate each brother's perception. Then discuss your interpretation of the *Amaryllis* in relation to their lives.

Related Works

1. Duncan, Lois (ed.). **Trapped! Cages of Mind and Body.** New York: Simon & Schuster Books for Young R   1998. 228p.

$16.00. ISBN 0 689 81335 X. [short stories] JS The short story by Gary Crew, "Tunnel Rat Dreaming," on pages 166 to 179, focuses on a homeless Viet Nam veteran waiting for his buddy who was killed in Viet Nam.

2. Eisner, Will. **Last Day in Vietnam: A Memory.** Milwaukie, OR: Dark Horse Comics, Inc., 2000. 80p. $10.95. ISBN 1 56971 437 1. [graphic] S/A Eisner tells and illustrates stories based on his encounters with people he met during his years involved with the military. Two apply specifically to Viet Nam.

3. Hobbs, Valerie. **Sonny's War.** New York: Farrar, Straus and Giroux/ Frances Foster Books, 2002. 215p. $16.00. ISBN 0 374 37136 9. [fiction] JS (See full booktalk in *Teen Genre Connections*, 2005, pages 230 to 233.) Fourteen-year-old Cory describes her life in a little California town after her father's death and her brother's decision to go to war.

4. Morales, Gilbert (ed.). **Critical Perspectives on the Vietnam War.** New York: The Rosen Publishing Group, 2005. 176p. (Critical Anthologies of Nonfiction Writing). $30.60. ISBN 1 4042 0063 0. [nonfiction] JS Articles and official papers from the Viet Nam period show the development of the war, the battlefield difficulties the soldiers faced, and the controversy surrounding it.

5. White, Ellen Emerson. **The Journal of Patrick Seamus Flaherty.** New York: Scholastic Press, 2002. 192p. (Dear America Book: My Name Is America). $10.95. ISBN 0 439 14890 1. [fiction] MJ ————. **Where Have All the Flowers Gone? The Diary of Molly MacKenzie Flaherty.** New York: Scholastic Press, 176p. (Dear America). $10.95. ISBN 0 439 14889 8. [fiction] MJ These companion books describe the Viet Nam War and its time period from a soldier's and a sister's viewpoints.

 C3 80

Holub, Josef. An Innocent Soldier.

New York: Arthur A. Levine Books, 2005. 240p. $16.99. ISBN 0 439 62771 0. [fiction] JS

Themes/Topics: Napoleonic War, war, orphans, family, loyalty, integrity, social class

Summary/Description

In November 1811, sixteen-year-old Adam Feuchter, after working three years as a farmhand, is falsely conscripted into Napoleon's army in place of his farmer's son, Georg. The army takes him even though he is only five-feet-two. Assigned to the horse artillery, Adam is bullied by Sergeant Krauter. Seventeen-year-old Lieutenant Count Lammersdorf sees the abuse and briefly takes Adam as his groom. When family servants report to take care of the Count, Adam returns to the abusive and dishonest sergeant until the servants, overwhelmed by the brutal conditions, desert the lieutenant. The lieutenant returns for Adam, who eventually cares for him through sickness, starvation, and exposure as Napoleon's attack on Russia deteriorates. Eventually Adam is promoted to corporal so that other officers cannot make him their servant. Cooperating as friends, the lieutenant and Adam make it back home where they are separated. Adam becomes a sergeant. As he prepares to rendezvous with Napoleon and a new army, he discovers the young Count recovering at the family estate. The family, who credit him with the Count's survival, welcomes him warmly. Among his own troops, he is considered a celebrity because of his service on the Russian front. The farmer, who falsely conscripted him, wanders the fields and mourns his own son's accidental death and Adam's absence. A "Historical Note" and maps introduce the novel.

Read Aloud/Reader Response

1. Chapter 1, pages 1 to 5. Adam dreams about the farmer killing him and receives unusual treatment on his last night in the farmer's house.
2. Chapter 2, pages 6 to 15. Adam experiences his horrible conscription.
3. Chapter 5, pages 27 to 31. The conditions drive him to consider desertion until he considers the consequences. The chapter's last paragraph presents rhetorical questions for discussion.
4. Chapter 15, pages 98 to 99, beginning "After that, . . . " and ending " . . . Lutherans or Papists." Adam kills and cooks the snake to feed the lieutenant. The author's choice of a snake and its relationship to religious references will promote class discussion.
5. Chapter 37, pages 215 to 221. Adam describes their return from Russia.

Booktalk

Adam Feuchter is almost sixteen, and he is about to get a birthday present from his farmer. Adam has worked for the farmer for three years. Now the farmer wakes him in the middle of the night. He lets Adam eat as much as he wants, and he tells Adam to hitch up the sleigh because they are riding into town. Adam knows something is up, something big. And he is right. Adam's birthday present is a paid trip to Russia. He is joining

Napoleon's army. They will march on Russia and defeat Czar Alexander. But of course we all know what happened to that plan. It was a major disaster. The farmer doesn't want his own son to be part of it, so he signs up Adam under his son's name and leaves as fast as he can. Adam doesn't have any family or friends, just the farmer. He has no choice. So he puts on the uniform. Then he does have a choice. He can volunteer to work with the horses. The horses love him, but his sergeant hates him. Adam spends most of his days doing what the sergeant says, picking up horse manure with his hands, and slogging through puddles. But luck shines. Seventeen-year-old Lieutenant Count Lammersdorf makes Adam his personal servant. Life is good. It doesn't last. Adam must return to his real life, the life with his sergeant's abuse and orders, the life with impossible choices, the life near death, the life of *An Innocent Soldier.*

Learning Opportunities

1. The biblical story of Adam, the first man, is central to the novel. Read the story of Adam and Eve. You may wish to use *Student Bible, New International Version* (Related Work 5). Then list every event, character, or object in the novel that relates to the story of Adam and Eve. Discuss how and why Holub used that allusion.
2. The farmer and the sergeant are central adult figures in the novel. Discuss their roles.
3. Using your library's resources, continue to research Napoleon's invasion of Russia. Discuss what the information adds to your appreciation of the story.
4. Using your library's resources, research the life of Napoleon (Related Work 1). Discuss what the information adds to your appreciation of the story.
5. The title of the novel can have several applications. Discuss the possibilities.

Related Works

1. Hausman, Gerald, and Loretta Hausman. **Napoleon and Josephine: The Sword and the Hummingbird.** New York: Orchard Books, 2004. 288p. $16.95. ISBN 0 439 56890 0. [fiction] MJS "The Hummingbird," the first ten chapters, details Josephine's life. "The Sword" explains Napoleon's rise to power, the couple's tempestuous relationship, their marriage's end, and Napoleon's defeat. A "Chronology" details the personal events of both lives and the significant historical events that influenced them. A "Bibliography" lists research sources.

2. Meyer, L. A. **Under the Jolly Roger: Being an Account of the Further Nautical Adventures of Jacky Faber.** New York: Harcourt Brace and Company, 2005. 318p. $17.00. ISBN 0 15 205345 X. [fiction] JS Jacky Faber becomes a privateer as England becomes more fearful of Napoleon's advance.

3. Morpurgo, Michael. **Private Peaceful.** New York: Scholastic Press, 2003. 202p. $16.95. ISBN 0 439 63648 5. [fiction] JS In this World War I novel, the Peaceful brothers, like Adam, suffer under a sadistic sergeant.

4. Morris, Neil, et al. (text). Paola Ravaglia et al. (illus.). **The Illustrated History of the World: From the Big Bang to the Third Millennium.** New York: Enchanted Lion Books, 2000. 288p. $29.95. ISBN 1 59270 019 5. [nonfiction] MJS In this chronologically and geographically organized history, short descriptions and extensive illustrations clearly show the relationships of world events happening sequentially and simultaneously. Pages 170 and 171 feature the Napoleonic Wars.

5. Yancey, Philip, and Tim Stafford (notes). **Student Bible: New International Version.** Grand Rapids, MI: Zondervan, 2002. 1440p. $32.99. ISBN 0 310 92784 6. [religion] JS This user-friendly version includes "Insights" (background information), "Guided Tour" (essays providing "bird's eye view"), and "100 People You Should Get to Know." The story of Adam appears in Genesis. Two essays clarify the story.

༼༽

McMullan, Margaret. How I Found the Strong: A Novel of the Civil War.

Boston, MA: Houghton Mifflin Company, 2004. 136p. $15.00.
ISBN 0 618 35008 X. [fiction] MJS

Themes/Topics: Mississippi, Civil War, 1861–1865, family life, slavery, respect

Summary/Description

Frank Russell, called Shanks because of his skinny legs, is ten years old when the Civil War begins. His father and fourteen-year-old brother, Henry, enlist. Frank, his mother, grandparents, and their slave, Buck, stay on the farm. The grandfather leaves the family to go West. The grandmother dies, and Frank's mother gives birth to a baby girl. Many of the family's supplies are seized for the army. Frank and Buck grow close working to keep the family alive. Maimed from the war, the father brings news that Henry is dead. As the Southern position deteriorates, many slaves leave, and local bullies harass those who stay. When two come for Buck, Frank and his father save him, but then walk Buck to the Strong River so that he can flee to the North. Returning home, Frank and his father are caught in a skirmish. A Confederate soldier bayonets the father. Frank kills the attacker, and saves his father's life. Frank realizes that his family respects him as a man even though he is the weaker brother who did not go to war.

Read Aloud/Reader Response

1. Chapter 1, pages 5 and 6, beginning with "What with all . . . " and ending with "They are just there." Frank reflects on the Southern attitudes toward slaves.
2. Chapter 3, pages 22 to 25, beginning with "They'll put slavery . . . " and ending with " . . . a little smile on her face." The conversation tries to justify slavery. Frank grows more uncomfortable with the attitudes.
3. Chapter 5, page 39, beginning with "Ma says everything . . . " and ending with the paragraph. Frank reflects on God's relationship with the world.
4. Chapter 13, pages 113 to 114, beginning with "I wonder if maggots . . . " and ending " . . . they must have had!" Seeing the maggots in a soldier's wounds, Frank reflects on Jesus' death.
5. Chapter 14, pages 124 to 125, beginning with "Ma, she reaches across . . . " and ending with the chapter. Frank reflects on how he has come to his new identity.

Booktalk

It is the spring of 1861. The Civil War just began. All able-bodied Southern men are signing up. They plan to scare those Yankees with their show of strength and be home by Christmas. Ten-year-old Frank Russell can't go. He has to be twelve even to be a drummer boy. But Henry, his fourteen-year-old brother, the favorite son, will march off to glory with their father. Frank, called Shanks because of his skinny legs, stays home with his mother, grandparents, and Buck, the family slave. But Frank fights a different war. Like the other one, it has starvation, hate, fear, and even death. But in this war, who is the enemy? Does he wear a Yankee uniform? Is he a neighbor? Someone called family? Or is this enemy Frank himself? How can anyone fight that war? Let Frank tell you himself in *How I Found the Strong.*

Learning Opportunities

1. Trace the relationship between Frank and Buck from the beginning to the end of the novel. Discuss how it changes and why.
2. List three minor characters. Explain how each affects the story.
3. One of the main events is the Emancipation Proclamation. Using your library's resources, research the end of slavery in the United States. You may wish to start your research with *Days of Jubilee* (Related Work 2). Share your findings with the group.
4. Choose what you feel is the most significant scene. Read it aloud to the group and explain your choice. Ask others in the group to choose scenes also. Compare the choices.
5. The Beall farm also suffers during the war. Beyond the romantic interest of Irene Beall, explain how its description affects the novel.
6. Choose an object mentioned in the story. Explain its significance.

Related Works

1. Bruchac, Joseph. **Sacajawea: The Story of Bird Woman and the Lewis and Clark Expedition.** New York: Harcourt, Brace and Company/Silver Whistle, 2000. 199p. $17.00. ISBN 0 15 202234 1. [fiction] MJS With the stories of his mother and Captain Clark, Sacajawea's son tells about the Lewis and Clark Expedition. In Chapter 4, Clark rationalizes his ownership of York. In Chapter 34, he frees York.
2. McKissack, Patricia C., and Fredrick L. McKissack. **Days of Jubilee: The End of Slavery in the United States.** New York: Scholastic Press, 2003. 144p. $18.95. ISBN 0 590 10764 X. [nonfiction] MJS Through Civil War diaries, letters, and slave narratives, the book describes how slaves gradually gained freedom through the Underground Railroad, rebellion, military service, the Emancipation Proclamation Act, and finally the Thirteenth Amendment to the U.S. Constitution.
3. Paulsen, Gary. **Soldier's Heart: Being the Story of the Enlistment and Due Service of the Boy Charley Goddard in the First Minnesota Volunteers.** New York: Delacorte Press, 1998. 106p. $15.95. ISBN 0 385 32498 7. [fiction] JS A young soldier enthusiastically enlists, but returns home physically and emotionally wounded.
4. Peck, Robert Newton. **Cowboy Ghost.** New York: HarperCollins Children's Books, 1999. 200p. $15.95. ISBN 0 06 028168 5. [fiction] MJ (See full booktalk in *Booktalks Plus*, 2001, pages 15 to 16.) The

younger, smaller son proves himself as brave or braver than his older, stronger brother.

5. Severance, John B. **Braving the Fire: A Civil War Novel.** New York: Clarion Books, 2002. 149p. $15.00. ISBN 0 618 22999 X. [fiction] MJS Jem Bridwell, whose family is divided by the Civil War, joins the Union army and is saved by the family slave, now an independent wage earner.

ध्र‍ध्

Spillebeen, Geert. Terese Edelstein (trans.). Kipling's Choice.

Boston, MA: Houghton Mifflin Company, 2005. 160p. $16.00.
ISBN 0 618 43124 1. [fiction] JS

Themes/Topics: World War I, John Kipling (1897–1915), Rudyard Kipling (1865–1936), Battle of Loos (1915), fathers and sons, class distinction

Summary/Description

Eighteen-year-old John Kipling, the youngest officer in the Irish Guards, is mortally wounded in his first day of battle. As John dies, he and the reader review his privileged but demanding life as the son of Rudyard Kipling, England's Poet Laureate. Inspired by Kipling's poetry, the English upper-class commits their sons to battles managed by inept officers facing new and terrifying technologies. Rudyard Kipling, unable to go to war because of poor eyesight, secures John's enlistment. John, whom his father sees as Mowgli, struggles with frail health and poor eyesight to meet his father's expectations. He embraces the opportunity to fight, endures rigorous training, conscientiously shepherds his men, and fatally risks his own life in battle. John's parents never find his body but glean the most information about their son from the men who fought under him. Rudyard Kipling dies a broken man questioning a life that extolled risk and patriotism. The epilogue describes Kipling's work with the Imperial War Graves Commission and his fruitless search for John's body, which may have been finally discovered in 1992.

Read Aloud/Reader Response

1. Pages 1 to 8, beginning with the novel and ending with " . . . boarding school in Rottingdean." John Kipling's swashbuckling approach results in the fatal wound, and the overwhelming agony that makes him fear that he will lose his dignity.

2. Pages 78 to 80, beginning "It has been rumored for weeks . . . "
    and ending " . . . a little club of merciless warlords." Poison gas,
    the new and horrifying World War I weapon, has horrible effects
    on the soldiers, but is merely a topic for conversation in the men's
    club.
3. Pages 96 to 97, beginning "Hey, Kipling!" and ending "Why do you
    do this to me Daddo?" John recalls himself as a ten-year-old trying
    to confront the overwhelming standards set by his father's writing.
4. Pages 104 to 105, beginning "A bullet in the leg, . . . " and ending
    "That would be acceptable." As Rupert and John think about battle,
    they try to calculate the wound that would allow them to live normal
    lives.
5. Pages 128 to 134, beginning "Suddenly two arms . . . " and ending
    "Dear love, John." The passage describes the final moments of
    John's death and the reaction of the Kiplings when they are notified.
    It is an appropriate selection for a multiple-part dramatic reading.

Booktalk

*Ask how many people in the group have heard of Rudyard Kipling. Then
read "If" or one of his military poems. Mention also that he wrote* The
Jungle Book. *After that information is presented, briefly discuss what
the writing reveals about the author and what it might have been like to
have him for a father.*

John Kipling was Rudyard Kipling's son. At eighteen, with his father's
influence, he was a World War I lieutenant in the Irish Guard. He was
killed in his first day of battle. According to his father, it wasn't supposed
to happen that way. John was supposed to come home a hero in spite of his
bad eyes and poor health. He was supposed to make his father proud. As
John lay bleeding to death from a wound in his neck, he recalls his life and
the father who pushed it to this point. Never fighting in battle himself, how
could Rudyard Kipling know what war was really like? He couldn't. So how
could he ever anticipate the terrible results of *Kipling's Choice?*

Learning Opportunities

1. Discuss how and why the author uses flashbacks.
2. Continue to research the life and work of Rudyard Kipling. Be sure
    to include the works that John mentions. Discuss these works in the
    context of today's world.
3. Technology is a major part of the novel. What technology is men-
    tioned? Discuss its significance in relation to the story.
4. Read *All Quiet on the Western Front* (Related Work 4) and *Kipling's
    Choice.* Do you feel they share a purpose?

5. "The Lost Son" and the "Epilogue" are small but significant parts of the book. Discuss what they add.
6. Why is the letter from Sergeant Cochrane important to the story?

Related Works

1. The Kipling Society. Available: http://www.kipling.org.uk. (Accessed May 2006). The Web site provides many of Kipling's poems as well as biographical information.
2. Morpurgo, Michael. **Private Peaceful.** New York: Scholastic Press, 2003. 202p. $16.95. ISBN 0 439 63648 5. [fiction] JS Private Peaceful waits for his older brother to be shot by a military squad and remembers how they came to this point.
3. Orr, Tamra (ed.). **Critical Perspectives on World War I.** New York: The Rosen Publishing Group, 2005. 176p. (Critical Anthologies of Nonfiction Writing). $30.60. ISBN 1 4042 0064 9. [nonfiction] JS In five chapters, articles and commentaries explain the 1914 European armies, America's entrance into the war, the war's media and propaganda machine, the people fighting and affected, and the battlefield action. The introduction explains the initial cavalier and romantic attitude of the time and "Memoirs & Diaries: The First Gas Attack" by Anthony R. Hossack, pages 137 to 145, describes another horrific scene from the war.
4. Remarque, Erich Maria. **All Quiet on the Western Front.** New York: Fawcett Crest, 1975. 296p. $4.95pa. ISBN 0 449 21394 3. [fiction] S/A A young German soldier, pressured to go to war and disillusioned by what he sees, tells this anti-war story, set in World War I and first published in 1928.
5. Winspear, Jacqueline. **Birds of a Feather.** New York: Soho Press, 2004. 311p. (A Maisie Dobbs Novel). $25.00. ISBN 1 56947 368 4. [fiction] JS/A Hired to find a missing socialite, Maisie discovers a series of murders related to a pro-World War I feminist group.

Defining Leaders and Events

છ૦

Allen, Thomas B. **George Washington, Spymaster: How the Americans Outspied the British and Won the Revolutionary War.**

Washington, DC: National Geographic, 2004. 184p. $16.95.
ISBN 0 7922 5126 1. [nonfiction] MJS

Themes/Topics: espionage, American Revolution, Secret Service, generals, presidents

Summary/Description

Beginning with Washington's early life and his gathering of intelligence for the French and Indian War, Allen portrays Washington as a spymaster who eventually defeats the British with wit rather than might. The book chronicles the beginnings and interactions of American spy networks; the codes, techniques, and equipment used by both sides; the contributions of allies; the volunteer roles of common men and women; treachery; and the deception that determines the Battle of Yorktown. A map shows the "Major Battles of the Revolution." Appendix I is a "War Time Line." Appendix II is a glossary of spy terms. Appendix III is Tallmadge's code and methods of deciphering it. Appendix IV expands chapter information with text notes. Appendix V lists source notes for each chapter. Appendix VI includes books and Web sites for further reference. The subject index highlights illustrations with italics.

Read Aloud/Reader Response

1. Chapter 1, pages 4 to 13, beginning "George was 11 ..." and ending with the chapter. Washington's early life and his completion of an assignment illustrate the many skills needed to complete his task.
2. Chapter 2, pages 21 to 23, beginning "Boston papers ..." and ending "... important secret agents." Propaganda and spin helped launch the revolution.
3. Chapter 3, pages 41 to 43, beginning "When Washington asked ..." and ending "... lose for my country." Nathan Hale's bravery influences Washington to use civilian spies.
4. Chapter 5, pages 66 to 70, beginning "Another rider ..." and ending "... intercepted the letter." Small coincidences, details, and connections impact a spy operation.
5. Chapter 7, pages 102 to 109, beginning "Lydia Darragh ..." and ending "... never once complained of fear." Lydia Darragh's story shows both the value of volunteer help and the difficulty of separating fact from fiction in spy legends.

Booktalk

Spies. What does that word make you think about? James Bond, CIA, terrorists? All these names conjure images of high-tech, glamour, and a fast, exciting life. What is a gray-haired man with bad teeth doing in that group? George Washington, the father of our country and the first president, achieved his place in history because he was a spymaster. His army couldn't match the English firepower, but he believed that American brains could. While still in his teens, Washington learned the power of enemy information. He gathered enough evidence on a trip to Pennsylvania and Ohio to convince the British to start the French and Indian War. When the colonies, the Patriots, decided to take on England, he used those lessons well. Here is the story of the network that changed the world and the man who overcame fear and treachery to build that network, *George Washington, Spymaster.*

Learning Opportunities

1. Using your library's resources, continue to research the spies of the Revolutionary War. You may wish to start with *Come All You Brave Soldiers* (Related Work 1) and *Women Soldiers, Spies, and Patriots of the American Revolution* (Related Work 4) or one of the sources listed in Appendix VI. Share the information that you find with the group.
2. Using your library's resources, research the role of Samuel Adams in the Revolutionary War. You may wish to start with *Samuel Adams: The Father of American Independence* (Related Work 2).
3. Using your library's resources, research modern spy organizations around the world. Share your information with the group.
4. Using your library's resources, continue to research spy methods such as those listed in Chapter 5, "Tools of the Spymaster." You may wish to start with *Top Secret: A Handbook of Codes, Ciphers, and Secret Writing* (Related Work 3).
5. After reading *George Washington, Spymaster,* discuss the elements that you think make up a successful spy organization or operation.

Related Works

1. Cox, Clinton. **Come All You Brave Soldiers.** New York: Scholastic Press, 1999. 182p. $15.95. ISBN 0 590 47576 2. [nonfiction] JS (See full booktalk in *Booktalks Plus,* 2001, pages 155 to 157.) Cox describes the contribution that black soldiers made to both sides of the Revolutionary War and discusses extensively the contribution of James Armistead, the slave assigned to Lafayette.
2. Fradin, Dennis. **Samuel Adams: The Father of American Independence.** New York: Clarion Books, 1998. 182p. $18.00. ISBN 0 395 82510 5. [nonfiction] MJS (See full booktalk in *Booktalks Plus,* 2001, pages 234 to 236.) *Samuel Adams* portrays Adams, the financially poorest patriot, as both a manipulator and a hero who twisted facts and forged alliances so that the colonies would break from the English.

3. Janeczko, Paul B. Jenna LaReau (illus.).**Top Secret: A Handbook of Codes, Ciphers, and Secret Writing.** Cambridge, MA: Candlewick Press, 2004. 144p. $16.99. ISBN 0 7836 0971 4. [nonfiction] MJ Janeczko includes extensive codemaking, codebreaking, and concealment techniques with examples and exercises. He also includes a list for further reading.

4. Kneib, Martha. **Women Soldiers, Spies, and Patriots of the American Revolution.** New York: The Rosen Publishing Group, 2004. 112p. (American Women at War). $21.95. ISBN 0 8239 4454 9. [nonfiction] MJS Kneib includes women who fought, spied, and supported the war financially. Chapter 3 is the story of Lydia Darragh, whose story is extensively discussed in *George Washington, Spymaster.*

5. West, David, and Jackie Gaff. Ross Watton (illus.). **George Washington: The Life of an American Patriot.** New York: Rosen Central, 2005. 48p. (Graphic Nonfiction). $26.50. ISBN 1 4042 0236 6. [graphic] MJS This biography focuses on dangerous mutinies during the revolution.

ᎏᎏ

Aronson, Marc. **The Real Revolution: The Global Story of American Independence.**

New York: Clarion Books, 2005. 238p. $21.00. ISBN 0 618 18179 2. [nonfiction] JS

Themes/Topics: American Revolution, 1775–1783, politics, government, economics, East India Company

Summary/Description

Framing the American Revolution in world events, Aronson begins with the stories of three soldiers: Robert Clive, George Washington, and James Wolfe. Each fights for England against France: Clive in India, George Washington in the American frontier, Wolfe in Quebec. Their victories and defeats characterize eighteenth-century British expansionism. Aronson explains the legal, military, and mob challenges to British ambitions and the London response to those challenges. The dynamics of slavery, communication, Indian relations, American Western expansion, financial movement, economic booms and busts, and the developing American character all contribute to a revolutionary mindset that births a nation and changes the world. The "Cast of Characters" lists and classifies all British, French, Americans, and East Indians mentioned. "To My Readers" explains Aronson's perspective.

"To My Readers, Again" reinforces some of the lessons America, as a world power, might learn. Endnotes discuss the research and suggest various sources. The bibliography and Web sites list extensive sources. The "Timeline" includes interrelated world events from 1600 to 1955. The index includes page numbers in italic type that indicate numerous maps, sketches, and photographs throughout the text. At several points, text and picture descriptions refer to related material on specific pages.

Read Aloud/Reader Response

1. Chapter 2, "The Half King's Gamble," pages 33 to 35, the passage in italics. Washington and Tanaghrisson, a local Seneca leader, combine a youthful way of fighting and Native American thinking to achieve political power.

2. Chapter 6, "The Spirit of Freedom," pages 80 to 83, beginning "Grenville's plan . . ." and ending " . . . in your defense." British perspective and American perspective conflict.

3. Chapter 6, "Slavery," pages 83 to 90. A revolution for freedom was financed by slavery.

4. Chapter 7, "Mobs," pages 95 to 97, beginning "The stamp tax . . ." and ending "He agreed." The Sons of Liberty intimidated their enemies by mob violence.

5. Chapter 7, "Networks," "Franklin Addresses Parliament," pages 101 and 103, beginning "Like Washington . . ." and ending " . . . what you were born into." Franklin verbalizes the American belief that each man controls his destiny.

Booktalk

Ask what the audience knows about the American Revolution. Then ask what further questions they might have wondered about.

Marc Aronson had a very simple question about the American Revolution. "Why tea?" Tea was central to the Boston Tea Party, the no-turning-back event that launched the American Revolution. Americans could afford the tea and tax better than any other country in the world. Why were they upset enough to take on a world superpower? His questions and their answers led him to bigger questions and answers that few people have ever considered. *Read pages xvi to xvii, beginning "When did the American . . ." and ending "all over the world."* In this book Aronson tells about a very small revolutionary movement in a world as big and as complicated as today's. Forget all those stories about old men in white wigs. Read instead about those teenagers who built ideas and empires. Read about a huge revolution that Americans got going, and maybe will never finish, *The Real Revolution.*

Learning Opportunities

1. Aronson talks about "transnational" history. Using your library's resources, continue to research the concept and its importance. Share your findings with the group.
2. Starting with Aronson's source notes and bibliographies, choose one other source. Read it, and share the information that you find with the group.
3. List as many economic issues from the period as you can.
4. Examine the list of economic issues. Find one parallel in today's American economy. Research that parallel. Share your information and discuss its implications with the group. You might want to consider the essay, "The Roots of Muslim Rage" in *Critical Perspectives on Islam and the Western World* (Related Work 5).
5. Choose one other "American" event. Using your library's resources, find other world events occurring at the time. Discuss how one of them is related.

Related Works

1. Adler, David A. **B. Franklin, Printer.** New York: Holiday House, 2001. 126p. $19.95. ISBN 0 8234 1675 5. [nonfiction] MJS (See full booktalk in *Teen Genre Connections,* 2005, pages 243 to 245.) This biography describes Franklin's life of hard work, self-improvement, and government service.
2. Aronson, Marc. **John Winthrop, Oliver Cromwell, and the Land of Promise.** New York: Clarion Books, 2004. 205p. $20.00. ISBN 0 618 18177 7. [nonfiction] JS (See full booktalk in *Teen Genre Connections,* 2005, pages 245 to 247.) Aronson explains the seventeenth-century social context that produced two men who sought an idyllic government and subsequently helped shape American thinking. It is the second book in the trilogy that concludes with *The Real Revolution.*
3. Aronson, Marc. **Sir Walter Ralegh and the Quest for El Dorado.** New York: Clarion Books, 2000. 205p. $20.00. ISBN 0 395 84827 X. [nonfiction] MJS (See full booktalk in *Booktalks and More,* 2003, pages 232 to 235.) The life of the historical figure Aronson calls the first modern man begins the trilogy that concludes with *The Real Revolution.*
4. Cox, Clinton. **Come All You Brave Soldiers.** New York: Scholastic Press, 1999. 182p. $15.95. ISBN 0 590 47576 2. [nonfiction] JS (See full booktalk in *Booktalks Plus,* 2001, pages 155 to 157.) This source describes how slaves and indentured servants tried to choose the side that would give them liberty and, after the war, had freedom denied.

5. Johansen, Jonathan (ed.). **Critical Perspectives on Islam and the Western World.** New York: The Rosen Publishing Group, 2006. 182p. (Critical Anthologies of Nonfiction Writing). $30.60. ISBN 1 4042 0538 1. [nonfiction] JS The articles give an overview of modern development and thinking in the Middle East. "The Roots of Muslim Rage," by Bernard Lewis, pages 44 to 69, presents a different perspective on the American Revolution.

ॐॐ

Freedman, Russell. **Children of the Great Depression.**
New York: Clarion Books, 2005. 118p. $20.00. ISBN 0 618 44630 3. [nonfiction] MJS

Themes/Topics: children, the Great Depression, 1930s

Summary/Description

Using memoirs, diaries, letters, and extensive pictures taken by photographers employed by the Farm Security Administration, Freedman graphically portrays the impact of the Great Depression on children. The chapters examine how parental crises, extreme poverty, disrupted schooling, child labor, population migration by car and train, entertainment, and hope shaped this generation and prepared them for another huge challenge, World War II. The "Chapter Notes" and "Selected Bibliography" guide the reader to additional print and nonprint sources. An index provides easy access to information.

Read Aloud/Reader Response

1. "The Sight of My Father Crying," pages 3 to 4, beginning "We had owned . . . " and ending " . . . the coal bin." The son sees his father, an adult who had made a good living, devastated by not being able to provide for his family.
2. "In and Out of School," page 35, beginning "In the impoverished . . . " and ending " . . . turn to eat." The brief story illustrates Appalachian poverty.
3. "Kids at Work," pages 43 and 44, beginning "A girl who started . . . " and ending " . . . hoping for work." A fourteen-year-old girl describes going to work.
4. "Kids at Work," page 51, beginning "Years later, . . . " and ending with the chapter. Hardship produces personal pride.
5. "Okie, Go Home!" pages 55 to 57, beginning "Almost half the nation's . . . " and ending " . . . taking turns in one pair." Two economists meet Tom, a twelve-year-old sharecropper.

Booktalk

Ask how many in the group listen to parents and grandparents telling them how much luckier they are growing up than the parents and grandparents were.

That kind of talk gets old, doesn't it? Especially when teenagers are confronted today with war, diseases, and hard choices about careers, drugs, and relationships. Life for young people now is not easy. But there was another time in America when the whole world seemed about to collapse. It took place in the 1930s and was called the Great Depression. Money was so scarce that in many families, not everyone ate everyday, had a place to sleep, or a pair of shoes. Adults, who once had money, lost it, along with their homes and their jobs. Some killed themselves; some walked away; and some took their families and hit the road. If you were over five, wherever you were, you pitched in to help and to survive. If you were a teenager, you might be the family's only wage earner. You had to be physically strong too because many families couldn't afford sturdy clothes, good food, soap, or medicine. Germ warfare had a whole different meaning. Where was the government? It trusted in the "survival of the fittest." There was no safety net or government aid. Each family was supposed to care for itself. How did they make it? They trusted their future, and that future was the *Children of the Great Depression*.

Learning Opportunities

1. Using your library's resources, continue to research one New Deal program. Share your information with the class.
2. Interview one person old enough to have lived during the Great Depression. Share your information with the group.
3. Choose one source described by Russell Freedman. Read or examine it. Share your findings with the group.
4. Compare the challenges described in *Children of the Great Depression* with the challenges that teenagers face today.
5. Create a photo essay depicting an important social movement or problem that in your community.

Related Works

1. Cooper, Michael L. **Dust to Eat: Drought and Depression in the 1930's.** New York: Clarion Books, 2004. 81p. $15.00. ISBN 0 618 15449 3. [nonfiction] MJS In a format similar to *Children of the Great Depression,* Cooper focuses on the conditions and implications of the Dust Bowl.
2. Griffin, Adelle. **Hannah, Divided.** New York: Hyperion/Disney Press, 2002. 208p. $15.99. ISBN 0 7868 0879 9. [fiction] MJ (See full

booktalk in *Teen Genre Connections,* 2005, pages 223 to 225.) In the middle of the Depression, thirteen-year-old, illiterate Hannah Bennett takes advantage of a scholarship to an elite Philadelphia school.

3. Hartnett, Sonya. **Thursday's Child.** Cambridge, MA: Candlewick Press, 2000. 261p. $15.99. ISBN 0 7636 1620 6. [fiction] JS (See full booktalk in *Teen Genre Connections,* 2005, pages 276 to 278.) Harper Flute, living through the Depression in Australia, relates the story of her younger brother who becomes a feral child.

4. Kupperberg, Paul (ed.). **Critical Perspectives on the Great Depression.** New York: The Rosen Publishing Group, 2005. 176p. $30.60. ISBN 1 4042 0061 4. [nonfiction] JS This collection of articles depicts the people, government, institutions, culture, and end of the Great Depression. "Cows and Horses Are Hungry," pages 15 to 23, and "Pea-Pickers' Child Dies," pages 23 to 30, are poignant accounts of the dire times. "Keeping an Eye on America: The Contradictions," pages 131 to 137, discusses the difficulty of and the controversy surrounding the pictures taken by Farm Security Administration photographers.

5. Partridge, Elizabeth. **Restless Spirit: The Life and Work of Dorothea Lange.** New York: Viking Press, 1998. 122p. $12.50. ISBN 0 670 87888 X. [nonfiction] MJS Dorothea Lange was one of the most famous photographers of the Great Depression. This photographic biography deals with both her personal life and professional work.

ದ ಜ

McClafferty, Carla Killough. **Something Out of Nothing: Marie Curie and Radium.**

New York: Farrar, Straus and Giroux, 2006. 134p. $18.00.
ISBN 0 374 38036 6. [nonfiction] MJS

Themes/Topics: radium, Marie Curie, Poland, women chemists

Summary/Description

Born in Russian-dominated Poland in 1877, Marie faced prejudice against Poles and women all her life. This includes her experiences as an underground student, governess, wife, mother, widow, and Nobel Prize winner. She dealt with poverty, grief, loneliness, personal scandal, a World War, the Great Depression, and the knowledge that her greatest discovery caused her death. The author includes source notes, a selected bibliography, and recommended Web sites. Extensive pictures and documents give a sense of her lifetime. An index makes information readily accessible.

Read Aloud/Reader Response

1. "Pierre," pages 22 to 23, beginning "In March 1892 . . . " and ending " . . . of my sister-in-law's life." The passage describes Marie's first rental in Paris.
2. "Discovery," page 37, beginning "Marie described . . . out of nothing." The statement shows how little the Curies had to start their world-changing undertaking.
3. "Fame," pages 54 to 59, beginning, "Not only were . . . " and ending with the chapter. Radium becomes a fad product and panacea.
4. "War," page 90, beginning, "*Sometimes by courage* . . . " and ending with the chapter. Currie realizes that no matter how weak and ill she becomes, she needs the laboratory.
5. "Danger," pages 95 to 100. "It seemed radium could . . . " and ending " . . . it was a small one." The Radium Girls, shop girls who painted watches, raise doubts about radium.

Booktalk

Most people would have told Marie Curie that she didn't have a chance in life. She was born in Warsaw, Poland, in 1877. Her country was under Russian domination. She wasn't even permitted to study her native language. But she did. The family had little money. No one thought she would ever have the means to study at the Sorbonne in Paris. But she did. Even with education, a woman rarely could find any man who would take her seriously. But she did, and she married him. They had no money, so how could they or she make any important discovery? But they did. With determination, drive, and discards, Marie Curie became internationally famous and changed the world. She had one great talent. She had the ability to make *Something Out of Nothing*.

Learning Opportunities

1. Choose one book or Web site listed by the author. Investigate it and share your findings with the group. You may find the Web sites helpful for the following Learning Opportunities.
2. Write a self-help book based on Marie Curie's life and success. List the personal qualities and her methods that you think made her successful. Share your conclusions with the group.
3. Using your library's resources, research three modern uses of radium. Share your findings with the group.
4. Using your library's resources, choose another famous woman scientist from the twentieth or twenty-first centuries. Share her contribution with the group.

5. Using your library's resources, find out more about the Nobel Prize. Share the information with the group.

Related Works

1. Coleman, Penny. **Adventurous Women: Eight True Stories about Women Who Made a Difference.** New York: Henry Holt and Company, 2006. 186p. $18.95. ISBN 0 8050 7744 8. [nonfiction] JS Coleman writes about uncommon women born in the nineteenth century who refused the stereotypes of their times, and made a difference.
2. Nelson, Marilyn. **Carver: A Life in Poems.** Asheville, NC: Front Street, 2001. 103p. $16.95. ISBN 1 886910 53 7. [biography in poems] MJS (See full booktalk in *Teen Genre Connections,* 2005, pages 42 to 44.) Born in 1864, Carver also battled poverty and prejudice to make something out of nothing.
3. Orr, Tamra (ed.). **Critical Perspectives on World War I.** New York: The Rosen Publishing Group, 2005. 176p. (Critical Anthologies of Nonfiction Writing). $30.60. ISBN 1 4042 0064 9. [nonfiction] JS In five chapters, articles and commentaries explain the 1914 European armies, America's entrance into the war, the war's media and propaganda machine, the people fighting and affected, and the battlefield action.
4. Updale, Eleanor. **Montmorency and the Assassins: Master, Criminal, Spy?** New York: Orchard Books, 2006. 416p. $16.99. ISBN 0 439 68343 2. [fiction] MJS In this second sequel, the ambitious Dr. Farcett causes the death of the woman he loves when he asks her to work with an X-ray machine.
5. Zindel, Paul. **The Gadget.** New York: HarperCollins Publishers, 2001. 184p. $15.99. ISBN 0 06 028255 X. [fiction] MJ (See full booktalk in *Teen Genre Connections,* 2005, pages 151 to 154.) The son of an American scientist, working at Los Alamos to build the atom bomb, becomes involved with Russian spies.

ᘉᘓ

Partridge, Elizabeth. **John Lennon: All I Want Is the Truth.**

New York: Viking Press, 2005. 231p. $24.99. ISBN 0 670 05954 4. [nonfiction] JS

Themes/Topics: rock musicians, England, Beatles, protest

Summary/Description

Partridge traces Lennon's life from his birth during a bombing raid, through his tumultuous childhood, into his successful collaboration with the Beatles, and then on to his post-Beatles contemplations and marriage to Yoko Ono. Lennon deals with his dysfunctional family, his mercurial and impulsive personality, his own romances, and his sons in a culture of war and drugs. The biography includes many full- and double-page photographs, extensive source notes and bibliography, a "Further Reading List," and a detailed index.

Read Aloud/Reader Response

1. Chapter 7, page 108, beginning "Before each show . . . " and ending " . . . to put the others on alert." Disabled children and adults appear thinking that the Beatles have curative power.
2. Chapter 12, page 195, " . . . you're an idealist . . . saint cry." John's Aunt Mimi characterizes Lennon.
3. "Afterword," page 201, "For John . . . his life." George Martin characterizes Lennon.
4. "Afterword," page 204, beginning, "His contradictions . . . " and ending " . . . the next time." The paragraph describes John Lennon's contradictions.
5. "Afterword," page 206, beginning "In an interview . . . " and ending with the book. John and the author reflect on life in the sixties.

Booktalk

Ask how many people in the group know about the Beatles. Ask them to share what they know. John Lennon was a Beatle, maybe the most famous one. He didn't have the most talent, good training, or the best personality. Neither his mother nor father wanted to take the time to raise him. He should have been a failure, a nobody. But Rock and Roll gave him a new family, school, and neighborhood. He had money, fame, praise, friends, and love almost in an instant. Was he happy? He still didn't know that when he died. He was still trying to make sense of what happened to him when he and three of his friends became a part of history. And if you asked John Lennon what he really wanted from his short life, he might have answered, *"All I Want Is the Truth."*

Learning Opportunities

1. List the titles of songs written by John Lennon. Choose your favorite piece and explain your choice to the group.
2. Using your library's resources, research the Viet Nam War. Share your information with the group.

3. Choose one book from the "Further Reading List." Explain to the group what it adds to your knowledge of John Lennon or The Beatles.
4. Choose a music star today. Research that person's life. Compare that star to John Lennon.
5. After reading *John Lennon: All I Want Is the Truth,* explain your reaction to John Lennon, the man.

Related Works

1. Aronson, Marc. **Art Attack: A Short Cultural History of the Avant-Garde.** New York: Clarion Books, 1998. 192p. $20.00. ISBN 0 395 79729 2. [nonfiction] JS Aronson traces literature, art, and music that rebelled against traditional standards. It is the movement embraced by Lennon and Yoko Ono.
2. Denenberg, Barry. **All Shook Up: The Life and Death of Elvis Presley.** New York: Scholastic Press, 2001. 288p. $16.95. ISBN 0 439 09504 2. [nonfiction] JS Tracing Presley's life from an impoverished childhood to phenomenal success, the biography suggests that Elvis's life choices compromised his talent and personal happiness.
3. Morales, Gilbert (ed.). **Critical Perspectives on the Vietnam War.** New York: The Rosen Publishing Group, 2005. 176p. (Critical Anthologies of Nonfiction Writing). $30.60. ISBN 1 4042 0063 0. [nonfiction] JS The articles include official statements about the war as well as essays revealing the protest against it.
4. The Rock and Roll Hall of Fame and Museum, Inc. Rock and Roll Hall of Fame and Museum, 2005. Available: http://www.rockhall. com. (Accessed May 2006). The Web site gives biographical information on all the inductees into the hall of fame. Lennon's heroes are included.
5. White, Katherine. **Elton John.** New York: Rosen Central, 2003. 112p. (Rock & Roll Hall of Famers). $34.25. ISBN 0 8239 3641 4. [nonfiction] J This biography of John Lennon's contemporary talks briefly about their friendship.

Multiple Cultures

"Multiple Cultures" also examines universal problems in new contexts. The books in "Learning from Other Countries" present worlds facing the challenges of change that we may share. "Learning from the Cultures within Our Country" reminds us how the distinct and separate communities within our blended culture influence our lives.

Learning from Other Countries

Ellis, Deborah. **The Heaven Shop.**
Narkham, ON, Canada: Fitzhenry & Whiteside, 2004. 192p. $16.95.
ISBN 1 55041 908 0. [fiction] MJ

Themes/Topics: Malawi, AIDS, orphans,
family, sharing, sacrifice

Summary/Description

Thirteen-year-old Binti Phiri attends St. Stephen's School for Girls and stars on a local radio show. Her fourteen-year-old brother, Kwasi, is a talented artist, and her sixteen-year-old sister, Junie, is engaged. Their mother died six years ago. Their father supports them with his coffin shop, Heaven Shop Coffins, but sends money to less fortunate family members. The father weakens and dies of AIDS. The father's brothers and sisters divide the property. Junie's fiancé breaks the engagement. One uncle takes Binti and Junie and another takes Kwasi. The sisters live in slave conditions. Junie runs away, and Binti decides to find their maternal grandmother, whom she discovers is forming a family of AIDS orphans and victims once supported by Binti's father. With the help of Jeremiah, an AIDS counselor, Binti reunites with her sister, now living as a prostitute, and her brother, sent to jail for stealing food from the uncle who was starving him. Led by Binti, they make coffins, and continue the grandmother's community after her death. The "Author's Note" explains AIDS, how it has spread through Sub-Saharan Africa, and how poverty encourages the epidemic. In "About the Author," Ellis answers questions about her work and *The Heaven Shop*.

Read Aloud/Reader Response

1. Chapter 7, pages 63 to 69, beginning with the chapter and ending ". . . had liked Binti's father" on page 69. This passage shows the children's grief, the community support, and the grabbing attitude of the relatives.
2. Chapter 7, pages 69 to 70, beginning "Two of the uncles . . . " and ending " . . . of burying my children." The grandmother speaks about AIDS and her son's death.
3. Chapter 13, pages 131 to 132, beginning, "Can we borrow your blazer . . . ," page 131, and ending " . . . do better the next time." Binti is in a role-play drama in the Orphan's Club.
4. Chapter 14, pages 136 to 137, beginning, "Binti went for . . . " and ending " . . . like Memory." Memory reveals how she became a mother and AIDS victim.
5. Chapter 17, page 151, beginning with the chapter and ending " . . . children of mine!" The grandmother reacts to her children's treatment of their orphaned nieces and nephew.

Booktalk

Thirteen-year-old Binti lives in Malawi. *(Show a map of the country.)* She is a radio star. Her father has his own business, Heaven Shop Coffins. She attends St. Stephen's School for Girls. Her mother died six years ago, but Binti still has a strong, tight family with her father, older sister, and brother. Life is good. Something not so good, however, is happening. Every day her father seems a little weaker and a little thinner. Some say he has "the Slim," what we know as AIDS, and that he will die soon. Binti knows they are wrong. AIDS is a disease for people who do disgraceful things. Her father isn't one of them. He buries those people. And yet he is sick, and he dies. Now his three children have to bury him and build a new life. They are strong. They believe in themselves. Unfortunately, their aunts and uncles don't. They own all the children's property. Binti's world of love and praise suddenly is full of greed and fear. *The Heaven Shop* made death sound so good. Now it all seems so wrong, and who can ever be strong enough to make it right?

Learning Opportunities

1. Discuss how Binti's real life parallels or fails to parallel her radio life.
2. Using your library's resources, research the background of Malawi. You may wish to start with *The Book of Rule: How the World Is Governed* (Related Work 1). Share the information that you find with the group.
3. How do Binti and Junie cope with their cruel treatment? Can either girl be successful?
4. Discuss the character of Jeremiah. Explain how he is important to the story.
5. Trace the change in Binti's character from the beginning to the end of the story. Consider the change in relation to the other characters in the story.

Related Works

1. Cain, Timothy (ed.). **The Book of Rule: How the World Is Governed.** New York: DK Publishing, Inc., 2004. 320p. $30.00. ISBN 0 7894 9354 3. [reference] MJS Cain includes the governments of 193 countries. Malawa appears on page 249.
2. Ellis, Deborah. **The Breadwinner Trilogy.** Toronto, ON, Canada: Groundwood Books. [fiction] MJ (See full booktalks in *Teen Genre Connections*, 2005, pages 272 to 276.) **The Breadwinner.** 2000. 170p. $5.95pa. ISBN 0 88899 416 8. When the Taliban take away Parvana's father, Parvana masquerades as a boy so that she can support her family. **Parvana's Journey.** 2002. 199p. $5.95pa. ISBN 0 88899 519 9. With her father dead and her family missing, thirteen-year-old Parvana journeys to relocate her family and gathers a new one. **Mud City.** 2003. 164p. $5.95pa. ISBN 0 88899 542 3. Shauzia, Parvanna's friend who wished to escape Afghanistan's devastation, decides to stay and help her fellow countrymen.
3. Mankell, Henning. Anne Connie Stuksrud (trans.). **Secrets in the Fire.** Toronto, ON, Canada: Annick Press LATD, 2003. 166p. $17.95. ISBN 1 55037 801 5. [fiction] MJS Sophia, a young refugee from war-torn Mozambique, builds a new life after losing her sister and her legs in a land mine explosion.

ℭℨℭℨ

Hosseini, Khaled. **The Kite Runner.**

New York: Riverhead Books, 2003. 371p. $14.00pa. ISBN 1 59448 000 1. [fiction] S/A

Themes/Topics: Afghanistan, male friendship, social class, honor, redemption, bullies, evil

Summary/Description

Thirty-eight-year-old Amir receives a call telling him "There is a way to be good again." The call brings back memories of Amir's life in Afghanistan thirty years before. His best friend, Hassan, was the son of a servant in their household. Amir's father admired Hassan. Amir, jealous, committed small cruelties against Hassan that Hassan ignored. When Hassan, Amir's kite runner, retrieved the last kite in a tournament that Amir won, a group of bullies raped him. Amir did nothing. His guilt drove him to frame Hassan for stealing. Amir's father forgave Hassan, but the servant and son left. As Afghanistan deteriorated, Amir and his father emigrated to America. Amir married. His father died. The caller, a lifelong friend of Amir's father, tells him that the Taliban executed Hassan and his wife and that Hassan was Amir's half-brother. Hassan's son is in an orphanage. Amir travels to Afghanistan and discovers that the orphanage sold the boy to a Taliban official, the bully who raped Hassan. The man demands that Amir fight him for the boy. Sohrab, Hassan's son, saves Amir by driving a brass ball into the official's eye with a sling shot. Amir adopts Sohrab, but fearing a delay might send him back to an orphanage, Sohrab attempts suicide. Although he lives, he remains sullen and withdrawn until Amir introduces him to kite flying. Some of the graphic descriptions and issues may be considered controversial for young adult readers.

Read Aloud/Reader Response

1. Chapter 4, pages 24 to 25, beginning with the chapter and ending with "Nothing." Amir relates the history of the relationship between the two fathers and sons.
2. Chapter 6, pages 54 to 55, beginning with "Would I ever lie . . . " and ending with " . . . outstretched arms." Amir recalls taunting Hassan about eating dirt for him. The passage anticipates the rape and the discovery that Hassan is his half-brother.
3. Chapter 17, page 221, beginning " . . . a boy who won't . . . " and ending with " . . . up to anything." Rahim challenges Amir to have the courage to bring back Hassan's son.
4. Chapter 19, pages 231 to 232, beginning "I feel like a tourist . . . " to " . . . you just didn't know it." Amir's driver sees the resentment that those who stayed to fight the war feel about those who fled to America.

5. Chapter 19, pages 239 to 240, beginning "His hands are . . ." and ending " . . . the man in the herringbone vest." Amir's dream reveals that he feels responsible for Hassan's death.

Booktalk

(*Read Chapter 1 aloud.*) This is a story about Afghanistan, but more important, it is a story about a life's small events and decisions. It is about how what we are taught affects those events and decisions, and how they build our lives. But most important, it is a tale that declares that it is never too late in life, never too late to appreciate something as small, or as beautiful, as a kite or perhaps the almost mystical power of a boy called *The Kite Runner.*

Learning Opportunities

1. Discuss how Hosseini unifies this novel with details.
2. Bullies are central to the novel. List each bully and explain how he affects the story.
3. Discuss how bullying relates to ethnic cleansing.
4. Using your library's resources, research the Taliban's history. Share the information with the class. You may wish to start with *Critical Perspectives on Al Qaeda* (Related Work 2).
5. What role do personal responsibility and redemption play in the novel?

Related Works

1. Cain, Timothy (ed.). **The Book of Rule: How the World Is Governed.** New York: DK Publishing, Inc., 2004. 320p. $30.00. ISBN 0 7894 9354 3. [reference] MJS. This source explains 193 governments and the challenging situations that they face. Afghanistan is on page 310.
2. Isaacs, April. **Critical Perspectives on Al Qaeda.** New York: The Rosen Publishing Group, 2006. 182p. (Critical Anthologies of Nonfiction Writing). $30.60. ISBN 1 4042 0542 X. [nonfiction] JS This anthology of articles explores the history of Al Qaeda and its relationship to the Taliban and the history of Afghanistan.
3. Nafisi, Azar. **Reading Lolita in Tehran: A Memoir in Books.** New York: Random House, 2003. 368p. $23.95. ISBN 0 375 50490 7. [nonfiction] S/A A professor at a Tehran university resigns her job and recruits seven of her students to share a discussion class centered on books banned by the government. The discussions explore family life under strict Islam rule. The content requires skilled and mature readers.

4. Romano, Amy. **A Historical Atlas of Afghanistan.** New York: The
    Rosen Publishing Group, 2003. 64p. (Historical Atlases of South
    Asia, Central Asia, and the Middle East). $30.95. ISBN 0 8239
    3863 8. [nonfiction] MJS The combination of maps, illustrations,
    pictures, and diagrams explains the history of the tumultuous area
    now called Afghanistan.
5. Satrapi, Marjane. **Persepolis.** New York: Random House/Pantheon,
    2003. 153p. $11.95pa. ISBN 0 375 71457 X. [graphic memoir] JS/A
    The great-granddaughter of one of Iran's emperors, Satrapi recounts
    her life from age six to age fourteen that witnessed the overthrow of
    the Shah, the Islamic Revolution, and the war with Iraq.

Lekuton, Joseph Lemasolai. **Facing the Lion: Growing Up Maasai on the African Savanna.**
Washington, DC: National Geographic, 2003. 123p. $15.95.
ISBN 0 7922 5125 3. [nonfiction] MJS

Themes/Topics: Masai, Kenya, nomadic life, bravery, conflicting
cultures, changing Africa

Summary/Description

Joseph Lekuton describes his nomadic life as a Maasai. In Chapter 1,
he relates an unsuccessful lion encounter that teaches him to confront
the other "lions" in his life. Subsequent chapters explain his birth, family,
tribal customs and responsibilities, as well as a successful school career,
and the support of Kenya's president via a soccer game. Eventually, he
completes his education in the United States, teaches in an American private school, and returns to Kenya with expertise and financial support. The
book offers two Web sites. The Web site, http://www.nkcef.org, explains
the Nomadic Kenyan Children's Educational Fund, which established
the Joseph Lekuton Scholarship Program for nomadic students. The Web
site, http://www.maasaierc.org/specialprojects.html, explains the development projects in Maasai communities of Kenya and Tanzania that hope
to preserve the Maasai culture, increase access to education and financial
opportunities, and protect the land rights of the Maasai.

Read Aloud/Reader Response

Mr. Lekuton is an excellent story teller, and his entire book is a captivat-
ing read aloud. The following five passages are just a few possible focus
points.

1.   Chapter 1, pages 9 to 18. Joseph describes the lion hunt.
2.   Chapter 3, pages 26 to 28, beginning "Cows are our way . . . " and ending " . . . sleep on its hide either." Joseph explains the tribe's relationship to cows.
3.   Chapter 5, pages 55 to 56, beginning "I think the toughest part . . . " and ending with the chapter. Joseph explains the conflicts between home and school.
4.   Chapter 6, pages 59 to 60, beginning "Soon I was old . . . " and ending " . . . the hyena is." Joseph relates the methods, expectations, and dangers of herding.
5.   Chapter 8, pages 78 to 79, beginning "Even though I . . . " and ending " . . . the next challenge." Joseph explains how Maasai teachings help him in school.

Booktalk

Show pictures of the Maasai. Ask if anyone in the group knows about the Maasai. Ask them to share what they know.

Joseph Lemasolai Lekuton was born Maasai. He grew up in a hut made of sticks and cow dung. He ate cow milk and blood. When drought made him thirsty, he licked the noses of cattle to survive. But the government moved him from the cow herd to the classroom. Many boys like him ran away from school. It was too confining, too different. Joseph stayed. His decision meant that he had to travel dangerous miles in the jungle—avoiding snakes, insects, wild animals, and poachers—as he tried to reconnect with his nomadic tribe during his school vacations. While he studied, they moved to survive. Joseph has not had an easy life, but, through his eyes, it has always been a beautiful one. He still lives in two different worlds. Each day these worlds grow farther apart. (*Show the pictures of Joseph from the inserts. In the first picture, he is dressed as a Maasai warrior. In the last picture, he is wearing Western dress.*) He still loves both. And he knows that in either one, on a moment's notice, he could find himself *Facing the Lion.*

Learning Opportunities

1.   Using your library's resources, continue to research Kenya and share your information with the group. You might wish to begin with *The Book of Rule: How the World Is Governed* (Related Work 1).
2.   Using your library's resources, continue to research the Maasai and share your information with the group.
3.   Joseph starts with the lion story even though it is not entirely flattering to him. What does the incident tell about him? Why do you think he tells the story?

4. List each "lion" that Joseph encounters. Discuss what he learns from each.

5. Joseph mentions that warriors make up songs about bravery. Choose someone you think is brave. Compose and sing an appropriate song for that person.

Related Works

1. Cain, Timothy (ed.). **The Book of Rule: How the World Is Governed.** New York: DK Publishing, Inc., 2004. 320p. $30.00. ISBN 0 7894 9354 3. [reference] MJS This reference for world government explains the governments of 193 countries. Tanzania appears on page 236. Kenya, and Moi's tenure as president, appears on page 237.

2. Eisner, Will. **Sundiata: A Legend of Africa, The Lion of Mali.** New York: NBM, 2002. 32p. $7.95. ISBN 1 56163 340 2. [graphic interpretation of African epic] MJS After his father and brothers are killed, a crippled child grows up to become the liberator and founder of Mali. Mali's government is also explained in Related Work 1, *The Book of Rule: How the World Is Governed,* page 181.

3. Kessler, Cristina. **Our Secret, Siri Dang.** New York: Philomel Books, 2004. 218p. $16.99. ISBN 0 399 23985 5. [fiction] JS As twelve-year-old Namelok approaches Maasai womanhood, she begins to challenge her tribe's customs.

4. Peet, Mal. **Keeper.** [fiction] JS (See full booktalk in "Contemporary"/"Competing," pages 75 to 77.) The main character, born in the rainforest, finds fame and success in soccer. Like Joseph, he uses that success to help his people.

5. Williams-Garcia, Rita. **No Laughter Here.** New York: HarperCollins Publishers, 2004. 133p. $15.99. ISBN 0 688 16247 9. [fiction] MJS Akilah slowly realizes that her best friend, a girl from Nigeria, was subjected to genital mutilation in her coming-of-age ceremony.

(ℨℨ

Staples, Suzanne Fisher. Under the Persimmon Tree.

New York: Farrar, Straus and Giroux/Frances Foster Books, 2005. 275p. $17.00.
ISBN 0 374 38025 2. [fiction] MJS

Themes/Topics: Afghan war, Afghanistan history, refugees, Peshawar, twentieth century, family, loss, hope, duty

Summary/Description

The lives of Najmah, a village girl, and Nusrat, an American married to an American-educated Afghan doctor, intertwine during the Afghan war in 2001. After losing her father and brother to the marauding Taliban and her mother and newborn brother to the American bombing, Najmah is rescued by a neighbor's brother. Dressed like a boy, she travels with her rescuer's family to a refugee camp, but runs away to Peshawar where she hopes to find her father and brother. Nusrat, waiting for her husband's return, opens a school for refugee children in her home. Najmah, unable to speak since seeing her mother and brother killed, is brought to the school. Nusrat guesses she is a girl, shelters her in her home, and teaches her. Eventually, Najmah's uncle, who wants the family land to grow poppies, locates Najmah. Najmah's brother, Nur, also arrives at Nusrat's home. Nusrat hides both the children from the uncle. Nur tells Najmah how the Taliban executed their father, and brings a rumor to Nusrat that an American doctor was killed in bombing. Accepting her husband's death, Nusrat decides to return to America and offers to take Najmah. Najmah and Nur, however, choose to return to their land to prevent the uncle from claiming it. A map of Afghanistan and an "Author's Note" set the story's context. A "Glossary" defines Dari words used in the text.

Read Aloud/Reader Response

1. Chapter 6, pages 78 to 81, beginning "Nusrat goes out . . . " and ending with the chapter. Even a simple trip holds difficulty and danger.
2. Chapter 7, pages 82 to 86, beginning with the chapter and ending with " . . . which I refuse." The passage describes the horror Najmah experiences when her brother and mother are killed.
3. Chapter 8, pages 96 to 99, beginning "Shortly after Faiz returned . . . " and ending " . . . talib who harassed Asma." The passage illustrates Taliban terrorism.
4. Chapter 12, pages 133 to 140, beginning "Nusrat converted . . . " and ending " . . . it had changed her life." Nusrat (Elaine) explains her conversion to Islam.
5. Chapter 23, pages 269 to 270, beginning "There are few happy endings . . . " and ending with the chapter. The characters make decisions truest to their hearts and beliefs.

Booktalk

Najmah lives with her family in Afghanistan. She is a shepherd. If the four members of her family work together all day, they can survive on the land. But the Taliban come and take her father and brother. Then an air raid kills her mother and newborn brother. Now she is alone. And alone, she could die. Elaine is an American. She travels with her husband to Peshawar, Pakistan. Her new Muslim name is Nusrat. Her husband is a doctor. He returns to Afghanistan, his homeland, to set up field hospitals, a task that may take his life. While she waits for his return, Nusrat sets up a school for refugee children. The war separates Najmah and Nusrat from their families, but the stars join their lives. The humble shepherd girl watches the stars for signs and omens. The wealthy, educated American sees the stars through scientific eyes. What can two people who see so differently have in common? As bombs and death surround them, they soon find out, in Nusrat's garden, *Under the Persimmon Tree.*

Learning Opportunities

1. Discuss how stars support the author's purpose.
2. Using your library's resources, research one aspect of Afghan history. Share your information with the group.
3. Chapters 1 and 2 introduce the two very different worlds of Najmah and Nusrat. How does the author make their friendship and mutual loyalty believable?
4. *The Breadwinner Trilogy* (Related Work 2) also tells about the war in Afghanistan. After reading the *Trilogy* and *Under the Persimmon Tree,* discuss the likenesses and differences in the perceptions.
5. Discuss the ending. Do you agree with the writer's choices and reasoning?

Related Works

1. Deuker, Carl. **Runner.** [fiction] JS (See full booktalk in "Contemporary"/"Competing," pages 70 to 73.) High school senior Chance Taylor becomes involved with terrorists, sees his father die fighting them, and enlists in the service rather than join an affluent American family who offer to make him part of his family.
2. Ellis, Deborah. **The Breadwinner Trilogy.** Toronto, ON, Canada: Groundwood Books. [fiction] MJ (See full booktalk in *Teen Genre Connections,* 2005, pages 272 to 276.) **The Breadwinner.** 2000. 170p. $5.95pa. ISBN 0 88899 416 8. When the Taliban destroy her family, Parvana begins her life as a boy. **Parvana's Journey.** 2002. 199p. $5.95pa. ISBN 0 88899 519 9. Parvana, with other orphans, finds a refugee camp and her mother. **Mud City.** 2003. 164p. $5.95pa. ISBN 0 88899 542 3. Shauzia, Parvana's friend, leaves the refugee camp, but decides that her responsibility lies with her people.

3. Johansen, Jonathan (ed.). **Critical Perspectives on Islam and the Western World.** New York: The Rosen Publishing Group, 2006. 182p. (Critical Anthologies of Nonfiction Writing). $30.60. ISBN 1 4042 0538 1. [nonfiction] JS This series of selected documents, essays, and articles explains the background of East/West relations and the rise of Islamist or Islamic fundamentalist movements.

Whelan, Gloria. **Chu Ju's House.**
New York: HarperCollins Publishers, 2004. 227p. $16.89.
ISBN 0 06 050725 X. [fiction] MJS

Themes/Topics: China, 1976, Cultural Revolution, runaways, gender roles, duty

Summary/Description

Fourteen-year-old Chu Ju knows that her parents will give her baby sister to an orphanage so that they can, as tradition dictates, try to have a boy. To save her sister, she runs away. Chu Ju works on a fishing boat, tends silkworms, and finally finds a home with an old woman who plants rice. The woman's son wishes to live in the city. When he sees that Chu Ju can maintain their land and write letters to communicate with him, he leaves. Ling, a young, local entrepreneur, befriends her, introduces her to new planting methods, and shares his books and revolutionary ideas. Chu Ju improves the land and saves both the woman's son and Ling from the authorities. The woman leaves her house and land to Chu Ju, now eighteen. Chu Ju reunites with her family and pledges to support them, but keeps her property and independence. She returns to her land and looks forward to a deeper relationship with Ling.

Read Aloud/Reader Response

1. Chapter 1, pages 4 to 10, beginning "During the years . . . " and ending " . . . no further chance for a son." Chu Ju explains tradition in relation to the Cultural Revolution. The passage also reveals the grandfather's relationship with Chu Ju.
2. Chapter 4, pages 80 to 81, beginning "My days were chewed . . . " and ending " . . . not the home I dreamed of." Chu Ju finds a family, and a new way of thinking, with her peers.
3. Chapter 5, pages 96 to 102, beginning "Together we walked . . . " and ending with the chapter. Chu Ju learns about Ha Na's house and the turmoil within it.

4. Chapter 7, pages 132 to 135, beginning "I blushed . . . " and ending " . . . remind me of failure." Ling and Chug Jug develop a caring relationship.
5. Chapter 12, pages 224 to 227, beginning "Ba Ba said, . . . " and ending with the novel. Chu Ju tries to find the balance of family, love, and independence.

Booktalk

In China of 1976, fourteen-year-old Chu Ju is a worthless girl. Her mother is about to have a baby. All will be well if the baby is a boy. According to tradition, a boy takes care of his parents in their old age. According to tradition, a worthless girl leaves the family to live with her husband. A family does not need to give a girl even a burial space. But misfortune strikes. The baby is a girl. The government will fine the family if they have three children. Chu Ju's parents decide that this girl will go to an orphanage. Chu Ju disagrees. If one girl must leave, it will be her, not a helpless baby. She runs away with only the lessons of her wise grandfather to support her. Homeless and poor, she worries about survival, not tradition. She learns about the world—the dangers and wonders it holds. And she finds that her own skills and strengths make her not so worthless after all. Chu Ju's journey is long and hard, but there is refuge, hope, and strength in a place she never imagined, a place called *Chu Ju's House*.

Learning Opportunities

1. Using your library's resources, continue to research the Cultural Revolution of China. Share the information with the group.
2. Chu Ju enters Ha Na's house and sees it as similar to her own. Discuss the similarities and differences.
3. List the characters in the novel. Discuss the degree of trust that you would give to each character if you were Chu Ju.
4. Discuss the role tradition plays in the novel.
5. Do you agree with Chu Ju's final decision to keep her own house?

Related Works

1. Cain, Timothy (ed.). **The Book of Rule: How the World Is Governed.** New York: DK Publishing, Inc., 2004. 320p. $30.00. ISBN 0 7894 9354 3. [reference] MJS This reference for world government explains the governments of 193 countries. The explanation of China's government appears on pages 290 to 299 and includes references to the post-Cultural Revolution period, which has encouraged economic expansion.

2. Namioka, Lensey. **Ties That Bind, Ties That Break.** New York: Delacorte Press, 1999. 154p. $15.95. ISBN 0 385 32666 1. [fiction] JS (See full booktalk in *Booktalks and More*, 2003, pages 22 to 24.) Born in the early twentieth century, Ailin challenges Chinese traditions and eventually emigrates to the United States, where she marries and inspires her husband, James Chew, to challenge tradition as well.

3. Whelan, Gloria. **Homeless Bird.** New York: HarperCollins Publishers, 2000. 216p. $15.95. ISBN 0 06 028454 4. [fiction] MJS (See full booktalk in *Booktalks and More*, 2003, pages 215 to 217.) Thirteen-year-old Koly marries to free her family of the burden of supporting her. Suffering the abuse and abandonment of her mother-in-law, she rebuilds her life in a more modern India through her embroidery talent.

4. Yan, Ma. Pierre Haske (ed.). Lisa Appignanesi (trans.). **The Diary of Ma Yan: The Struggles and Hopes of a Chinese Schoolgirl.** New York: HarperCollins Publishers, 2004. 176p. $16.89. ISBN 0 06 076496 1. [nonfiction] MJS Written in 2000 to 2001, the diary records the frustration of a Chinese girl living in abject poverty. She wishes to go to school even though her brothers, according to tradition, should be educated and she should stay home.

5. Yen Mah, Adeline. **Chinese Cinderella and the Secret Dragon Society.** New York: HarperCollins Publishers, 2005. 242p. $16.99. ISBN 0 06 056735 X. [fiction] MJ In World War II, a girl loses her traditional home and joins the Chinese Resistance.

Zenatti, Valérie. Adriana Hunter (trans.). **When I Was a Soldier: A Memoir.**
New York: Bloomsbury Children's Books, 2005. 235p. $16.95.
ISBN 1 58234 978 9. [nonfiction] JS

Themes/Topics: women soldiers, Israel, Jews, French, Armed Forces, coming-of-age

Summary/Description

On her eighteenth birthday, according to Israeli law, Valérie Zenatti becomes a soldier. For two years, she experiences "rigorous training" and "harsh living conditions." Opening chapters describe her final exams and high school graduation. The military responsibilities mature her. When she returns home, she no longer lives as a child. She questions

Israel's romantic self-characterizations, and she has less in common with younger friends who have not experienced military service. Under the pressure of extreme discipline and demanding studies, she seeks psychiatric help, but in completing her duty tour, she makes a significant contribution to her country's safety. Her last chapter describes the feeling of rebirth that accompanies her army discharge.

Read Aloud/Reader Response

1. "Countdown to the Army," pages 39 to 41, beginning with the chapter and ending with " . . . a foreigner." Valérie explains the meaning of Israeli military service.
2. "To Arms, Etc.," pages 67 to 68, beginning "We're each . . . " and ending " . . . poets, dear girl." Valérie describes the impact of being issued a dog tag.
3. "Prohibited to Under 18s," pages 108 to 113, entry of 4th October, 9 P.M. The group explores the place of Israel in the world and in the hearts of Jews.
4. "Corporal, and Proud of It," page 185, beginning "In Israel . . . " and ending " . . . reply the others." Valérie describes the many conflicting factions within Israel itself.
5. "When an Old Man Dies It Is Like a Library Burning (African Proverb)," pages 223 to 225, beginning "And here I am . . . " and ending with the chapter. An old woman tells her story of persecution by the Germans and inspires Valérie to continue her role as a soldier.

Booktalk

Show a series of headlines and pictures dealing with Palestine versus Israel or Palestine versus Lebanon. Be sure to include pictures of Israeli soldiers.

Valérie Stevens is part of those pictures and headlines. Every Israeli, on his or her eighteenth birthday, has to sign up for military service. On her eighteenth birthday, after passing high school exams, Valerie becomes a soldier. She doesn't expect to like it, but she doesn't anticipate how powerful the guns and the uniform will make her feel. She doesn't anticipate how much affection, attention, and respect that uniform brings her—someone who was just a schoolgirl in civilian life. Still doubts linger. Is Israel the oppressed or the oppressor? Can peace, stability, or safety come from war? Are the Palestinians monsters or just humans, as persecuted as the founders of her country? All these questions come to her. Then work, fear, pressure, and the numbing military routine push them aside—almost. Valérie just entered Life University.

The lessons are lasting and potentially lethal. They unite a country and a nation. Let Valérie tell you her story. Let her tell you what these lessons teach her in *When I Was a Soldier.*

Learning Opportunities

1. Organize a debate on the pros and cons of compulsory military service.
2. Using your library's resources, research the founding of Israel. Share the information with the group.
3. Using your library's resources, research *Masada.* Share the information with the group.
4. Using your library's resources, research the Holocaust of World War II. Share the information with the group.
5. Using your library's resources, continue to research the issues in the conflicts between Israel and its neighbors. Share the information with the group.
6. Trace Valérie's change and growth throughout her memoir. Identify what you think are the most important things she learned during the two years.

Related Works

1. Byers, Ann. **The Holocaust Camps.** Berkeley Heights, NJ: Enslow Publishers, Inc., 1998. 128p. (The Holocaust Remembered Series). $20.95. ISBN 0 89490 995 9. [nonfiction] MJS Byers explains how the German camps, which began as prison and labor camps with torture and high death rates, ended as extermination camps.
2. Miklowitz, Gloria D. **Masada: The Last Fortress.** Grand Rapids, MI: Eerdmans Books, 1998. 188p. $16.00. ISBN 0 8028 5165 7. [fiction] MJS (See full booktalk in *Booktalks Plus,* 2001, pages 162 to 164.) The seventeen-year-old son of Zealot leader Eleazar be Yá ir tells about holding the fortress for seven months against the Romans.
3. Müller, Melissa. Rita Kimber and Robert Kimber (trans.). **Anne Frank: The Biography.** New York: Henry Holt and Company, 1998. 330p. $14.00pa. ISBN 0 8050 5997 0. [nonfiction] S/A Müller places Anne Frank in a family, social, and political context.
4. Provost, Anne. John Nieuwenhuizen (trans.). **In the Shadow of the Ark.** New York: Arthur A. Levine Books, 2004. 368p. $17.95. ISBN 0 439 44234 6. [fiction] S/A In this retelling of Noah and the Ark, Ham's concubine and her father help to build the Ark and realize they will be left to die. Controversial topics like ethnic cleansing, mercy killing, and homosexuality require a mature audience also

familiar with sustained allusion. It speaks directly to the conflict in the Middle East and the problems of imperfect men directed to build a perfect world.

5. Webster, Matt. **Inside Israel's Mossad: The Institute for Intelligence and Special Tasks.** New York: The Rosen Publishing Group, 2003. 83p. (Inside the World's Most Famous Intelligence Agencies). $20.00. ISBN 0 8239 3815 8. [nonfiction] MJS In explaining Mossad's development, Webster also explains Israel's development.

Learning from the Cultures within Our Country

ભૈૺ

Carvell, Marlene. **Sweetgrass Basket.**
New York: Dutton Children's Books, 2005. 243p. $16.99.
ISBN 0 525 47547 8. [fiction, poetry] JS

Themes/Topics: Indian school, sisters, identity, Pennsylvania history, prejudice

Summary/Description

Sent to an off-reservation school after their mother's death, Mattie and Sarah Tarbell find their Mohawk heritage and their own self-respect challenged by the white world's cruelty, prejudice, and ignorance. Mattie, the older sister, clashes with the head supervisor, Mrs. Dwyer, who sees Mattie's Native expression and her independent behavior as unacceptable. Eventually, she accuses Mattie of stealing her broach. Without proof Mrs. Dwyer harasses Mattie until she runs away. The escape fails. Mattie, sick from exposure, is returned to the school, held in the institution's stockade, released by her teacher, and left untreated. She tries to work but dies in her sister's arms, and is buried at the school instead of in her ancestral burial ground. Later, Sarah finds that the broach slipped behind the laundry room pipes. Although the discovery proves her sister's innocence, Sarah fears that Mrs. Dwyer will interpret it as collusion. Sarah throws the broach away. The story is told in "prose, poetry and alternating voices." A pronunciation guide for Mohawk words and an explanatory "Author's Note" appear at the beginning of the novel.

Read Aloud/Reader Response

Although the passages below are particularly singled out, the entire book could be adapted for a dramatic reading performance.

1. "Sarah," pages 12 to 15. New students receive a cold and cruel welcome.
2. "Mattie," "Sarah," pages 50 to 51. Paired poems illustrate the girls' feelings about their new home and their determination not to show their emotions.
3. "Mattie," pages 100 to104. Mrs. Dwyer scolds Mattie for opening Mrs. Dwyer's door and delivering her laundry, but Mattie recalls how doors are regarded in the Mohawk culture.
4. "Mattie," pages 109 to 112. Sarah gives Mattie the basket their mother made for Mattie.
5. "Sarah," pages 134 to136. Naming two nouns, Sarah expresses the despair she shares with the other students.
6. "Mattie," pages 227 to 230. Mattie speaks from the grave and explains why her body should have been sent home.

Booktalk

Ask how many in the group have ever heard of schools for Native Americans. Ask if they know where these schools were.

Most people think that Native American schools were established on reservations, but in 1879, the Carlisle Indian Industrial School in Carlisle, Pennsylvania, was our country's first off-reservation school for Native Americans. The author dedicates her story to the three-hundred-fifty Native American students who attended that school. The story is told by two sisters, Mattie and Sarah, whose father sends them to the school after their mother dies. The sisters belong to the Mohawk tribe. Their father wants them to earn their way in the white man's world. Together, they take the train to the off-reservation school. Together they find more hate and ignorance than they ever dreamed could exist. Most of these white people don't want to hear the girls' language, or see their clothes, or hear about their ways of life. The school will teach them to think, talk, and act white. Then they won't offend whites when cleaning their houses or washing and mending their clothes. Mattie and Sarah hide their Indian names. They put on new clothes, and speak almost not at all. They try to be good—the way white people see good—but they still are brown. Their color won't change. Every move they make is watched. Every word they say is a suspected lie. Everything they own is dangerous and threatening—even something as small, fragrant, and precious as a *Sweetgrass Basket*.

Learning Opportunities

1. Using your library's resources, research off-reservation schools for Native Americans. Share your information with the group.
2. Using your library's resources, research Mohawk spiritual and cultural beliefs. Share your information with the group.
3. Discuss how the information from Learning Opportunities 1 and 2 support your understanding of the novel.
4. List each time the sweetgrass basket appears. Then discuss what it reveals.
5. Characterize each sister. Be sure to discuss how they are alike and different.
6. How might you rewrite, replace, or add to "Labor Conquers All Things"?

Related Works

1. Bruchac, Joseph. **Code Talker: A Novel about the Navajo Marines of World War Two.** New York: Dial Books, 2005. 231p. $16.99. ISBN 0 8037 2921 9. [fiction] MJS In this novel about the Navajos in World War II, Bruchac also includes the prejudice and hate encountered at the white man's school.
2. Noël, Michel. Shelley Tanaka (trans.). **Good for Nothing.** Toronto, ON, Canada: Groundwood Books, 2004. 322p. $18.95. ISBN 0 88899 478 8. [fiction] JS In 1959, fifteen-year-old Nipishish, a Métis or half-breed, returns to the Indian reserve in northern Quebec after being thrown out of residential school and discovers the government's plots against his people.
3. Olsen, Sylvia. **White Girl.** Winlaw, BC, Canada: Sononis Press, 2004. 235p. $9.95. ISBN 1 55039 147 X. [fiction] S When her mother marries an Indian, fifteen-year-old Josie Jessop moves to the reservation and discovers a new family, a new love, and her own prejudices. Some language might be considered controversial.
4. Orenstein, Denise Gosliner. **Unseen Companion.** New York: HarperCollins Publishers/Katherine Tegen Books, 2003. 357p. $16.89. ISBN 0 06 052057 4. [fiction] JS In 1969 Bethel, Alaska, four teenagers tell their stories about a beaten half-breed teenage rebel, Dove Alexie, who, after being arrested, suddenly disappears.
5. Philip, Neil. **The Great Mystery: Myths of Native America.** New York: Clarion Books, 2001. 145p. $25.00. ISBN 0 395 98405 X. [nonfiction] MJS In defining and explaining the myths and their evolutions, Philip emphasizes how the Native American relationship to nature influences human interaction.

ℭ℥

Nelson, Marilyn. Pamela Espeland (notes and annotations). **Fortune's Bones: The Manumission Requiem.**

Asheville, NC: Front Street, 2004. 32p. $16.95. ISBN 1 932425 12 8. [nonfiction] JS

Themes/Topics: slavery, Connecticut, poetry

Summary/Description

Following the explanations of *manumission* and *requiem,* the volume presents six poems spoken by the following: general narrator; Fortune's wife; Dr. Porter, who stripped the bones; the people who encounter the bones in the home and museum; and Fortune. The concluding poem declares us all to be Fortune. The notes and pictures accompanying the poems give the factual background. Fortune, one of the last slaves in Connecticut, died about 1798 at the age of sixty. His owner, Dr. Porter, boiled the body, stripped the bones, and used the reconstructed skeleton to study the human body. Eventually, a descendent of the doctor contributed the bones to a local museum. In 1996, the community investigated the bones, then designated as "Larry," and searched for information about his history and circumstances.

Read Aloud/Reader Response

All the poems are suitable for choral reading.

1. "Preface," page 13. Fortune is placed in the context of slavery.
2. "Dinah's Lament," page 15. Fortune's wife laments cleaning the room where Fortune's bones hang.
3. "On Abrigador Hill," pages 17 and 19. The doctor ponders cutting Fortune's body.
4. "Kyrie of the Bones," pages 21 and 23. All those encountering the bones react.
5. "Not My Bones," pages 25 and 27. Fortune distinguishes between the body and the man.
6. "Sanctus," page 29. The general narrator concludes that each of us is Fortune.

Booktalk

Ask how many people in the group know the definitions of Manumission and Requiem. After establishing the meaning of the words, show the cover of the book.

The freeing of a slave is usually a time for celebration. A burial is usually a time for sadness. If we look at the cover, we can see celebration and sadness blending. The man on the left is a slave. The skeleton on the right are his bones. A Connecticut doctor owned both. Even after most of the slaves in Connecticut were free, the doctor chose to keep his slaves. Fortune was one of them. Fortune's only path to freedom was death, but the doctor, the owner, wanted more. He wanted *Fortune's Bones.* And so he boiled the flesh from the dead man's body and kept them. It was a terrible secret hidden under a false name, "Larry," written on the skeleton's skull. The name trick worked so well for so many years that people even forgot that those bones ever belonged to a person. But one day those bones would speak, even sing. They would remind people that they had an owner. They would tell about a terrible tragedy and a wonderful celebration at the same time: escape and degradation entwined, all ready to explode from *Fortune's Bones.*

Learning Opportunities

1. Using your library's resources, research the traditional funeral mass. Share with the group the purpose of each part of the mass.
2. Using your library's resources, research the traditional New Orleans brass band jazz funeral. Try to recreate such a ceremony.
3. Several famous composers, including the composer of the music for *The Manumission Requiem,* are listed on page 8. Choose one requiem written by one of the composers. Listen to it and record your reactions.
4. Organize a choral reading of *The Manumission Requiem* written for Fortune.
5. Using your library's resources, research slavery in the North. Share the information that you find with the group. You might wish to start with the Web site listed on page 32: www.slavenorth.com/connecticut.htm.

Related Works

1. Hearn, Julie. **Sign of the Raven.** [fiction] JS (See full booktalk in "Fantasy/Science Fiction/Paranormal"/"Discovering Our Roots," pages 152 to 154.) In this time travel fantasy, the main character discovers "freaks" fearing that their bones and body parts will be kept as curiosities after their deaths.
2. Hesse, Karen. **Witness.** New York: Scholastic Press, 2001.176p. $16.95. ISBN 0 439 27199 1. [poetry] JS (See full booktalk in *Booktalks and More,* 2003, pages 180 to 183.) Eleven citizens describe the Ku Klux Klan's invasion of a small Vermont town in 1924.

3. Lester, Julius. **Time's Memory.** New York: Farrar, Straus and Giroux, 2006. 230p. $17.00. ISBN 0 374 37178 4. [fiction] JS Amma, the creator god and master of life and death, sends a young man to the New World on a slave ship so that he can quiet the souls of slaves improperly buried. He achieves his task by letting them tell their stories.

4. McKissack, Patricia C., and Frederick L. McKissack. **Days of Jubilee: The End of Slavery in the United States.** New York: Scholastic Press, 2003. 144p. $18.95. ISBN 0 439 10764 X. [nonfiction] MJS Using an overall historical description, personal narratives, and pictures, this book documents the sometimes chaotic and ambiguous end to slavery.

5. Nelson, Marilyn. **Carver: A Life in Poems.** Asheville, NC: Front Street, 2001. 103p. $16.95. ISBN 1 886910 53 7. [biography in poems] MJS (See full booktalk in *Teen Genre Connections*, 2005, pages 42 to 44.) This award-winning biography celebrates George Washington Carver's life in poems.

෴

Ryan, Pam Muñoz. **Becoming Naomi León.**
New York: Scholastic Press, 2004. 256p. $16.95. ISBN 0 439 26969 5. [fiction] MJS

Themes/Topics: Mexican culture, parental abuse, alcoholism, the physically challenged, family

Summary/Description

Naomi Soledad León Outlaw and her physically challenged brother Owen live in Avocado Acres Trailer Rancho with their think-positive grandmother and her supportive neighbors. Their alcoholic and abusive mother arrives at the trailer. She has a new boyfriend, a new name, and a plan for Naomi to care for the boyfriend's daughter. The children, at first charmed by their mother, slowly rediscover her abusive and manipulative nature that left them deserted, emotionally scarred, and in their grandmother's custody. The grandmother and her neighbors perceive the mother's intentions, and travel to a carving festival and competition in Mexico to find the children's father. The grandmother seeks permanent custody. As they wait for the father to appear, Naomi helps the carving team produce a prize winner and learns about her father and her Mexican heritage. When the father arrives, he supports the grandmother's custody claim and promises to become part of his children's lives. In California, the grandmother and children attend a custody hearing. Naomi, previously fearful, quiet, and shy, tells the truth about her mother and thwarts the mother's custody attempt.

Read Aloud/Reader Response

1. "a paddling of ducks," pages 3 to 6, beginning with the chapter and ending " . . . greatly disappointed." The passage highlights characteristics of Naomi, Owen, and Gram.
2. "a skulk of foxes," pages 17 to 19, beginning "She wore jeans, . . . " and ending " . . . strangely familiar." The mother arrives.
3. "a lamentation of swans," page 29. "One of her . . . sometimes the same." Naomi explains her grandmother's thinking.
4. "a passel of todays," pages 137 to 138. Naomi ponders finding their father.
5. "a crash of hippopotami," pages 234 to 237, beginning with "I heard the judge's words, . . . " and ending ". . . million times since Mexico." Naomi struggles to speak when she realizes that only her testimony will keep the family together.
6. "a murmuration of tomorrows," pages 244 to 246. Naomi realizes that she is growing into someone powerful.

Booktalk

(Read aloud "a rabble of yesterdays," on page 1.)

Ten-year-old Naomi saw her mother walk out the door six years ago. She never saw her walk back in. Her seven-year-old brother Owen was a baby then. He doesn't even remember their mother. Suddenly Mom *is* back, knocking on the door of the trailer Gram, Naomi, and Owen call home. Mother is beautiful. Some would say foxy. In fact, foxy describes both her looks and mind. She wants to make friends again, then take Naomi away but leave Owen, the cripple, the "funny looking kid," with Gram. Mom has a new boyfriend. They need Naomi to take care of his daughter and help them collect child support. Then neither of them will have to work too hard. Isn't that the least Naomi can do for her lovely, loving mother? Naomi learned early that keeping quiet as a mouse was her key to survival. Is silence still her best weapon, or is it time, in her journey to *Becoming Naomi León,* to roar like a lion?

Learning Opportunities

1. Each chapter title indicates an animal group. Discuss why Ryan made this choice.
2. Describe and evaluate how Owen, Naomi, and Gram cope with stress.
3. The father appears only briefly. Is he appealing?

4. By the end of the novel, how has Naomi changed? List the characters, situations, and settings that contributed to that change.
5. Read the chapter titles as a list. Discuss how the list tells the story.
6. Using your library's resources, research Mexican customs and stories that might appeal to Naomi and Owen. You might wish to start with *Horse Hooves and Chicken Feet: Mexican Folktales* (Related Work 4).

Related Works

1. Bertrand, Diane Gonzales. **Trino's Choice.** Houston, TX: Piñata Books, 1999. 124p. $9.95pa. ISBN 1 55885 268 9. [fiction] MJ (See full booktalk in *Booktalks and More,* 2003, pages 226 to 229.) Twelve-year-old Trino learns to choose study and work over street life to support his mother and their blended family.
2. Cameron, Ann. **Colibrí.** New York: Farrar, Straus and Giroux/ Frances Foster Books, 2003. 240p. $17.00. ISBN 0 374 31519 1. [fiction] MJS (See full booktalk in *Teen Genre Connections,* 2005, pages 269 to 271.) Twelve-year-old Colibrí finds the strength to flee her kidnapper and find her real parents.
3. Johnston, Tony. **Any Small Goodness: A Novel of the Barrio.** New York: The Blue Sky Press, 2001. 128p. $5.95. ISBN 0 439 18936 5. [fiction] MJS Eleven-year-old Arturo Rodriguez lives in the barrio of East Los Angeles where he struggles to hang on to the best of his culture.
4. Phillip, Neil (comp.). Jacqueline Mair (illus.). **Horse Hooves and Chicken Feet: Mexican Folktales.** New York: Clarion Books, 2003. 83p. $19.00. ISBN 0 618 19463 0. [fiction] MJS This collection of folktales includes "tale types" that are told with a distinctive Mexican flavor.
5. Ryan, Pam Muñoz. **Esperanza Rising.** New York: Scholastic Press, 2000. 272p. $15.95. ISBN 0 439 12041 1. [fiction] MJS (See full booktalk in *Booktalks and More,* 2003, pages 42 to 44.) Set in the Depression, this journey reveals the struggles of Mexican immigrant workers and one formerly wealthy girl among them who suddenly must join her fate and welfare with theirs.

Schmidt, Gary D. **Lizzie Bright and the Buckminster Boy.**

New York: Clarion Books, 2004. 219p. $15.00. ISBN 0 618 43929 3. [fiction] MJS

Themes/Topics: race relations, clergy, Maine, twentieth century, prejudice, forgiveness

Summary/Description

In the early 1900s, Turner Buckminster moves to Phippsburg, Maine. His father is the minister of Phippsburg's First Congregational Church. The family confronts rigid community expectations. Turner finds friendship with the smart and rebellious Lizzie Bright, who lives on Malaga Island, a poor community founded by former slaves, and Mrs. Cobb, a lonely and bitter old woman for whom he plays the organ each day to make up for hitting her fence with a stone. The town fathers see Phippsburg and Malaga Island as ripe for tourism and want Turner's father to help them drive out the islanders. Turner and Lizzie's relationship is controversial. Turner's father initially supports the evacuation and turns on his son because of town pressure. But as the town greed becomes obvious, Turner's father respects Turner's independence and shares with him his own controversial reading material, the work of Darwin. Turner invites Lizzie to hear his organ music with Mrs. Cobb, who develops affection for both teenagers. When she wills her house to Turner, he plans to give it to Lizzie, but the officials commit all Malaga residents to the insane asylum. Turner's father dies defending Turner. Turner and his mother move into Mrs. Cobb's home, and by the time Turner tries to retrieve Lizzie, she is dead. The tourist development plan is a scam, and Turner and his mother help one of their worst persecutors to regain solvency and respect. The "Author's Note" explains the story's historical base.

Read Aloud/Reader Response

1. Chapter 1, pages 1 to 7, beginning with the chapter and ending with the first division mark in the chapter. The Buckminsters' introduction reveals the town attitudes.
2. Chapter 1, pages 14 and 15, beginning "Mrs. Elia Hurd . . . " and ending " . . . smell sweet grass." Turner meets Mrs. Elia Hurd and decides that she is his soul mate.
3. Chapter 2, pages 22 to 30, beginning "Turner was right . . . " and ending with a chapter section division. Turner reads to Mrs. Cobb and fights with Willis Hurd.
4. Chapter 8. Set in September, this chapter contains some significant changes in the novel. Mrs. Cobb encourages Turner to find Lizzie. Lizzie's grandfather is dying. Turner chooses to let Willis strike him out. Against his father's wishes, Willis repaints the shutters of his grandmother's house, and Turner helps him.

5. Chapter 12, pages 215 to 217, beginning "And that was when . . . " and ending with the chapter. Turner decides to share his whale encounter with Willis.

Booktalk

The year is 1912, and Turner Buckminster's father is the new minister at the First Congregational Church in Phippsburg, Maine. After six hours of Phippsburg, Turner doesn't think he can stand much more. The Phippsburg citizens know everything. They know how the minister's family should talk, dress, and think. They even have a one-way-to-play baseball game with a sneaky high pitch that fools Turner every time. And what they don't know they make up from their spying and gossiping. It's their town, their rules, and their game. Turner is ready to leave, anytime. Then he meets Lizzie Bright Griffin. She is sassy and smart, but she is also black. Friendships between teenagers like Turner and Lizzie are against the Phippsburg rules. Besides, the town fathers want to take Lizzie's home, Malaga Island, and turn it into a money-making tourist attraction. They want Turner's father to help them. Turner doesn't like this game either. Lizzie tells him that's the way it is. Turner figures it isn't that way if he can help it. The lines are drawn. The town fathers and Turner's father on one side. *Lizzie Bright and the Buckminster Boy* on the other. Win or lose, Turner vows that the rules in Phippsburg are going to change forever.

Learning Opportunities

1. Both Turner's father and Lizzie's grandfather are ministers. How would you describe the differences in their religions?
2. List every appearance of a Hurd family member in the novel. Then discuss how the family helps the author accomplish his purpose.
3. Choose one of the following words: stubborn, cantankerous, annoying, and evil. Discuss how it applies to the novel.
4. Choose one of the following words: faith, hope, and love. Discuss how it applies to the novel.
5. Whales are central to the story. List where they appear and where they are mentioned. Then discuss their relationship to the author's purpose.
6. Charles Darwin is a significant allusion. Using your library's resources, find out as much as you can about Darwin and his controversial ideas.

Related Works

1. Hesse, Karen. **Witness.** New York: Scholastic Press, 2001. 176p. $16.95. ISBN 0 439 27199 1. [fiction] JS (See full booktalk in

Booktalks and More, 2003, pages 180 to 183.) Hesse describes the Ku Klux Klan invasion of a small Vermont town through the eyes of eleven of its citizens.

2.   Ketchum, Liza. **Where the Great Hawk Flies.** New York: Clarion Books, 2005. 264p. $16.00. ISBN 0 618 40085 0. [fiction] MJ Thirteen-year-old Daniel Tucker and eleven-year-old Hiram Coombs overcome their heritages and their families' prejudices to become friends in eighteenth-century Vermont.

3.   Lynch, Chris. **Gold Dust.** New York: HarperCollins Publishers, 2000. 196p. $15.95. ISBN 0 06 028174 X. [fiction] MJ (See full booktalk in *Teen Genre Connections,* 2005, pages 260 to 262.) Set during the Boston busing of the 1970s, the novel recounts the interracial friendship between seventh graders of radically different backgrounds.

4.   Murphy, Jim. **Gone A-Whaling: The Lure of the Sea and the Hunt for the Great Whale.** New York: Clarion Books, 1998. 208p. $18.00. ISBN 0 395 69847 2. [nonfiction] MJS (See full booktalk in *Booktalks Plus,* 2003, pages 108 to 110.) Spanning the history of whaling, the book explains how whaling has changed from hunting to observing.

5.   Taylor, Mildred D. **The Land: Prequel to Roll of Thunder, Hear My Cry.** New York: Penguin Putnam/Phyllis Fogelman Books, 2001. 275p. $17.99. ISBN 0 8037 1950 7. [fiction] JS (See full booktalk in *Teen Genre Connections,* 2005, pages 267 to 269.) The friendship between a biracial boy and an older African-American boy ends in the tragic death of the African-American as the two strive for success in the post-Civil War world.

Son, John. **Finding My Hat.**
New York: Scholastic Press/Orchard Books, 2003. 185p. (First Person Fiction). $16.95. ISBN 0 439 43538 2. [fiction] MJS

Themes/Topics: Korean Americans, family life, grief

Summary/Description

In a series of essays, Jin-Han Park tells about his American life. His first memory, losing his hat to the Chicago wind, is a metaphor for his search for a place in America. The last essay concerns his grief over losing his mother to cancer. The father and mother, because of their limited English, operate their own wig business rather than trusting corporate promotion in American-owned enterprises. Searching for more prosperous markets throughout America, they encounter friends, happiness, personal heartache, and prejudice. Jin-Han knows how his family's life differs from his American counterparts. As a teenager with an intelligent, concerned girlfriend, he is balancing the two cultures as well as his grief and happiness.

Read Aloud/Reader Response

Each essay is appropriate for a "Read Aloud/Reader Response" activity, but the following might be especially useful.

1.   "Losing My Hat," pages 1 and 2. This opening essay describes the first memory that Jin-Han has of losing his hat, one that his mother made for him, and her loving reaction.
2.   "American as Apple Pie," pages 19 to 23, beginning with the chapter and ending with " . . . get along fine." An invitation to the Parks from a Polish American neighbor illustrates the difficulty that both sides have understanding each other.
3.   "Powerful Rays," pages 47 to 59, beginning, "There were six . . . " and ending with the chapter. In kindergarten and with his little sister, Jin-Han explores the power of a kiss.
4.   "The Tree of Life," pages 130 to 133, beginning "When we got back . . . " and ending with the chapter. Jin-Han explains how he learns to expand his reading.
5.   "Day of Rest," pages 135 to 140. Jin-Han explains his mother's hard work and ambition on Sunday, her only day of rest, and his parents' expectations for their children.

Booktalk

Bring several hats and discuss the associations the group has with each one.

Just a hat—that's all that two-year-old Jin-Han loses on a windy Chicago day. His mother can buy him another, easily. But some other things aren't as easy for him or his parents. Jin-Han's parents are from Korea. Their English, their food, and their ways are not American. Jin-Han spends his after-school time taking care of his little sister in their wig store. He doesn't know any American kids who do things like that. So will his hat be Korean or American? Will it be a fireman's hat, a surgical cap, a snow hat with flaps, or maybe a sun visor? He doesn't know, but he tells us about part of his journey to find it and about the many hats he wears in the search. Afro wigs to fast food visors seem to fit other people well enough, but none is just right for him. And believe him when he tells you that his past and future are both all about *Finding My Hat*.

Learning Opportunities

1. Choose one piece of clothing that holds significance for you. Write a short essay that explains or illustrates its importance. Share it with the group.
2. Using your library's resources, continue to research the Korean cultural heritage. Share the information with the group.
3. Read both *Finding My Hat* and *A Step from Heaven* (Related Work 2). Both are about Korean American families. Discuss the similarities and differences between the two.
4. Reread the essays. Try to classify Jin-Han's experiences as Korean, American, or universal. Discuss your classifications with other members of the group who have completed the same exercise.
5. Choose one incident that Jin-Han relates. Tell it again from the point of view of another character in the essays.

Related Works

1. Bagdasarian, Adam. **First French Kiss and Other Traumas.** New York: Farrar, Straus and Giroux/Melanie Kroupa Books, 2002. 134p. $16.00. ISBN 0 374 32338 0. [fiction] JS (See full booktalk in *Teen Genre Connections*, 2005, pages 73 and 74.) In five groups of essays, a fictional character tells his traumatic and sometimes humorous life experiences in becoming a man.
2. Na, An. **A Step from Heaven.** Asheville, NC: Front Street, 2001. 156p. $15.95. ISBN 1 886910 58 8. [fiction] JS (See full booktalk in *Booktalks and More*, 2003, pages 33 to 35.) Young Ju, a Korean immigrant, relates her family's entry to and life in the United States.
3. Nam, Vickie (ed.). **Yell-Oh Girls!** New York: HarperCollins/Quill, 2001. 294p. $13.00pa. ISBN 0 06 095944 4. [nonfiction] JS (See full booktalk in *Booktalks and More*, 2003, pages 262 to 264.) In essays and poetry, Asian-American females express their joy, frustration, and determination in relation to their ancestry.
4. Park, Linda Sue. **When My Name Was Keoko: A Novel of Korea in World War II.** New York: Clarion Books, 2002. 199p. $16.00. ISBN 0 618 13335 6. [fiction] JS (See full booktalk in *Teen Genre Connections*, 2005, pages 235 to 237.) Told though the eyes of Sun hee and her older brother Tae yul, the story, spanning five years, recounts the Japanese assault on Korean culture during World War II.

5. Turner, Ann. **Hard Hit.** New York: Scholastic Press, 2006. 176p. $16.99. ISBN 0 439 29680 3. [poetry] JS Mark Warren, a talented high school pitcher, finds his life upended when his father is diagnosed with pancreatic cancer. Like Jin-Han, he feels both distant and overwhelmed.

♋♋

Weaver, Will. **Full Service.**
New York: Farrar, Straus and Giroux, 2005. 232p. $17.00.
ISBN 0 374 32485 9. [fiction] JS

Themes/Topics: service stations, farm life, Minnesota, 1965, faith, family, redemption, judgment

Summary/Description

Fifteen-year-old Paul Sutton's family belongs to a nondenominational, religious community. The members own their own farms but share labor and restrict their socializing to that religious community. Paul's mother suggests that Paul work in town so that he will better understand the rapidly changing world. A service station job gives him contact with local sports heroes, gangsters, law breakers, and hippies. He learns about romantic love, smoking, drugs, beer, and the ease of compromising one's personal integrity. His experiences lead him to question religion, especially his own. He learns the importance of personal responsibility, holds on to his love for his family, and develops his own faith in a power greater than man.

Read Aloud/Reader Response

1. Chapter 2, pages 14 to 20, beginning with the chapter and ending with " . . . you the back room." The gas station is a place of belief, and Kirk is one source of temptation.
2. Chapter 6, pages 63 to 69, beginning "After my mother . . . " and ending with the chapter. This passage describes the meal with the prisoners hired to bale the hay.
3. Chapter 14, pages 134 to 142, beginning with "At four-thirty . . . " and ending with the chapter. Because Paul does not heartily agree with the controlling barber's beliefs, he receives a brutalizing military haircut.
4. Chapter 21, pages 202 to 205. Paul is forced to attend the Sunday Meeting after passing out in the barn for the night where he lay covered with cow dung.

5.   Chapter 23, pages 211 to 212, beginning "And suddenly it was time . . . " and ending " . . . all that I had gained this summer." Paul has gone to "Convention" every year, but this year he sees it as boring and threatening.

Booktalk

Ask the audience if they know what a Full Service gas station is. If not, distinguish between today's self-serve low contact stations and older full service stations. You might want to list the seven points of Shell Full Service on pages 17 and 18: "Cheerful greeting," "Fill with ethyl," "Check oil," "Check water," "Check radiator and fan belt," "Wash windshield," and "Provide extra service."

Fifteen-year-old Paul Sutton is going to spend his summer providing "the public" with *Full Service.* Paul lives in Hawk Bend, Minnesota, population 1,750. But Paul spends most of his time on his parents' farm. They belong to a religious group that shares equipment, labor, and social life. Paul's world is smaller than even Hawk Bend. But this is 1965. Nobody's world can stay small. The Viet Nam War is raging. Civil rights marches are regular events. And a president has been assassinated. Paul's mother suggests that Paul get a town job. She thinks that if Paul meets "the public," he will have a better chance of finding a place in this changing world. It sounds good to Paul. Paul agrees to pump gas and clean restrooms at the local Shell station. The job seems simple enough. Paul knows hard work and engines. But the "public" includes hippies, gangsters, prisoners, and jealous lovers. The "public" comes with beer, cigarettes, and more temptation than Paul ever thought about. This summer job does more than put money in his pocket and a few new ideas in his head. Everything changes when life teaches Paul about *Full Service.*

Learning Opportunities

1.   Weaver locates the Shell station on one corner of the intersection and churches on the other three corners. Discuss the Shell station in religious terms. Be sure to consider the role of Mr. Shell in the story.
2.   Using your library's resources, research one significant event of the 1960s. Share the information with the group. Discuss how it adds to your understanding of the story.
3.   Do you agree with the story's ending?
4.   The title can be applied to the story in several ways. Explain how you would apply it.
5.   "The Convention" is a significant event in Paul's life. Describe the events that take place and Paul's reaction to them. Then discuss what Paul's reactions reveal about him.

Related Works

1. Bauer, Joan. **Hope Was Here.** New York: G. P. Putnam's Sons, 2000. 186p. $16.99. ISBN 0 399 23142 0. [fiction] MJS (See full booktalk in *Booktalks and More,* 2003, pages 258 to 260.) Waiting tables at the Welcome Stairways Diner in Mulhoney, Wisconsin, involves sixteen-year-old Hope in politics and love.

2. Bauer, Joan. **Rules of the Road.** New York: G. P. Putnam's Sons, 1998. 201p. $15.99. ISBN 0 399 23140 4. [fiction] MJS (See full booktalk in *Booktalks Plus,* 2001, pages 114 to 116.) Sixteen-year-old Jenna Boller's summer job transforms her into a poised business woman who can speak her mind and confront her alcoholic father.

3. Ching, Jacqueline. **The Assassination of Martin Luther King Jr.** New York: The Rosen Publishing Group, 2002. 64p. (The Library of Political Assassinations). $19.95. ISBN 0 8239 3543 4. [nonfiction] MJS Like the other books in the series, which includes volumes on the assassinations of John F. Kennedy and Malcolm X, this volume opens with a description of the assassination and then explains King's life and beliefs.

4. Hobbs, Valerie. **Sonny's War.** New York: Farrar, Straus and Giroux/Frances Foster Books, 2002. 215p. $16.00. ISBN 0 374 37136 9. [fiction] JS (See full booktalk in *Teen Genre Connections,* 2005, pages 230 to 233.) Fourteen-year-old Dory lives in a small California town in 1967. Her father dies. Her mother becomes a business woman. Her brother goes to Viet Nam, and Dory falls in love with her pacifist English teacher.

5. Myers, Walter Dean. **The Greatest: Muhammad Ali.** New York: Scholastic Press, 2000. 192p. $16.95. ISBN 0 590 54342 3. [nonfiction] MJS This biography about this famous and controversial fighter contains many of the civil rights conflicts of the sixties.

INDEX

About the Author

Photo by June Gebhardt.

LUCY SCHALL, a former middle school and high school English teacher, is a book reviewer for *VOYA*, and the author of three other acclaimed booktalking guides, including *Teen Genre Connections* (Libraries Unlimited, 2005).